THE VAULT GUIDE TO THE TOP 2
Banking Employ
is made possible through the generous su

CW01021670

 ABN·AMRO

INSEAD

The Business School
for the World

BARCLAYS CAPITAL

LEHMAN BROTHERS

 **BARCLAYS WEALTH**

London Business School

 **BNP PARIBAS**
CORPORATE & INVESTMENT BANKING

 **Merrill Lynch**

 CREDIT SUISSE

NOMURA

 ***Fidelity*** ™
INTERNATIONAL
choose wisely

 Teach First
LEARNING TO LEAD

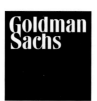
Goldman Sachs

 **UBS**

Creative, flexible and always open to fresh thinking, BNP Paribas is a global investment bank that likes to do things its own way. That's why we give our graduates so much responsibility so early on. We want to hear what our future leaders have to say sooner rather than later, so you'll be doing a real job and making genuine commercial decisions from the outset. You'll also be encouraged to draw inspiration from colleagues across the business as you share your ideas and work in a team to generate new ones. And with a training plan that's bespoke to you, you'll have a true say in how you progress.

To learn more about a career with an investment bank that's not like all the rest, go to **www.graduates.bnpparibas.co.uk**

It's <u>not</u> business as usual

It's for putting your ideas on

Not getting your feet under

Teach First's graduate programme is a unique opportunity to be different and to make a difference. It's an innovative combination of teaching with management skills training and leadership development, plus unparalleled internship, networking and coaching opportunities.

Whatever you aim to do with your career, Teach First.

I taught first

www.teachfirst.org.uk

Teach First
LEARNING TO LEAD

Where do you
see yourself in

10 years?

5 years?

2 years?

MBA Programme

It's the question we will all hear at least once in our career. With an MBA from London Business School, it is a question that has no limitations.

The London Business School MBA provides the skills, opportunities and global connections for you to achieve your career goals.

Our direct access to London's impressive finance and consulting recruiter base, excellent relationships with over 50 private equity firms and connections with 100 major corporations ensure you have the opportunities you need to satisfy your ambition.

Only the most talented are invited to attend our global classroom, for a learning experience that is both character forming and life changing.

Could this be you?

London Business School
Regent's Park
London NW1 4SA
Tel +44 (0)20 7000 7505
Fax +44 (0)20 7000 7501
Email mba1@london.edu
www.london.edu/mba/ambition/

To download a brochure on our MBA programme visit www.london.edu/mba/ambition/

London experience. World impact.

Great minds don't always think alike.

At Goldman Sachs, we welcome people from more than 100 different countries, each with talents as unique as their goals. Here individuality is an asset. You can be, too.

Goldman Sachs is a leading global investment banking, securities and investment management firm that provides a wide range of services worldwide to a substantial and diversified client base that includes corporations, financial institutions, governments, non-profit organisations and high-net-worth individuals.

We offer career opportunities for new analysts and associates. To find out more about our career paths and to complete an online application, please visit **www.gs.com/careers**

Application deadlines
Full Time: 19 October
Summer Internship: 28 December

You have one year to
challenge your thinking,
change your outlook and
choose your future.

INSEAD

The Business School
for the World

The MBA Programme
www.insead.edu/mba

At ABN AMRO we look for people who can think laterally and act decisively to develop effective solutions for our clients. This brainteaser will get you thinking.

Two American racing drivers were rivals to become CEO of a major car firm owned by a businessman in Chicago. The businessman didn't like either man, so came up with a plan – a race to decide who'd take over the firm. Both men had to drive from New York to Chicago, and the one whose car arrived last in Chicago would become CEO. The racers realised this could take a long time, so they went to a wise man and explained the situation. The wise man spoke four words and the two drivers left his office prepared to race. What did the wise man say?

INDIVIDUAL IN OUR THINKING,
GLOBAL IN OUR OUTLOOK.

Global graduate opportunities in corporate and investment banking

Our graduate development programme offers opportunities across Europe, North America and Asia Pacific. Wherever you join us you'll enjoy the scope to think innovatively, take early responsibility and tackle a variety of complex challenges. A place where you'll appreciate a culture that values your work/life balance as much as your skills.

For the answer, as well as details of our global graduate development programme, go to
www.graduate.abnamro.com

Making more possible   **ABN·AMRO**

Some think
steel and glass.

**We think
meeting
of minds.**

Mention global finance and people will often think of big buildings of glass and steel, marble halls and swift lifts. But offices are only offices and we have to work somewhere. It's what we do inside those offices that matters. Banking adds value, creates wealth and makes things happen in the world. The people at Credit Suisse do important, exhilarating, rewarding work, but they are still just people. So if you're thinking that the high-rise world of global finance is not for you, give us the benefit of the doubt and visit the website. You might feel right at home.

www.credit-suisse.com/careers

Thinking New Perspectives.

CREDIT SUISSE

Fidelity say: Choose a job you love and you will never have to work a day in your life.

Investment Management Graduate and Intern Careers

At Fidelity* we look after over $280.7 billion in managed funds worldwide, making us the UK's largest mutual fund manager. It's not surprising then, that when we make decisions they are carefully researched and considered. In fact, we have the largest Research and Development team in the industry. It's this intellectually rigorous approach to finance that has helped us become an acknowledged leader in our field.

That means we can now offer graduates some of the most exciting and challenging financial careers around. If you place a premium on intelligence and considered judgement too, we'll give you everything you need to become a recognised expert in your field. To help you make a wise choice why not find out more about us?
Visit **www.fidelityrecruitment.com**

choose wisely

global reputation

[limitless potential]

growth and success

inspiring colleagues

Merrill Lynch is one of the world's leading wealth management, capital markets and advisory companies. Our iconic brand and global capabilities offer you the chance to realise your potential whilst working side-by-side with thought leaders on projects of breathtaking scope and complexity. Join us and you can also benefit from a performance-based culture of excellence, where respect for the individual, commitment to breakthrough, big-picture thinking and enduring values create an environment for your continued growth and success.

For more information or to apply online, visit
ml.com/careers/europe

Merrill Lynch is an equal opportunity employer.

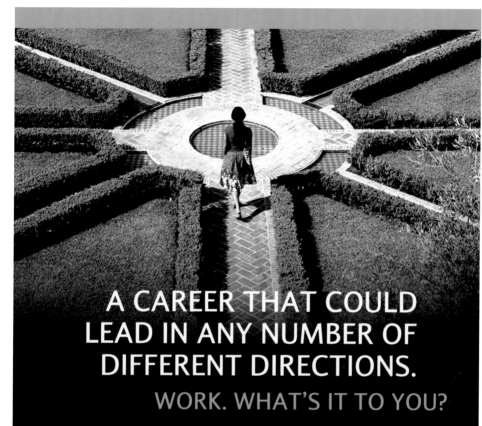

A CAREER THAT COULD LEAD IN ANY NUMBER OF DIFFERENT DIRECTIONS.

WORK. WHAT'S IT TO YOU?

As a graduate with Barclays Wealth, you can keep your options wide open. One of the leading wealth managers in the UK, we serve affluent and high net-worth personal and corporate clients with a complete end-to-end wealth management service on a global basis.

This includes private banking, brokerage, financial planning and advisory services. All of which makes this a great opportunity to gain broader exposure to the world of financial services. Our three-year graduate programme will give you exposure to clients from day one. As well as an overseas placement at one of our international offices, you can expect unprecedented career development opportunities and access to senior mentors to help you make the most of them. To find out more and to apply, please visit

barclayswealth.com/think

We are. Are you?

We'll judge you on your ability and nothing else.

The media's watching Vault!
Here's a sampling of our coverage.

"[Vault tells] prospective joiners what they really want to know about the culture, the interview process, the salaries and the job prospects."
- *Financial Times*

"Thanks to Vault, the truth about work is just a tap of your keyboard away."
- *The Telegraph*

"The best place on the Web to prepare for a job search."
– *Fortune*

"For those hoping to climb the ladder of success, [Vault's] insights are priceless."
– *Money* magazine

"A killer app."
– *The New York Times*

"To get the unvarnished scoop, check out Vault."
– *Smart Money* magazine

"Vault has a wealth of information about major employers and job-searching strategies as well as comments from workers about their experiences at specific companies."
– *The Washington Post*

VAULT
> the most trusted name in career information™

VAULT GUIDE TO THE **Top 25**

BANKING
EMPLOYERS

2008 EUROPEAN EDITION

VAULT GUIDE TO THE **Top 25**

BANKING
EMPLOYERS

2008 EUROPEAN EDITION

BY SABA HAIDER
and the staff of vault

Library of Congress CIP Data is available.

ISBN 13: 978-1-58131-493-9

ISBN 10: 1-58131-493-0

Printed in the United Kingdom by Athenaeum Press Ltd., Gateshead, Tyne & Wear

ACKNOWLEDGEMENTS

There are many, many people to whom we are (deeply) grateful for their assistance with this guide.

Thanks to everyone at Vault, and to the wonderful group of journalists in the UK who helped with this guide, for their help in the editorial, production and marketing efforts for this guide. Special thanks to Marcy Lerner, Derek Loosevelt, Thomas Nutt, Stephanie Myers, Anu Rao, Amanda Woolf, David Nicholson, Jeff Beer, John Fuller, Mary Phillips-Sandy, Harmandeep Singh, Graeme Buscke, Laurie Pasiuk, Leandro Lafuente, Katherine Epstein, Luke Teegarden and Adnan Haider.

We are especially grateful to the staff at all of the firms who helped with this book, and to the banking professionals who took the time out of their busy schedules to do our survey, to be interviewed, or to answer any and all of our questions.

Finally, the editorial team that worked on this guide (in all five languages involved with researching a book on European banking) would like to make a special thank you to Google Translate. What a fantastic tool.

It's Lehman Brothers...

Not just for
their superior
results, but for the
way they achieve them.

Whether you're interested in investment banking, capital markets,
investment management, finance, operations or information technology,
visit us online at www.lehman.com/careers.

LEHMAN BROTHERS

Capital Markets | Investment Banking | Investment Management

Table of Contents

Visit the Vault Finance Career Channel at **www.vault.com/finance**—with insider firm
profiles, message boards, the Vault Finance Job Board and more.

V/\ULT   CAREER
        LIBRARY   **ix**

THE BEST OF THE REST   145

APPENDIX   286

Visit **Vault Europe's Finance Career Channel** at **www.vault.com/europe** for insider firm profiles, employee surveys of finance professionals in Europe, message boards, job listings, expert finance career advice, insider salary information and more.

VAULT CAREER LIBRARY   **xi**

Introduction

Europe's banking and finance industry has long been a hallmark of history and pride. Alongside the dramatic evolution of the social and cultural landscape of Europe over the past century, this key economic sector has also experienced its share of growth, trials and tribulations.

Today, the world of banking in Europe is at perhaps the most interesting point in its own history. Jumbo takeovers, mergers and acquisitions have defined this era. It's a more exciting time than ever to be working in the sector that is literally changing the world's economic landscape every day.

In the fall of 2006, Vault published the first edition of the 2007 *Vault Guide to the Top European Banking Employers*. For the second edition, we are featuring 58 of Europe's top firms and are including prestige rankings for the top 25 firms, as selected by the employees of the banks who participated in our survey. The Vault Guide to the Top 25 Banking Employers in Europe profiles both European banks and the European operations of leading international banks. The profiles in our guide are based on our industry surveys, research and extensive feedback from employees about everything from company culture to compensation, training, management, perks and benefits. They also offer their valuable perspective about interviews, internships and diversity at their firms.

Since 1996, Vault has been the leading career information publisher in North America. The *Vault Guide to the top 50 Banking Employers* is now in its 11th edition. In addition, graduates and young professionals worldwide have found our online resource www.Vault.com, to be a valuable tool offering employee surveys and insider information on more than 5,000 employers and 4,500 universities, including the world's top business schools, as well as hundreds of industries and professions.

In the spring of 2006, Vault Europe was launched, offering European graduates and young professionals with relevant career information based on the successful model in the US. With a pan-European headquarters based in Europe, in less than two years Vault Europe has made brilliant progress in developing European guides as well as our online resource of surveys and profiles on Europe's top employers. And we're growing very fast.

Working on the second edition of Vault's guide to the top banking employers in Europe has been a brilliant experience which could not have been done without the enormous support and assistance of the banks being profiled in this guide. These banks are proving their commitment to ensuring that today's graduates know about the opportunities available to them.

Good luck in your career.   — Saba Haider, Editor

Visit **Vault Europe's Finance Career Channel** at www.vault.com/europe for insider firm profiles, employee surveys of finance professionals in Europe, message boards, job listings, expert finance career advice, insider salary information and more.

VΛULT CAREER LIBRARY

1

A Guide to This Guide

All of the company information and profiles in this guide are organised in a way that allows you to get a snapshot of all the basic information about and key stats of a firm.

To help you understand how the company information in this guide is presented, here is a useful guide to understanding the information featured in each profile.

Firm facts

Locations: A listing of the company's offices, with the city (or cities) of its headquarters bolded. We have only listed cities within Europe. If the firm is a non-European firm headquartered outside of Europe, the headquarters listed is the company's European headquarters. Most, if not all, of the firm's profiled in this guide have operations outside of Europe. However as this guide is Europe-focused, we are only including European locations.

Departments: Major departments and/or divisions of a firm distinguished by their role in the firm's operations. Departments are listed in alphabetical order, regardless of their size and prominence.

Employment Contact: The individual contact, email address or website that the firm identifies as the best place for interested applicants to send their CVs, or the appropriate contact to answer questions about the recruitment process. Sometimes more than one contact is given. Generally companies list all of this information in a specified section of their website.

The stats

Employer Type: The firm's classification as a publicly traded company, privately held company or subsidiary.

Ticker Symbol: The stock's ticker symbol for a public company, as well as the exchange on which the company's stock is traded.

Chairman, Chief executive, CEO, etc.: The name and title of the leader(s) of the firm.

Employees: The total number of employees, including bankers and other staff, at a firm in all of its offices (unless otherwise specified). Some firms do not disclose this information. Figures, if included, are from the most recent year the information is available.

No. of Offices: Worldwide except where otherwise stated.

Revenue: The gross sales (in the reported currency) that the firm generated in the specified fiscal year(s). Clearly some privately held firms do not disclose this information. Numbers from the most recent year the information is available (if at all) are included. Revenue is worldwide except where otherwise stated.

The profiles

Company profiles are divided into three sections: The Scoop, Getting Hired and Our Survey Says.

The Scoop: The firm's history, clients, recent developments and other points of interest.

Getting Hired: General qualifications that the firm seeks in new associates, tips on getting hired and other noteworthy aspects of the hiring process at the firm.

Our Survey Says: Actual quotes from surveys and interviews with current employees of the firm on such topics as a firm's culture, hours, travel requirements, salaries, training and more. Profiles of some firms do not include an Our Survey Says section.

Pluses and Minuses: The best and worst things, respectively, about working at the firm. Pluses and minuses are taken from the opinions of insiders based on our surveys and interviews.

The Buzz: When conduction our prestige survey, we asked respondents to include comments about the firms they were rating. Survey respondents were not able to comment on their own firm. We collected a sampling of these comments in The Buzz. We tried to include quotes that represented the common outside perceptions of a given firm. The quotes may not always reflect what insiders say in our surveys and interviews. We think The Buzz is a way of gauging outside opinion of a company

The State of European Banking

By the end of 2008, the map of European banking is likely to be radically different from how it was at the time of press, in the summer of 2007.

By then, a new European law will almost certainly be in place to prohibit EU states from discriminating against bidders for any of their national banks.

For the moment, Europe remains marked by protectionism and political championing of industries and banks, despite the gradual rise in the number and value of banking mergers and acquisitions that take place. This year has already seen what could become the largest banking merger in history, with the UK's Barclays Bank competing with Royal Bank of Scotland for control of Dutch bank ABN Amro, each with bids of more than €60 billion on the table.

Such a deal is a rarity in European banking, with the last similar events — Spanish bank Santander's $17 billion acquisition of UK's Abbey and Unicredit's acquisition of Germany's HBV — taking place in 2004 and 2005 respectively. In the meantime, European regulators and the banking industry in general has been faced by a series of smaller skirmishes at the margins.

A shopping frenzy: European M&A

In Italy, the former governor of the national bank, Antonio Fazio, was taped discussing the details of a deal in which Banco Popolare Italiana was given an unfair advantage in an M&A deal over a foreign bidder. Last year, Fazio was replaced by the more liberal and internationally experienced Mario Draghi, who has explicitly said he will allow free market forces to determine the outcome of banking transactions. There is plenty of appetite among other European banks to acquire Italian counterparts, partly because Italian banking customers pay exceptionally high fees. A typical basket of banking services will cost an Italian €250 per year, against €34 per year in the Netherlands.

In Spain, the market is similarly diffuse, with each of the country's 17 autonomous regions having a collection of savings banks, altogether accounting for around 50 per cent of the country's banking sector. As Spain moved from dictatorship to democracy in the 1980s, the savings banks took on the role of representing their local societies. Banks developed voting rights for political blocs, leading to Spanish companies forming close ties with the banks and discouraging outsiders from buying them. Today, this provincial attitude is increasingly out of step with the best interests of customers, who are more likely to value a competitive mortgage rate or a large credit facility above the noise of local politics.

It is also out of step with the direction of the European Union, which is mounting a sustained campaign to break down monopolies and create a fully functioning single market, for financial services as well as other aspects of trade. The EU Competition Commissioner Charlie McCreevy and his colleague Neelie Kroes have regularly come to blows with European central bankers and industrialists who are trying to hang on to national champions. Over the next year, we are likely to see France's new President Nicolas Sarkozy push the boundaries of his country's protectionist envelope. He has already attacked the European Central Bank, arguing that France should have more control over its financial affairs.

In some respects, Europe is merely trying to do — as a continent — what individual countries have done for centuries. Now that Europe has a single currency, an expanded political and geographical entity and a far more free flow of money across its borders, there is a significant momentum to challenge the largest global banks. Barclays or RBS and ABN would together enter the world's top five largest banks, enabling the combined entity to compete at the highest level in the global sector.

The forthcoming EU regulations preventing discrimination in banking takeovers could well lead to a spurt of M&A activity among European banks in the coming months, as they rush to join together now, rather than wait until they could be the targets of hostile activity. Italian giant UniCredit has been linked with French bank Société Générale (SocGen), a deal that would potentially exceed the Barclays/ABN merger. France's President Sarkozy may in turn encourage fellow French bank BNP Paribas to bid for SocGen as a way of keeping things in-house.

Good times

All this talk (and some action) has sprung from the extremely healthy economic conditions that Europe has experienced over the past few years. As credit has remained cheap, companies have profited from outsourcing their manufacturing to low-cost economies and the rewards of IT automation have flowed into balance sheets. For banks, the astonishing length of the M&A bull run, now in its fourth year and with no immediate signs of an end, has kept their profit margins at historic highs.

The banks' ability to combine M&A advice with bond issuance and direct investment has put them in a lucrative position as the run has surged onwards. Despite regular warnings of an imminent crash, at the time of writing (May 2007), such fears appear premature. Lending criteria have certainly relaxed, and the willingness of the major banks to put their

Visit **Vault Europe's Finance Career Channel** at www.vault.com/europe for insider firm profiles, employee surveys of finance professionals in Europe, message boards, job listings, expert finance career advice, insider salary information and more.

VAULT CAREER LIBRARY

5

own money into transactions — sometimes in the form of an 'equity bridge' which would leave the banks very exposed in the event of a crash — is rising.

The shift towards banks taking an active trading role and taking equity in deals stems from a natural ambition to get as much of a cut of the pie as they can, yet many financial experts are uncomfortable about this. The International Monetary Fund warns that, as syndication of loans can take several months, banks that provide 'equity bridge' finance are at risk during this period and "could suffer large losses".

Some banks have launched private quity units. One example of this is Deutsche Bank that, with its DB Investment Partners has launched private equity units, helping to provide $3.5 billion financing for the $29 billion bid from private equity firm KKR in the US for payments services firm First Data. This was the first time that the bank has used its balance sheet to support a leveraged buyout.

Understanding the players

Clearly, the distinction between lenders and investors is starting to blur and anyone aiming to make a career in banking would do well to understand both sides of the equation. In large company acquisitions today, there are likely to be numerous players, each contributing levels of investment and debt, each with different levels of recourse.

Those who are seeking work in European banking in 2007 are in a fortunate position. The expansion of financial services in general, and of investment banks in particular, has tipped the supply and demand curve sharply in candidates' favour. There is now a so-called 'war for talent' going on in the City of London and other European financial capitals, with 27 per cent more jobs on offer in mid-2007 than for the same period in 2006. Salaries rose by between 10 and 15 per cent in some sectors, with newly-qualified accountants in London able to command around £55,000 per year, while experienced accountants in investment banking can expect more than £80,000 a year, according to financial executive headhunters company WoodHamill.

The positions of the main players in the finance industry have remained relatively static for some years, with Goldman Sachs, Morgan Stanley and JP Morgan at the top of the M&A table, Citigroup, Lehman Brothers and Deutsche Bank heading the global underwriting lists and Credit Suisse, Morgan Stanley and Goldman Sachs all prominent in handling IPOs.

None of the major US banks are interested in making large European acquisitions for the moment, partly because of the weak dollar and partly because they have as much market share and deal flow as they can handle, with income and profits rising steadily without the need for time-consuming and potentially messy mergers. It is the Europeans themselves who are intent on reaching such critical mass that they can compete more squarely with the American giants.

The impact of technology

New technology has played a critical role in facilitating cross border activity, both in M&As and the regular business of banking. Payment methods, mortgages, insurance and a great range of financial services can be offered across national borders at the click of a mouse, particularly in the eurozone, making transnational bank mergers far more practical and appealing. Banks which have traditionally sat within their own national boundaries are now waking up to the potential to diversify beyond their slow-growing, saturated home markets. A new spirit of adventure is replacing the old inhibition, based on differences in culture, laws, tax systems and language.

In the space of a generation, careers in banking have been transformed from a steady, long-term progression up the company ladder, from tea making to deputy branch manager and so on, to today's fast-paced, global industry where UK graduates can easily be working in New York, Frankfurt or Hong Kong before they are 25. The management structure is flatter, the opportunities to travel and to specialise in specific areas (tax, M&A, derivatives etc) are more plentiful than ever, and the bonuses paid to top level employees run into millions of pounds. The pace of change in the coming few years is only going to increase. So, prepare for an exciting ride.

Visit **Vault Europe's Finance Career Channel** at **www.vault.com/europe** for insider firm profiles, employee surveys of finance professionals in Europe, message boards, job listings, expert finance career advice, insider salary information and more.

V/\ULT   CAREER LIBRARY   7

Decrease your T/NJ Ratio
(Time to New Job)

Use the Internet's most targeted
job search for finance professionals.

Vault Finance Job Board

The most comprehensive and convenient job board for finance
professionals. Target your search by area of finance, function,
and experience level, and find the job openings that you want.
No surfing required.

To search jobs, go to **www.vault.com/europe**

THE VAULT
PRESTIGE
RANKINGS

TOP 25

BANKING EMPLOYERS

Ranking Methodology

The Vault Guide to the Top 25 Banking Employers, 2008 European edition, rates 58 firms either based or with significant operations in Europe, in the realm of banking and financial services. Our editors selected the 58 featured firms based on previous Vault surveys that gauged opinions of industry insiders and employed various factual data, including the size of a firm in terms of its revenue or assets, to determine if the firm qualifies as a top European banking employer.

The firms identified were asked to distribute our online survey to relevant employees and a fantastic number of banks agreed to participate. The survey consisted of questions about life at the respective firm (or former firm) and asked participants to rate all of the listed firms being featured in the guide in terms of prestige. Participants were asked to rate companies with which they were familiar on a scale of 1 to 10, with 10 being the most prestigious. They were not allowed to rate their own employer.

All surveys were completed anonymously by participants throughout the UK and Europe. For those companies that did not participate, Vault reached out to employees at the respective firm (s) through other proprietary sources. Those professionals took the same survey as the employees at firms that participated.

In all, 543 banking and finance professionals in the UK and Europe took Vault's 2007 Top European Banking Employers Survey from February 2007 through May 2007. Vault averaged the prestige scores for each firm and ranked them in order, with the highest score belonging to our No. 1 firm, Goldman Sachs. Banking giant Goldman received a score of 8.519, nearly one full point higher than the No. 2 firm, Morgan Stanley (7.978). Rounding out the top five were Blackstone Group (7.787) at No. 3, JP Morgan (7.563) at No. 4 and UBS (7.265) at No. 5.

Visit **Vault Europe's Finance Career Channel** at **www.vault.com/europe** for insider firm profiles, employee surveys of finance professionals in Europe, message boards, job listings, expert finance career advice, insider salary information and more.

VΛULT CAREER LIBRARY

1 1

The Vault 25 • 2008

[The 25 most prestigious banking employers in Europe]

RANK	FIRM	SCORE	EUROPEAN HEADQUARTERS/ LARGEST EUROPEAN OFFICE
1	Goldman Sachs	8.520	London
2	Morgan Stanley	7.978	London
3	Blackstone Group	7.787	London
4	JPMorgan Investment Bank	7.563	London
5	UBS Investment Bank	7.266	Zurich
6	Merrill Lynch	7.181	London
7	Lehman Brothers	7.120	London
8	Deutsche Bank	7.085	Frankfurt
9	Citi	6.794	London
10	Lazard	6.708	London
11	Credit Suisse	6.655	London
12	N.M. Rothschild & Sons	6.629	London
13	Barclays Capital	6.290	London
14	Macquarie Group	5.901	London
15	Bear Stearns	5.724	London
16	BNP Paribas	5.680	Paris
17	HSBC	5.652	London
18	Royal Bank of Scotland	5.649	Edinburgh
19	Dresdner Kleinwort	5.453	Frankfurt/London
20	Bank of America	5.386	London
21	Greenhill & Co.	5.369	London
22	Société Générale	5.170	Paris
23	ING Group	5.106	Amsterdam
24	Nomura	4.750	London
25	Calyon	4.695	Paris

THE VAULT
25

TOP 25

BANKING EMPLOYERS

1

Goldman Sachs

Peterborough Court
133 Fleet Street
London, EC4A 2BB
United Kingdom
Phone: +44 (0) 20 7774 1000
Fax: +44 (0) 20 5552 7090
www.gs.com

EUROPEAN LOCATIONS

London (European HQ)
Dublin
Frankfurt
Geneva
Madrid
Milan
Moscow
Paris
Stockholm
Zurich

DEPARTMENTS

Asset Management & Securities
Services
Investment Banking
Trading & Principal Investments

THE STATS

Employer Type: Public Company
Ticker Symbol: GS (NYSE)
Chairman and CEO: Lloyd C. Blankfein
2006 Revenue: $37.67 billion
(FYE 12/06)
2005 Revenue: $24.78 billion
(FYE 12/05)
2006 Employees: 26,467
No. of Offices: 45 (Worldwide)

PLUSES

Utterly prestigious; tremendous
opportunity

MINUSES

Not easy to get in; very competitive

EMPLOYMENT CONTACT

www.gs.com/careers

THE BUZZ
WHAT EMPLOYEES AT OTHER FIRMS ARE SAYING

- "Miles ahead of the rest"
- "Too institutionalised"
- "Still the banking brand to beat"
- "Extremely difficult to get hired"

THE SCOOP

The Goldman standard

Goldman Sachs was founded in the US in 1869 and opened its first European office in London in 1970. Additional European offices later opened in Frankfurt, Paris, Madrid, Geneva, Zurich, Milan, Dublin, Moscow and Stockholm. Goldman's London office is the hub for its European operations and employs more than 4,000 people.

The firm's business arms include investment banking, trading and principal investments, and asset management and securities services. The investment banking division serves clients in the industrial, consumer, natural resources, health care, financial institutions, real estate, special products, technology, media and telecommunications industries. Goldman offers financial advisory services for mergers, acquisitions, divestitures and debt and equity capital.

In 2006, most of Goldman's M&A power stemmed from its work in the United States. In European mergers and acquisitions it slipped slightly, falling behind Morgan Stanley and Citigroup. Previously, Goldman had been No. 1 in European M&A for four consecutive years.

Absolutely fabulous

Goldman's great performance in 2006 meant one thing for its employees: big bonuses. And no one profited more than Chairman and CEO Lloyd C. Blankfein, who at year's end had only held his position for six months. According to a December report, Blankfein received a $53.4 million bonus in 2006, the highest ever given to a banking executive. The windfalls varied between Goldman's American and European employees, however. Like most US-based banks in Europe, Goldman pays bonuses in US dollars and many European staffers who didn't link their bonuses to average exchange rates saw their total haul slip behind their American counterparts' year-end gifts, as the dollar further weakened against the Euro and the British pound.

Musical executive seats

Continuing the shakeups that started with Blankfein's arrival at the top in June 2006, November and December 2006 brought several changes at Goldman's executive offices. Scott Kapnick, one of the bank's three co-heads of investment banking, stepped down from his post at the end of November. Kapnick had, until July 2006, been co-CEO of Goldman's European business (Richard Gnodde was his replacement). The bank's remaining investment bank co-heads, David Solomon and John Weinberg, will continue in their roles. Also in November 2006, Goldman announced that it would strengthen its London office,

Visit **Vault Europe's Finance Career Channel** at www.vault.com/europe for insider firm profiles, employee surveys of finance professionals in Europe, message boards, job listings, expert finance career advice, insider salary information and more.

VAULT CAREER LIBRARY **15**

because the bank was seeing relatively faster growth in Europe and Asia than in the Americas. More than 100 top European bankers were simultaneously invited to join the partnership pool and 262 more were promoted to managing directors.

A month later, in December 2006, Vice Chairwoman Suzanne Nora Johnson, Goldman's highest-ranked woman executive and a 21-year veteran of the company, announced her retirement. Next to move was Philippe Altuzarra, a senior banker who was shifted from Paris to London.

Analysts watched these changes carefully to see if the new Goldman, under CEO Blankfein, would swing more toward the trading or the investment banking side. While Blankfein got his start at Goldman as a trader, his predecessor, Henry Paulson, was a banker. Many wondered if Blankfein would favour his trading staff over bankers when he took his post, but the investment bank's excellent performance in 2006 was impossible to ignore.

Also in December 2006, the European Commission gave Goldman and Kohlberg Kravis Roberts permission to jointly buy forklift giant Kion for $5.1 billion. Many analysts suggest that by purchasing European utilities, banks like Goldman will assure steady revenue streams to fuel their investment banking and financing businesses.

Titans of trade

Seven of the world's biggest investment banks — Goldman Sachs, Citigroup, Credit Suisse, Deutsche Bank, Merrill Lynch, Morgan Stanley and UBS — announced in November 2006 that they were working together to launch a European trading platform designed to compete with other regional stock exchanges. The banks' trading system will offer high-speed trades and rates well below those of the Deutsche Borse, Euronext and the London Stock Exchange. While no numbers have been released, each bank will be a shareholder in the new project entity and will be represented on its board.

Performance rewarded

The annual Thomson Financial International Financing Review awards are among the most coveted in the banking business, and at the IFR Awards ceremony in London in December 2006, Thomson/IFR named Goldman Sachs its Bank of the Year. "Goldman Sachs's performance in 2006 was extraordinary," stated the citation. "The firm used the quality and depth of its client relationships to develop a unique strategy of being an advisor, financier and co-investor to and with its clients. This strategy paid real dividends in 2006." Goldman Sachs also picked up Leveraged Finance House of the Year and Equity House of the Year awards.

GETTING HIRED

Cream of the crop

Goldman Sachs is fairly selective when choosing full-time employees and summer interns. The firm uses a number of methods to find the best candidates. Between 2005 and 2006 the firm increased its global workforce by almost 4,000 people — from 22,425 in 2005 to 26,467 in 2006.

One associate says, "We look for the best and brightest applicants. Academic excellence, business acumen, great communication skills, drive and motivation are essential qualities." Another source notes, "The selection process is quite thorough and includes a long string of interviews." An insider describes the interview process as being "rigorous" and involving a number of meetings with various individuals.

There is also the advantage that a coveted GS internship provides. One analyst describes the work as being fairly comprehensive. He says, "[It's] the same as all the jobs that one would do as a first-year analyst day to day, plus many presentations and learning events." Another adds, "I worked on the fixed income trading floor shadowing sales people, participating in trading games and preparing presentations for clients. I was given a full-time offer on the basis of my performance during my internship." An associate confirms, "[It's] definitely easier to get hired following this internship."

That said, one Goldman Sachs source says that almost half of the hiring done at the graduate level each year comprises candidates who did not do the firm's summer internship.

OUR SURVEY SAYS

A sense of community

The word most used by insiders about the culture within Goldman Sachs is "teamwork." A third-year associate says, "The organisation tends to be quite flat, and team-based. Everyone from the analyst to the partner is an integral member of the team and contributes to the process and the discussions. The attitude is also one of help. If you're in need, just raise your hand and someone will help you — always — whichever office in the world he or she is in." An executive director adds, "Goldman Sachs is typified by a unique culture emphasising teamwork and the importance of the firm's most valued asset — its people. This comes through in our approach to everything."

Visit **Vault Europe's Finance Career Channel** at **www.vault.com/europe** for insider firm profiles, employee surveys of finance professionals in Europe, message boards, job listings, expert finance career advice, insider salary information and more.

VAULT CAREER LIBRARY 17

Another London source says the firm is "very people-orientated with an open environment. Everybody works hard but is rewarded for getting results." A fellow analyst notes, "There is an open-door policy where you are free to speak with anyone in the department at ease. It is also a culture towards benefiting the community and I participate in mentoring at a deprived school in London."

Money is time and time is money

Employees rate the firm's compensation fairly high. Analyst bonuses generally range from £4K to £9K. One respondent said he received a signing bonus of £5,500 when he took the job. Associates generally earn approximately £200K in bonuses, while executive directors can earn much more. In addition, the firm offers stock options, evening meal allowances, night car service and what one contact sums up as "great facilities all round."

Although long hours are part of the job, Goldman Sachs insiders aren't always thrilled with the amount of time spent at the office. An associate reflects, "The work often requires a lot of stamina and the job needs to excite you." Another contact says, "This is not a culture where people work 40 hours a week and take lunch breaks. Whilst some divisions' hours can be less daunting than, say, IBD, nobody works less than 50 hours a week." However, one Londoner says, "There can be long hours but [they] usually are fairly flexible if you have personal commitments." But, despite the long haul, one analyst says, "If you put in the effort, the work is well worth it." And regardless of how rewarding a career in banking can be, several sources pointed to the sometimes "stressful situations with clients" as being their least favourite part of the job.

They've got the right stuff

Management at Goldman Sachs is rated highly and managers are known for their ability to communicate and offer feedback. One associate says, "They know their job very well. They are solution finders and know how to get the deals and people they work with to the finish line." Another source adds, "The best thing is that people are always providing you with feedback."

As for office attire and a dress code, dressing smart is important.One insider says, "Every day seems to sway between formal and business casual depending in which area you work and how much client contact the job requires." But an associate adds that "it is increasingly becoming more formal."

Training and diversity

Sources applaud the firm's "focus on excellence" and training at Goldman Sachs is given high priority. The firm's training programme, aptly named "Goldman Sachs University

(GSU)", allows staffers to consistently keep learning. An associate says, "GSU is excellent, with new live training proposed every week as well as online courses to be accessed at all times." All aspects of diversity are given a high priority at the firm.

Overall, Goldman Sachs sources are very satisfied with the firm. As one associate in London says, "It's an awesome place to work, learn and grow."

Visit **Vault Europe's Finance Career Channel** at **www.vault.com/europe** for insider firm profiles, employee surveys of finance professionals in Europe, message boards, job listings, expert finance career advice, insider salary information and more.

VAULT CAREER LIBRARY 19

Morgan Stanley

25 Cabot Square
Canary Wharf
London, E14 4QA
United Kingdom
Phone: +44 (0) 20 7425 8000
Fax: +44 (0) 20 7425 8990
www.morganstanley.com

EUROPEAN LOCATIONS

London (European HQ)
France • Germany • Hungary •
Italy • Netherlands • Russia •
Spain • Sweden • Switzerland •
Turkey and the UK

DEPARTMENTS

Asset Management
Discover Cards & Services
Global Wealth Management
Investment Banking
Sales & Trading

THE STATS

Employer Type: Public Company
Ticker Symbol: MS (NYSE, Pacific
Exchange)
Chairman & CEO: John J. Mack
2006 Revenue: $33.9 billion
(FYE 11/06)
2005 Revenue: $26.7 billion
(FYE 11/05)
2006 Employees: 53,870
No. of Offices: 600 (Worldwide)

KEY COMPETITORS

Citigroup Global Markets
Credit Suisse
Deutsche Bank
Goldman Sachs
JP Morgan
Merrill Lynch
UBS

PLUSES

Very prestigious

MINUSES

Extremely competitive

EMPLOYMENT CONTACT

www.morganstanley.com/careers/recr
uiting/europe/index.html

THE BUZZ
WHAT EMPLOYEES AT OTHER FIRMS ARE SAYING

- "Involved in high-profile deals"
- "Slipped a little"
- "Top-tier bank; really good
  reputation"
- "Not what it used to be"

Yes, those Morgans

From its official beginning in 1935, Morgan Stanley has grown to become a powerful global investment bank. But its roots go back even further, to 1854, when Junius S. Morgan took a job with a London bank. The Morgans were Americans, and Junius' son, J. Pierpont Morgan, became one of the world's first celebrity financiers, helping to build the American rail system and forming General Electric and US Steel. Morgan Stanley was built by former employees of JP Morgan & Co., and the bank arrived in Europe in 1967 when it opened an office in Paris. London followed in 1975, and today the New York-based bank has approximately 600 offices in 31 countries worldwide. London has become its European headquarters.

Today, Morgan Stanley is comprised of three business arms: institutional securities, global wealth management and investment management. The firm's Discover cards and services division is set to be spun off into a standalone business in the third quarter of 2007.

A new Discover

In December 2006, Morgan Stanley announced plans to spin off its credit card unit, Discover. Commenting on the spinoff, John J. Mack said, "Given the record results and significant momentum both in our securities business and our cards and payments business, we have concluded, after our most recent strategic review, that they can best execute their growth strategies as two stand-alone, well-capitalised companies with independent boards of directors focused on creating shareholder value. The spin-off will allow Discover to continue building on its strong brand and significant scale."

The Discover card spin-off, which remains subject to regulatory approval, is expected to take place during the third quarter of 2007, according to the firm. When the deal is finalised, Morgan Stanley shareholders will receive tax-free Discover shares. In its 2006 year-end report Morgan Stanley explained that Discover has improved well enough to be a stable standalone — the unit reported net revenue of $4.3 billion for the year and boasted more than 50 million card members. It also launched a new debit card program, broadening the scope of its offerings in the UK and improving its credit position, with loan losses at a 10-year low.

C'est tout!

After four years of litigation, Morgan Stanley finally prevailed in a massive lawsuit taken to French courts. In the summer of 2006 a Parisian appeals court overturned a prior decision by the country's commercial court, which had ruled against Morgan Stanley in a $118 million suit brought by luxury goods company LVMH in 2002. The French company alleged that analysts in Morgan Stanley's UK offices had provided flawed research in a

Visit **Vault Europe's Finance Career Channel** at www.vault.com/europe for insider firm profiles, employee surveys of finance professionals in Europe, message boards, job listings, expert finance career advice, insider salary information and more.

VAULT CAREER LIBRARY

21

deliberate attempt to benefit one of the bank's other major clients - Gucci. The latest and final decision found that while research errors had been made, they were not intentional.

Eyes on the prizes

Morgan Stanley landed a pile of banking awards in 2006, many of which reflected its strength in Europe. The magazine *Euromoney* dubbed it Best M&A House in Central and Eastern Europe; *Global Finance* called it Best Equity Bank in Western Europe and London's *Sunday Times* newspaper ranked it the No. 5 Best Big Company to Work For. At the International Fund Investment Global ETF Awards, Morgan Stanley took home the prize for Most Useful ETF Research in Europe.

The bank's financial strength showed, too. It reported a record net revenue of $33.9 billion for the year ended November 2006, a 26 per cent rise from the previous year. Much of this increase came from growth in the bank's commodities, credit products, and interest rate and currency products, and equity sales and trading growth in Europe and Asia.

Giving global advice

A number of Morgan Stanley's European offices participated in newsworthy deals in 2006. Morgan Stanley Paris served as advisor to Suez in its proposed €37 billion merger with GDF. Its German offices worked as lead arranger to Linde on its €15 billion syndicated acquisitions facility and to RAG on its €6.2 billion acquisition facility. Morgan Stanley was the joint lead manager to the Republic of Austria on a €4 billion benchmark bond issue. The bank was also involved with one of Europe's biggest leveraged lending deals in 2006, advising Cinven and Warburg Pincus on their €4.4 billion secondary leveraged buyout of Casema.

In keeping with the firm's strategy of staking claims in European emerging markets, Morgan Stanley announced in November 2006 that it would open an office in Istanbul. Turkish authorities and regulators have approved the plan and the Istanbul office is set to open in 2007. Jonathan Chenevix-Trench, chairman of Morgan Stanley International, described the move as, "an important strategic step for Morgan Stanley", noting that the bank has served Turkish clients since 1990.

You buy some, you sell some

In November 2006 Morgan Stanley said that it would acquire a 19 per cent stake in London-based Lansdowne Partners, a boutique investment manager and hedge fund with more than $12 billion in assets under management. Lansdowne, founded in 1998, includes European equity, UK equity, global financials, macro services and emerging markets services. In December 2006 Morgan Stanley announced its decision to sell Quilter

Holdings Ltd., its standalone UK mass affluent business, to Citigroup. That deal is expected to be completed sometime during the first quarter of 2007.

GETTING HIRED

It's all online

The application process for a job at Morgan Stanley begins either by filling out an online application that can be found on its web site (www.morganstanley.com/about/careers/index.html), or during one of the firm's many campus recruitment events. The prestigious employer is open about seeking "very focused" employees and has a popular internship programme that often leads to full-time employment.

One first-year analyst says that "About 50 per cent of equity interns make it onto the full-time payroll." Another insider, and ex-intern, explains that at the end of the internship, all interns are interviewed about their experience and have a feedback session with their manager. That information is then used to decide if an intern will be offered a graduate position. Insiders do point out that if you're interested in a role in the coveted investment banking division, the firm expects you to have incredible marks on your transcript — and if you haven't interned for the firm, you must simply be "very good".

The interview-athon

If you're one of the lucky ones that lands an interview, make sure you thoroughly express your interest in both the firm and role as the interviewers are "very perceptive to enthusiasm levels", say insiders. Staffers across all divisions say they had two rounds of interviews. One source, who first interviewed for a summer analyst position, says the first interview was on campus with "a professional" from the firm. Questions that are "typical of an investment bank interview" were asked — "except it was very friendly and not particularly technical". The second round, he says, was in London over what he describes as "a full day called 'assessment centre', starting with some tests and group discussion over some imaginary problems and ending with three interviews in the afternoon with senior people." He adds, "One of these interviews was very technical, pushing me to where I could not answer correctly. The other two were more of the behavioural type, trying to see what I was interested in and whether there was good fit."

An ex-intern says both of the assessment day interviews were "quite relaxed" adding, "I didn't feel like they were trying to catch me out. I was made to feel relaxed throughout the assessment process." One analyst, who interviewed for a role in the popular investment banking division, describes the two round interview process: "The first round is fit-based

Visit Vault Europe's Finance Career Channel at www.vault.com/europe for insider firm profiles, employee surveys of finance professionals in Europe, message boards, job listings, expert finance career advice, insider salary information and more.

VAULT CAREER LIBRARY 23

whereas the second round is organised as a one-day assessment centre which involves group exercises, one-on-one IB interviews, a numerical/reasoning test and a one-on-one case study."

He adds, "The group exercise involves the discussion of a business situation where candidates simulate a board meeting. There is not much room for preparation, as the teamwork ability is what seems to matter here. Those who got the offers contributed creative ideas directed to the core issues, not those who tried to be the great leaders without making effective contributions."

Interviews in the first round are personality-based, say employees, adding: "Nonetheless, those with previous experience got a lot of technical questions. Some also reported consulting questions, such as market sizing, where simple calculations had to be done." Our source, rather relevantly slips in some advice: "Those who have read the *Vault Guide to Finance Interviews* should not have any problems."

Quantitative elements

Maths-phobes need not fear, as "The numerical test is very easy." Our insider's advice for the test is simple: "Answer questions correctly rather than rushing through it — nobody in my group finished it! Go to the Morgan Stanley careers page to get an idea of how such tests look like. Practise your school maths — percentages, multiplying and dividing, fractions etc. That's it. "The case study is very simple and involved a business disposal situation where various alternatives for the seller have to be evaluated. It is essential that you ask the interviewer loads of questions and that you prepare a good structure for your analysis — as in consulting interviews."

An ex-intern reflects on his experience of getting hired with satisfaction: "I believe that Morgan Stanley's recruitment process was very good. It was best to have most of the selection stages on one day in the form of an assessment centre. In addition, I agree with having two interviews on the day as this provides a fairer assessment of an individual's suitability."

"I was made to feel relaxed throughout the assessment process"

Blackstone Group International, The

40 Berkeley Square
London, W1J 5AL
United Kingdom
Phone: +44 (0) 20 7451 4000
Fax: +44 (0) 20 7451 4001
www.blackstone.com

EUROPEAN LOCATIONS

London (HQ)
Hamburg
Paris

DEPARTMENTS

Advisory Services
Corporate Advisory Services
Corporate Debt
Distressed Securities Advisors
India/Asia Closed-End Funds
Long/Short Equity Investments
Marketable Alternative Asset
Investments
Private Equity
Private Placement Advisory
Real Estate
Restructuring & Reorganisation

THE STATS

Employer Type: Private Company
Chairman & CEO: Stephen A. Schwarzman
No. of Employees: 750
No. of Offices: 12 (Worldwide)

KEY COMPETITORS

Apax
CVC
Carlyle Group
Goldman Sachs
KKR
Permira

PLUSES

Solid player with established name

MINUSES

Not a huge employer

EMPLOYMENT CONTACT

www.blackstone.com
(See "Careers" section)

THE BUZZ
WHAT EMPLOYEES AT OTHER FIRMS ARE SAYING

- "Aggressive, expanding"
- "Strong player but tends to have a negative reputation"
- "One of the best in class"
- "Very hard-nosed environment"

THE SCOOP

Simply smart investing

Founded as an alternative to traditional investment banking in 1985, The Blackstone Group has grown steadily over the past 22 years to become a major player in the industry. The firm currently operates in alternative asset investing such as private equity, real estate, corporate debt and hedge funds, and in advisory including corporate advisory and restructuring advisory.

As an investment group, the firm relies on core values that set it apart from its larger rivals — it maintains a small firm in order to give senior-level attention to clients, invests only in friendly takeovers rather than in hostile bids, grows through attracting professionals who create affiliated businesses, puts significant amounts of its own money into investments and avoids conflicts of interest in order to provide entirely objective advice. This model has proved more than successful. Since its inception and leading up to March 1, 2007, Blackstone invested in approximately 320 transactions for a total enterprise value topping $290 billion.

Modest beginnings

Stephen A. Schwarzman and Peter G. Peterson founded The Blackstone Group in 1985 after working in the investment banking industry for many years. The two had garnered high-level positions at Lehman Brothers investment bank, with Schwarzman serving as chairman of mergers and acquisitions and Peterson serving as CEO. Blackstone initially opened in New York with a staff of four and a balance sheet of $400,000. Through strategic investing and the application of its core beliefs, the group has greatly expanded its operations and balance sheet. Today Blackstone has offices in Atlanta, Boston, Chicago, Dallas, Los Angeles, San Francisco, London, Hamburg, Paris, Mumbai and Hong Kong, with its headquarters in Manhattan on Park Avenue.

A private equity star

The private equity group is Blackstone's primary investment vehicle, with more than $35 billion managed in six funds: Blackstone Capital Partners I, II, III, IV, V and Blackstone Communications Partners. Blackstone has proven to be especially successful at raising capital, with the most recent fund, BCP V, boasting commitments of over $19 billion.

The Blackstone Communications Partners Fund focuses on investments in the communications industry and closed at $2 billion in 2000. Upon closing, funds are invested in transactions which can include leveraged buyouts, joint ventures, partnerships, recapitalisations and growth capital investments. Investments are guided by several key

Visit **Vault Europe's Finance Career Channel** at www.vault.com/europe for insider firm profiles, employee surveys of finance professionals in Europe, message boards, job listings, expert finance career advice, insider salary information and more.

VAULT CAREER LIBRARY   27

factors: corporate partnerships, out-of-favour or underappreciated industries (past investments have included cable television, refining and automotive parts), value-oriented companies and active portfolio management.

Blackstone invests in transactions throughout the globe with investment levels between $250 million and $1.25 billion. Current holdings include such diverse companies as Celanese, CineWorld, Equity Office Properties, FGIC, Freedom Communications, Freescale, Graham Packaging, HealthMarkets, Orangina, SunGard, Travelport, TRW Automotive, TDC, United Biscuits, Universal Orlando, Vanguard Health Systems and VNU. Corporate partnerships account for approximately one-third of the equity capital invested by Blackstone. Corporate partners have included companies such as Time Warner, AT&T, Sony, Union Carbide, Union Pacific, USX and Vivendi.

Group by group

In addition to private equity, Blackstone contains eight other segments: real estate, corporate debt, marketable alternative investments, distressed security advisors, long/short equity, India/Asia closed-end mutual funds, corporate advisory services, and restructuring and reorganisation advisory services. The real estate group has grown assets under management from $3 billion to over $17 billion since 2002. The corporate debt group (BCD) handles over $9 billion of committed capital, investing in senior debt, subordinated debt, preferred stock and common equity. These investments are typically long-term-oriented, focused on assets with strong fundamentals and sustainable competitive advantages.

The marketable alternative investments group (Blackstone Alternative Asset Management — or BAAM) is Blackstone's funds of hedge funds division. This group, which was initially used to manage Blackstone's internal investments, is now open to clients. BAAM has become a leading fund of hedge funds, with more than $19 billion under management, and more than 90 per cent of BAAM's assets come from institutional investors. The newly formed long/short equity investment group, which was formed in 2006, invests primarily in long and short equity investments, using a research-driven approach to capitalise on mis-priced or misunderstood securities. The distressed debt group invests in the debt of financially distressed companies.

All around the world

Blackstone advisors are behind an increasing number of high-stakes mergers and acquisitions around the globe, having handled transactions worth more than $450 billion. The corporate advisory services division of Blackstone advises clients on challenging transactions ranging from distressed M&A to executive financings and fairness opinions. Clients have included AIG, Merck, Reuters, Sony, Suez, Verizon and the state of New York.

VAULTCAREER LIBRARY

Under its restructuring and reorganisation advisory services, Blackstone has participated in some of the largest restructurings in history, including Delta Airlines, Enron, Macy's, Transworld Airlines, Williams Communications and Xerox.

European biscuits

As the result of both increased opportunities in Europe and a desire to build a larger global presence, Blackstone has been increasing its European investments and expanding its European offices. In August of 2000, Blackstone created The Blackstone Group International, to be the centre of the firm's European operations. One of the firm's recent European deals was the 2006 purchase (with private equity firm PAI partners) of United Biscuits, a leading manufacturer and marketer of biscuits in the UK, for a price in excess of £1.6 billion ($3.1 billion).

Currently five business units operate in Europe: private equity investing, real estate investing, corporate debt, marketable alternative asset investing (BAAM) and corporate advisory services. Blackstone's European head office is located at Berkeley Square in London and boasts more than 120 employees, including roughly 60 professional staff. Blackstone's Hamburg office primarily handles private equity investments in German-speaking countries and Scandinavia. The French arm of Blackstone, located in Paris, only handles real estate investments at present.

GETTING HIRED

Fore more information about current vacancies, graduate opportunities and careers at Blackstone, check out the careers section of the company's web site at www.blackstone.com.

Visit **Vault Europe's Finance Career Channel** at **www.vault.com/europe** for insider firm profiles, employee surveys of finance professionals in Europe, message boards, job listings, expert finance career advice, insider salary information and more.

VAULT CAREER LIBRARY

29

VAULT 4 PRESTIGE RANKING

JPMorgan Investment Bank

10 Aldermanbury
London EC2V 7RF
United Kingdom
Phone: +44 (0) 207 742 4000
Fax : +44 (0) 207 325 8195
www.jpmorgan.com

EUROPEAN LOCATIONS

London (European HQ)
Belgium • Czech Republic • France
• Germany • Greece • Italy •
Netherlands • Portugal • Russia •
South Africa • Spain • Switzerland
• Turkey • United Kingdom

BUSINESSES

Advisory (M&A and Restructuring)
Debt & Equity Underwriting
Institutional Equities
Market Making
Trading & Investing
Research

THE STATS

Employer Type: Subsidiary of
JPMorgan Chase & Co. NYSE: JPM
Chairman & CEO: Jamie Dimon
2006 Net Revenue: $61.437 billion
(FYE 12/06)
2005 Net Revenue: $54.5 billion
(FYE 12/05)
Investment Bank 2006 Net Revenue:
$18,227 million (FYE 12/06)
Investment Bank 2005 Net Revenue:
$14, 613 million (FYE 12/05)
2006 Employees: 174, 360
(FYE 12/06)
No. of Offices: Offices in more than
100 countries globally

KEY COMPETITORS

Barclays Capital • Citigroup •
Deutsche Bank • Goldman Sachs •
Lehman • Merrill Lynch • Morgan
Stanley • UBS

PLUSES

• "Smart and genuine people"
• "Team spirit is outstanding"

MINUSES

• "Bureaucracy leads to
unpredictability of work flow"
• "Low turnover brings some
staleness"

EMPLOYMENT CONTACT

www.jpmorgan.com/careers
Click on "Careers" link

THE BUZZ
WHAT EMPLOYEES AT OTHER FIRMS ARE SAYING

• "Good benefits"
• "Elitist"
• "Sorting itself out well"
• "Too large"

30   V/\ULT CAREER LIBRARY   © 2007 Vault, Inc.

THE SCOOP

Growth of an empire

New York-based JPMorgan Chase & Co, a leading global financial services firm, has assets of more than $1.4 trillion and more than 170,000 employees in 100 countries around the world. JPMorgan Investment Bank serves more than 8,000 issuer and 16,400 investor clients globally.

The international banking powerhouse known as JPMorgan Investment Bank is a subsidiary of JPMorgan Chase & Co, with offices in most European countries. It also encompasses JPMorgan Cazenove, a joint venture that created one of the UK's heavyweight investment banks.

The JPMorgan brand encompasses six key business areas: investment banking, worldwide securities services, private banking, asset management, One Equity Partners and private client services. As a diversified financial services firm, JPMorgan serves the interests of clients who have complex financial needs such as corporations, governments, private firms, financial institutions, non-profit organisations, wealthy individuals and institutional investors.

Smells like team spirit

The investment banking division at JPMorgan is divided by teams — industry, M&A and capital markets. Industry teams include consumer health care and retail, diversified industries and transportation, natural resources, financial institutions, metals and mining, real estate and technology, media and telecommunications.

The firm proudly holds "global leadership positions" in the industry for all of its key product offerings such as M&A advisory, capital raising, restructuring, risk management and research. The firm deals in proprietary trading and investing, as well as "market-making in cash securities and derivative instruments around the world".

Continental Europe

JPMorgan Investment Bank has operations in Belgium, Czech Republic, France, Germany, Italy, Netherlands, Portugal, Russia, Spain, Switzerland, Turkey and Greece, as well as the UK. According to Thomson Financial, JPMorgan Investment Bank has an impressive leadership position in the European market, and is currently ranked in the year to date as No.1 in both EMEA Common Stock and Equity and Equity-related, as well as No. 2 in EMEA M&A Announced and No. 3 in EMEA IPOs. The firm also has a Middle Eastern presence with offices in Bahrain, Dubai, Saudi Arabia, Uzbekistan and Israel.

Visit **Vault Europe's Finance Career Channel** at www.vault.com/europe for insider firm profiles, employee surveys of finance professionals in Europe, message boards, job listings, expert finance career advice, insider salary information and more.

VAULT CAREER LIBRARY   31

Winning ways and celebrity mergers

In 2006, the bank's merger mania included some high-profile transactions. It advised Arcelor on its defence against Mittal Steel's $43.6 billion hostile takeover attempt, represented Endesa on its defence against bids from both E.ON AG and Enel and advised Suez on its $110 billion merger with Gaz de France.

The JPMorgan legacy is illustrated well by a number of prestigious industry awards it has received. IFR named JPMorgan the Best European Equity House as well as the Interest Rate and Commodities Derivatives House of the Year. *Euromoney* called it the Best Equity-Linked House and the Best Leveraged Finance House of 2006 and the Credit 2006 European Awards ranked JPMorgan Best in Credit, Best Structured Credit House, Best in Credit Derivatives and Best Trade Ideas in Research. The bank also won workplace kudos — in fall 2006, *BusinessWeek* called JPMorgan Investment Bank one of the Top 10 Best Places to Launch a Career and the *Times of London* hailed JPMorgan as one of the UK's Top 50 companies Where Women Want to Work.

At Credit's 2006 European Awards, JPMorgan Investment Bank scored four wins, namely Best in Credit, Best Structured Credit House, Best in Credit Derivatives and Best Trade Ideas in Research. Other recent awards for JPMorgan Investment Bank in Europe include No. 1 in the 2006 Institutional Investor European Fixed Income survey, for the fourth consecutive year, as well as No. 1 Emerging Markets Strategy in the US and Europe. Also in the 2006 Global Investor survey, the bank won No. 2 overall and No. 1 in EMEA and Asia in the annual FX Survey.

JPMorgan was ranked No. 1 in Institutional Investor's 2007 All-Europe Fixed-Income Research Survey. Anther award the firm won in 2006 is Euroweek's EMEA Sovereign Bond of the Year.

GETTING HIRED

Discerning taste

JPMorgan is considered very discerning and insiders maintain that the company goes out of its way to find the right candidates. One analyst says, "The best and brightest come in many shapes and forms, and our recruiting strategy reflects our desire to draw from the broadest possible pool of talent with a passion to exceed and work together in a spirit of partnership."

The interview process is described as "gruelling" and "rigorous." An associate says, "[The firm] tests everything from analytics to teamwork, and professionalism and communication skills are crucial." Another adds, "Candidates are reviewed and tested in multiple rounds by members of different business areas. Finally, senior management judges applicants during an assessment day." A vice president notes, "In my experience, only a fraction of the candidates in the final round assessment centres are given offers."

You've got the right stuff

An internship is, as always, a good way to land a job, but as one source says, "Many employees cite the internship as a key advantage in getting a full-time position but it is far from a sure thing." A first-year analyst says, "It is the review process completed by the members of the team you work with that counts the most."

Former interns speak highly of the program, explaining the internship work is quite involved, allowing interns to gain actual hands-on experience. One insider says, "We worked on marketing projects, helping to generate new ideas for clients, and helped with research and valuation assignments. Interns have the opportunity to work on live deals and often meet with clients from the start, quickly earning big responsibility. You learn a tremendous amount and it is a very realistic work experience for students."

And, considering day-to-day business involves working with clients and colleagues across Europe, speaking a second European language, while not necessary, is clearly an advantage.

OUR SURVEY SAYS

Where everybody knows your name

The firm culture is described as "extremely international and very relaxed" where "people are not expected to fit a mould." Overall, one associate says, "[The culture] makes for an open, productive work environment where most seem to be comfortable and happy. It also enhances creativity." An insider says the firm is "very teamwork focused", adding, "While every firm says this, the tenure of people h.ere shows genuine respect for your colleagues. [There are] remarkably few arrogant people or ego issues here for an investment bank."

An analyst notes, "For me the culture is about being around exceptional individuals with talent and passion for what they do. "'Work hard, play hard' is a common theme and taking lunch in the sun with a group is done regularly." One vice president adds, "Teamwork is at the heart of our culture. We play as a team both in times of success and failure. People work hard and are hugely driven as in any top-tier investment bank, but I have always felt that people respect each other and each other's time here, no matter what level of seniority. I have never experienced the concept of face time and I have always felt comfortable

Visit **Vault Europe's Finance Career Channel** at **www.vault.com/europe** for insider firm profiles, employee surveys of finance professionals in Europe, message boards, job listings, expert finance career advice, insider salary information and more.

VAULT CAREER LIBRARY

33

approaching even the most senior professionals. I think the people are ultimately the key competitive strength of [the firm]."

Tick, tick, tick

Long hours aren't highly regarded but are widely held as comparable to the industry norm. An insider says, "There is pressure to get the work done — not to be in the office per se. Because we work in teams, you can't operate remotely for long. My work hours are not massively different from those of my best clients, albeit more unpredictable. Hours are not used as an input into compensation or promotion decisions."

Love your boss

The management at JPMorgan is very highly rated. One longtime insider says, "I have had the same boss for 13 years and in that time I could have moved to any bank on the street. The reason I don't is because I still learn every day from my direct manager." A second-year analyst notes, "Managers are often very busy, so 'proactiveness' is required on behalf of team members to gain some of their time. However, this is generally given willingly when requested. Work distribution, in my experience, has been good and they are also keen to get juniors involved in all areas of the job as soon as possible."

One insider describes the firm's management as having great humility. He is impressed with how greatly management takes into consideration that there is life outside of work, saying, "At the end of the day we are all people with our own moments of happiness or sadness, when our private lives dominate our thoughts during our working days. The bank has been very accommodating to me and I have attempted to replicate that towards my own teams."

Food and shelter

Sources say that JPMorgan's London office's location and building is satisfactory. One analyst describes it as "fine but nothing luxurious" adding that it's "an open space, so there isn't a lot of privacy, but is better to ask questions and create a good atmosphere." Another associate in London says, "The trading floor is suboptimal with respect to temperature and availability of space, but not to a point where it hinders work." And for anyone concerned with food options, a contact discloses that the London office building has "two coffee shops, a canteen and a refreshment trolley service."

Look smart, be smart

The dress code, according to one insider, is "totally flexible". He says, "Most people are casual but ready to be smart quickly since you can't plan on when you have client meetings." An analyst discloses that staff can "dress down" on Fridays. To that, he adds, "Myself and the majority stick to a suit [with] no tie. Comfortable." Another analyst says the working wardrobe "varies hugely across the bank by business area. In my department the code is very smart/casual — or mixed as suits and ties are worn by some people and shirts without ties by others. But certainly no jeans nor chinos — [it is] always smart for client contact."

University of IB

Training at the firm is constant, strongly encouraged and described as "second to none." An analyst says, "Training is excellent and on offer all the time, although with the commitments at the desk it is not easy to get along to the sessions as often as one would like."

The firm's in-house training is dubbed "IB University" but "is not as formal as it sounds and involves hour-long sessions on a regular basis with, usually, senior bankers teaching a specific topic." One associate says, "[The courses] span technical, professional and management skills. These core courses are designed to match the stage of development and experience of the individual." An analyst notes, "As a graduate to IB you spend eight weeks on a specific training scheme in New York, after which training is ongoing at all levels."

In addition, JPMorgan provides its first-year analysts and trainees with a rotation scheme that is a tremendous opportunity to learn the tricks of the trade. An analyst says, "The graduate rotation scheme offered within my department has full support from senior management and allowed excellent personal development during my first three years at the firm."

Everybody welcome

Diversity across the board — gender, ethnic and sexual orientation — is given high priority throughout the firm. An insider says, "We are making a huge effort in this area and we also follow up with mentoring for our women to ensure they are given maximum support to be successful." A female analyst notes the firm has held "panel discussion events, training events and [offered] much support from senior management". Although she adds, "It is acknowledged the bank still has a way to go at the senior level as women remain underrepresented here."

Another insider points to the firm's Winning Women Event, explaining that JPMorgan hosts a two-day graduate event at its London office "for undergraduate women of all degree disciplines to learn about the industry, network and job shadowing our employees."

A contact adds, "[There is] an ethnic minority-specific mentoring program at the school level and a networking group for employees within the firm. However, the bank could still

Visit **Vault Europe's Finance Career Channel** at **www.vault.com/europe** for insider firm profiles, employee surveys of finance professionals in Europe, message boards, job listings, expert finance career advice, insider salary information and more.

VAULT CAREER LIBRARY **35**

do with seeing more numbers actually within the firm." One associate is quite impressed with the level of cultural diversity at the firm, saying, "In my old team we had 11 different nationalities in a group of 22, while in my new team we have five different nationalities in a group of five."

Sexual orientation does not influence treatment by managers, explain sources. One analyst says, "I know of a number of gay and lesbian members in my department and have seen no difference whatsoever in their treatment or development. There is a LGBT (lesbian, gay, bisexual and transgendered) networking group within the firm that is widely and openly advertised."

Minor hurdles

Budget cuts are hardly pleasant for anyone and an insider says, "some degree of cost-cutting 'from the top' has reduced funds for social events and caused the closure of the gym within the London office." However, following feedback from London staff, the gym, which had been closed last year, will be reopening in summer 2007, says a JPMorgan official.

While respondents admit that dealing with bureaucracy is just part of working at "a large firm", they do raise the point that it can contribute to the unpredictability of work flow. Nevertheless, perhaps some enjoy working at JPMorgan too much, as a newer hire explains that a low turnover of staff is perhaps a reason that staffers may not be able to move up as quickly as at other firms. He says, "There has been incredible staff tenure and low turnover at some levels. This is overall great, but maybe also brings some staleness into the way we operate at times."

Pleased as punch

When it all boils down, JPMorgan sources at all levels are very satisfied with the firm. As one insider puts it, "Great idea generation and technical skill levels make it rewarding and fun to work here." A vice president says, "It has been a fantastic experience for me during my six years here. I feel I have developed enormously by working in a place with so many talented and committed individuals, and I have had exposure to projects and people that I don't think I would have had in any other job at this age. It's been hard work, but not once have I had difficulties going to the office in the morning and not once have I felt bored."

Many sources say the people they work with are the best part of the firm. An insider notes, "When I compare my colleagues to those at competitor firms, I genuinely believe that we have a unique combination of people who are both smart and genuine rather than arrogant." The positive environment at the firm is highly regarded and mentioned by most JPMorgan respondents, who all say that the team spirit is outstanding. They add that there is a great diversity of team members and most insiders enjoy the intellectual atmosphere and working alongside highly-educated peers.

Visit **Vault Europe's Finance Career Channel** at **www.vault.com/europe** for insider firm profiles, employee surveys of finance professionals in Europe, message boards, job listings, expert finance career advice, insider salary information and more.

VAULT   CAREER
         LIBRARY   **37**

UBS Global Headquarters
Bahnhofstrasse. 45
P.O. Box CH-8098
Zurich Switzerland
Phone: +41 (0) 11 234 11 11
www.ubs.com

EUROPEAN LOCATIONS

Zurich, Switzerland (Global HQ)
London, UK (IB HQ)
Locations in Austria • Belgium •
Channel Islands • Cyprus • Czech
Republic • France • Germany •
Greece • Ireland • Italy •
Luxembourg • Monaco •
Netherlands • Poland • Portugal •
Russia • Spain • Sweden •
Switzerland and Turkey.

DEPARTMENTS

Global Wealth Management &
Business Banking • Global Asset
Management • Investment Bank
(Equities, Finance, Fixed Income &
Money Markets, Currencies &
Commodities, Global Asset
Management, Investment Banking
Department, Legal and
Compliance)

THE BUZZ
WHAT EMPLOYEES AT OTHER FIRMS ARE SAYING

• "High prestige and good
atmosphere"
• "Less overall cohesion than some
competitors"
• "Solid shop"
• "Not sure what direction it's
heading in"

THE STATS

Employer Type: Public Company
Ticker Symbol: UBS (NYSE, VTX)
Group CEO: Peter Wuffli
Investment Bank Chairman & CEO:
Huw Jenkins
2006 Net Profit: CHF 11.2 billion
(FYE 12/06)
2005 Net Profit: CHF 9.4 billion
(FYE 12/05)
2007 Employees: 80,000+
No. of Offices: Offices in more than
50 countries

PLUSES

• Supportive managers and a "social,
participative environment"
• Environmentally conscious and
proactive

MINUSES

• "Below street average"
compensation
• Lots of bureaucracy

EMPLOYMENT CONTACT

www.ubs.com/careers

THE SCOOP

Swiss giant

As an integrated and leading global financial firm, UBS creates added value for clients by drawing on the combined resources and expertise of all its businesses. UBS is a leading global wealth manager, a global investment banking and securities firm with a strong institutional and corporate client franchise and a key asset manager. The Swiss giant holds roughly a quarter of the Swiss lending market and is the market leader in Swiss corporate and individual client banking.

Globally, UBS employs more than 80,000 people. With headquarters in Zurich and Basel, Switzerland, UBS operates in over 50 countries and from all major international centres. UBS IB has three front-office business areas — investment banking; equities and fixed income, which includes money markets, currencies and commodities. It serves corporate, institutional, government and private clients worldwide, offering securities and commodities sales and trading, underwriting, mergers and acquisitions advice, debt and equity capital advice, research, risk management and a variety of foreign exchange transactions. It also provides access to a number of private equity and hedge funds.

UBS traces its roots to the early days of Swiss financing when a series of mergers, acquisitions and name changes brought a number of Swiss banks together as the Union Bank of Switzerland and the Swiss Bank Corporation. These entities merged in 1998 to form UBS AG, and in 2000, the reborn bank acquired a securities arm by purchasing New York-based PaineWebber. A rebranding effort in 2003 brought all of UBS' activities under one streamlined umbrella.

Sweet image

According to an August 2006 survey by *BusinessWeek* and global marketing and branding giant Interbrand, UBS's goal of creating a stronger brand is working. The bank's brand was valued at $8.7 billion in the 2006 survey, making UBS No. 42 in the list of most valuable global brands. UBS' first appearance on the list was in 2004 — at No. 45. "You & Us" — the firm's official tagline — was created to embody a single UBS brand identity around the world.

Who's the boss?

In August 2006, Jeremy Palmer, former head of UBS Wealth Management UK, was named CEO of the investment bank in the EMEA region. He replaced Robert Gillespie, who became vice chairman of the investment bank. Palmer, who reports to investment bank Chairman and Chief Executive Huw Jenkins, was charged with expanding UBS' presence in emerging EMEA markets as well as working to integrate the investment bank with UBS' other

Visit **Vault** Europe's Finance Career Channel at **www.vault.com/europe** for insider firm profiles, employee surveys of finance professionals in Europe, message boards, job listings, expert finance career advice, insider salary information and more.

VAULT CAREER LIBRARY

39

businesses. Meanwhile, Matthew Brumsen, former leader of UBS business sectors in the UK, became the new head of UBS Wealth Management for the UK and Northern and Eastern Europe.

The newsmakers

In January 2007, UBS announced its partnership with Bloomberg, the financial news service, in launching a global commodity index published in both dollars and euros. Through the UBS Bloomberg Constant Maturity Commodity Index, investors will be able to scan and diversify their investments in global commodities by viewing the up-to-date economic commodity environment which has been designed to be a global benchmark for investment in the sector. The new index has thus become a basis for a range of investment products offered by UBS, further strengthening the Swiss giant's product offering and international growth.

The Eco-bank

In April 2007, the FT reported that UBS launched the world's first "Global Warming index", initially based on 15 major US cities. The FT reported that the index would allow businesses "most affected by the uncertainty of climate change — from ice-cream salesmen to makers of winter coats — to hedge their profits against it in a simple and transparent fashion. Retail and institutional investors will also be able to buy exposure to, or short sell, the index in much the same way they would with the FTSE or Dow Jones stock indices. If temperatures rise, so will the value of the index."

Trading toward clean air

In November 2006, UBS unveiled the UBS World Emissions Index (UBS-WEMI), the first index for global emissions allowances markets. The index takes advantage of the rules implemented by the Kyoto Protocol, which 165 countries ratified in August 2006. Under these rules, industries that can easily reduce their emissions to regulatory levels can sell their unused emissions permits to other industries that need them. At its launch, UBS-WEMI covered several European emissions trading platforms, all of which are part of the European Emissions Trading Scheme — an early implementation of the Kyoto Protocols.

Business and community awards

At the end of 2006, UBS was named European Banking & Financial Institutions House of the Year at the Financial News European Awards for Excellence in Investment Banking. A month earlier, *Euromoney* had named UBS Best Bank for Debt Capital Market transactions in its real estate awards division. But UBS didn't just win awards for the way it did business — in October 2006 the bank won its fifth Dragon Award from the Lord Mayor of London, recognition of the firm's corporate community involvement in greater London.

GETTING HIRED

Crème de la crème

UBS seeks out the best candidates from the top European schools and conducts a comprehensive screening process that initially consists of an online application and test, followed by interviews and an assessment centre. Information about careers and graduate opportunities at the firm can be found on the company's web site at www.ubs.com/careers.

"We look for the best talent in experienced hires or graduate hires, but for all levels it's about potential and attitude as much as it is about existing achievements," explains one insider involved in recruiting. Besides doing well on the logical and numerical reasoning tests and interviews, being multilingual also helps candidates get the inside track; most new hires are fluent in more than one language.

That crucial internship

But the biggest advantage is definitely an internship. More than a quarter of UBS respondents who participated in the survey did internships and agreed that is what gave them the edge. Besides having a chance to impress potential supervisors, interns are paid about £500 a week. Many were hired by the departments in which they interned, and all of them seem to enjoy the programme. One recent hire explains, "I was given a variety of very engaging work, including modeling, sector analysis and deal coordination. It made it easier to be hired for a full-time position as it provides a greater opportunity to demonstrate your strengths than a short interview and case study."

Internships can also allow applicants who might not have scored the highest on the tests to shine. "The internship is what really got me hired, as it allowed the team to assess me on the job rather than on tests where I probably didn't have the best scores of all," tells one former participant. In fact, former interns seem to agree that they were given a fair amount of freedom and that staff was open to their suggestions.

An intern can expect to shadow various team members to learn and eventually take on some of their routines. Duties include helping with day-to-day work as well as special projects. The programme also includes networking events, such as sports days and events with senior directors, along with internal training courses and breakfast meetings presented by senior managers that explain their department's function within the firm. These meetings also cover global asset management and wealth management in order to educate investment bank interns about all areas of business at UBS and thus show them career path options at the firm. The internship's length varies by department, but usually lasts about ten weeks.

Visit **Vault Europe's Finance Career Channel** at www.vault.com/europe for insider firm profiles, employee surveys of finance professionals in Europe, message boards, job listings, expert finance career advice, insider salary information and more.

VAULT CAREER LIBRARY 41

OUR SURVEY SAYS

Team players

UBS sources describe their company as collegiate, meritocratic, professional and supportive. "You are given the opportunity to interact with clients at a very early stage and are offered more challenging opportunities based on your own merits. I have never in my time with the firm sought advice and not received it. People genuinely take time to further others' development," says one second-year analyst. UBS focuses on teamwork and results, but still manages to be a "social, participative environment which, although productive, is not solely results driven. Senior staffers interact with team members and new joiners regularly and act as a support mechanism."

Cool compensation

Insiders praise the bank's compensation package, including added perks such as discounts with gyms and stores. Sources say bonuses are a bit lower than at other firms, but UBS staffers receive Valueflex, an extra 15 per cent of base salary that they can invest in pension/private dental and medical insurance/life insurance or take as cash or additional holiday time. Staffers can also invest a proportion of their salary in UBS shares and receive two free 10-year stock options for each share purchased in this way.

The Valueflex scheme that offers various customised benefits, extra holiday, life/travel/dental insurance and car parking at "very good" rates that can be bought depending on the staffer's circumstances. Other perks such as discounts on home PCs, meals and taxis when working on weekends and after 9 p.m. are also available. Subsidised lunches, free fruit, coffee and tea, as well as gym and public transportation discounts are also perks. The most common complaint is that UBS doesn't have the prestige of other investment banks and offers "below street average" compensation, especially for junior employees. A new hire in debt capital markets (DCM) sees an "occasional inferiority complex," but acknowledges that "this is dissipating".

Putting in the time

Sources in most divisions claim to work between 50 and 60 hours a week, but rarely on weekends. The exception lies in banking, as corporate finance colleagues say they're putting in more hours — between 80 to 90 hours per week — as well as frequent weekends. One young go-getter says there are "many hours of work and very few weekends available," to which he adds, if you cannot live with that, you probably should not work in investment banking." Another junior investment banker reports, "The number of hours required to be in the office are excessive, even for investment banking, although mainly due to my team. Other teams do not work as much, especially on weekends. I rarely have more than one day off a week."

Bureaucratic mess

Clearly bureaucracy is a reality at any large organisation, but UBS sources say the daunting size of the firm and its bureaucracy and procedures make things run slowly. One points out that the largesse of the firm "makes it difficult to see where and how you can progress." However, a positive co-worker offers a counter-perspective, explaining, "Because we take our time to make decisions, we can sometimes be less nimble than other smaller firms. However, this has its upside in our loyalty to existing employees and commitment to strategy once in place."

Sources remind prospective hires to be prepared to work long hours and weekends if you want to work in corporate finance. Financial gain is a fantastic incentive, but if you like sleeping in on Saturdays or spending all your weekends skiing, golfing and spending your hard-earned cash, think again — working on the weekend is common. As one junior financier relates, "I would say that the only downside is the working hours and the disrespect that senior staff have of weekend and spare time in general — [it's a] cause and effect scenario."

Supportive management

Unlike a lot of firms where often bosses can be "too busy" for their own staff, UBS staff is happy overall with their managers, and praise the "flat hierarchical structure." Amusingly, however, one newly-hired credit analyst quips, "Most people are very nice, but it takes only one guy to ruin your time at work." But most staffers say the management is fairly friendly and supportive.

Another new hire tells us, "I have been given the opportunity to take on challenging work, but am given the support needed when asked for. Managers are always friendly and genuinely concerned by employees being overworked or badly treated. I have a great relationship with my manager, who I feel I can always go to for advice. Similarly, subordinates are seen as people, not resources." In addition, UBS has a "360" evaluation programme in which employees are evaluated by their supervisors, peers and subordinates to make sure junior employees are treated well and have their opinions taken into account.

The office dress code

Not surprisingly, investment banking boasts a suit and tie culture — so anything else would be considered a bit, well, unusual. By and large, the dress is "smart" casual, except for meetings with clients, and jeans are allowed on Fridays. One corporate finance insider reports, "In my department, it is easy to be called away for client meetings at the last second. As such, formal dress is required for the vast majority of the time, despite a business casual policy." As for office aesthetics, while it may be a banking powerhouse,

Visit **Vault Europe's Finance Career Channel** at **www.vault.com/europe** for insider firm profiles, employee surveys of finance professionals in Europe, message boards, job listings, expert finance career advice, insider salary information and more.

VAULT CAREER LIBRARY 43

UBS quarters aren't particularly posh, which could be due to renovation. "Clean, tidy and efficient" is how one staffer lukewarmly describes the functional digs.

Getting in shape

UBS values training, and both junior and senior sources give their training programmes top marks. Regularly structured training programs are de rigueur for all staff, so would-be slackers should be forewarned that attendance is not optional. Training for most new hires is either held in Zurich or London. Besides internal training, the firm also encourages its employees to get advanced degrees, depending on business need. "My firm invests a lot in initial and continuous training of its employees," divulges one new hire in research. "Since I started in September, I have had an internal graduate training program, and I have been enrolled and already completed the Level 1 of the CFA programme and am currently studying for the Level 2 — all at the expense of my employer."

There are weekly seminars for new hires to get them up to speed. "The format of the graduate training program for my entire intake was a little dull, but most of the basics we learned were useful," we're told. Most UBS respondents praise the training opportunities, but some lament the lack of free time available to take advantage of the full spread. This year will see the launch of a new two-year structured training programme for graduates.

All for one

UBS has made a noteworthy effort in promoting women and overall diversity, and the firm prides itself on having a respectful working culture that values the contribution of individuals. They run a series of networks that offer seminars and networking events. A female insider explains, "There is a great culture where men and women alike are treated as a person, not as a gender. I have been managed by women in both of the teams I have worked in." She adds, "Men have historically dominated investment banking, but there are an increasing number of women in top positions, although some say not enough, as women are becoming junior directors, yet there are fewer female senior directors."

With regard to minorities, one staffer observes, "It is often rare to have two people of the same nationality at any bank of desks." Another explains, "My employer is involved in a lot of programs aimed at increasing ethnic minority representation within investment. I am a beneficiary of such initiatives."

One happy family

Insiders say that culture at UBS is on the very functional side, and staff members seem to like their colleagues, the firm's diversity and, most importantly, their bosses. A new Italy-based contact in corporate finance says, "Compared with US bankers and stories I have heard, seniors treat juniors much nicer here." And praise for the positive management and team spirit at the firm transcends locations. A new staffer in research in London boasts that UBS is "very committed to its employees" adding that, "I sense a lot of effort on the part of my management to make the place of work as happy as possible for all employees."

Sources also state that UBS doesn't have the pressure-cooker environment of other firms. A senior sales staffer describes the firm's environment as being "relatively relaxed and un-pressured, despite high standards," and adds that, "People are expected to perform without having to be bullied into it."

Additionally, UBS co-workers praise the sense of cooperation and teamwork at the firm: "[There is] really a spirit of teamwork and collaboration." One contact describes the spirit among employees as being "competitive, but not cutthroat." Other sources praise their work/life balance, and one simply states, "By far the best thing is the culture."

Perhaps the showering of praise UBS respondents have bestowed upon the firm is best summed up by one, rather proud, human resources source who praises "the talent, respect, warmth and energy of the people" he is in contact with on a daily basis at the firm at his office and at others around the world.

Visit **Vault Europe's Finance Career Channel** at www.vault.com/europe for insider firm profiles, employee surveys of finance professionals in Europe, message boards, job listings, expert finance career advice, insider salary information and more.

VAULT CAREER LIBRARY 45

Merrill Lynch

Merrill Lynch Financial Centre
2 King Edward Street
London, EC1A 1HQ
United Kingdom
Phone: +44 (0) 20 7743 4457
Fax: +44 (0) 20 7743 1048
www.ml.com

EUROPEAN LOCATIONS

London (European HQ)
France • Germany • Ireland •
Italy • Luxembourg • Monaco •
Netherlands • Poland • Portugal •
Spain • Switzerland • Turkey • UK

DEPARTMENTS

Global Markets & Investment
Banking
Global Private Client

STATS

Employer Type: Public Company
Ticker Symbol: MER (NYSE)
Chairman, President & CEO: E. Stanley
O'Neal
2005 Revenue: $26.01 billion
(FYE 12/05)
2006 Revenue: $34.7 billion
(FYE 12/06)
2006 Employees: 55,300 (Worldwide)
No. of Offices: 900 (Worldwide)

KEY COMPETITORS:

- Citigroup Global Markets
- Goldman Sachs
- Morgan Stanley

PLUSES

- "Opportunities to work on several desks"
- "Team-oriented, accepting and tolerant"

MINUSES

- "A weak face time culture"
- "Things are not always moving as fast as they should."

EMPLOYMENT CONTACT

www.ml.com (Click on "careers" link)

THE BUZZ
WHAT EMPLOYEES AT OTHER FIRMS ARE SAYING

- "Much improved performer"
- "Bulge bracket firm with strong reputation"
- "Very American culture"
- "Has lost so much reputation"

Friends and founders

One of the world's biggest financial services firms, Merrill Lynch is divided into two core businesses: global markets and investment banking (GMI) and global private client (GPC). GMI provides institutional sales and trading, advisory and capital raising services to corporations, governments and institutions. Businesses within GMI include global markets, investment banking, global private equity and global leveraged finance. GPC, Merrill's second arm, offers wealth management services and products to individuals and businesses.

Charles E. Merrill arrived in New York City in 1907 and took a job at a textile company. He met Edmund C. Lynch in Manhattan at the 23rd Street YMCA — Lynch needed a roommate. The pair became fast friends, and Merrill went on to work in investment companies, finally opening his own firm in 1914. Lynch soon joined his comrade at the office and the firm was rechristened Merrill, Lynch & Co. in 1915. According to their contemporaries, they were a perfect match — Merrill liked to dream of what could be, and Lynch liked to dwell on what might go wrong. Decades after its founders' deaths and despite several mergers, Merrill Lynch continues to carry the two men's names into the frontlines of finance.

A prized Rock

In 2006, Merrill closed a massive deal with investment firm BlackRock. Under the terms of the agreement, Merrill Lynch Investment Managers (MLIM) merged with BlackRock to create one of the world's largest asset management firms, with nearly $1 trillion in assets under management. The sale of MLIM freed up a reported $2 billion in capital for Merrill Lynch, and Chief Executive Stan O'Neal indicated that these funds could be put toward principal investments and propping up trading activities. At present, trading accounts for close to 45 per cent of Merrill's revenue whereas at rival firm Goldman Sachs, that figure is more than 60 per cent. In October 2006, shortly before the BlackRock deal closed, Merrill also bought a minority stake in DiMaio Ahmad Capital, a hedge fund, and committed proprietary capital to several of that firm's funds.

The things they win

Merrill's GMI business won top awards in 2006, including three *Euromoney* citations: Global Investment Bank of the Year, Best CDO House and Best Equity House in India. The magazine described the banking powerhouse as "a force to be reckoned with in investment banking". Merrill also topped SmartMoney's 2006 Full-Service Broker Rankings, and in October, when Bloomberg unveiled a new ranking system that measured how well analysts picked — or didn't pick — stocks, Merrill took first place. Its analysts made 68 "winning calls" during 2006. Merrill also had something to celebrate at *EuroWeek* magazine's 2006 Celebration of Excellence Awards, picking up prizes in Financial Institutions, US High Grade Corporates, US Hybrid Bonds, Non-Core Currencies and Asian G3 Currency Bonds.

Visit **Vault Europe's Finance Career Channel** at www.vault.com/europe for insider firm profiles, employee surveys of finance professionals in Europe, message boards, job listings, expert finance career advice, insider salary information and more.

V/\ULT CAREER LIBRARY

47

Let's grow

In October 2006, Merrill announced that it would acquire niche investment bank Petrie Parkman & Company, a boutique mergers and acquisitions firm with offices in London, Denver and Houston. That month, Merrill also poached four BNP Paribas executives, giving them top spots in London and New York and charging them with boosting the firm's global metals trading business.

The great Exchange

Merrill Lynch, along with Citigroup, Credit Suisse, Deutsche Bank, Goldman Sachs, Morgan Stanley and UBS, is part of a consortium to build a high-speed European trading platform to rival the London Stock Exchange, Euronext and Deutsche Börse. The plan, revealed in November 2006, will allow each bank to hold shares and participate on the board of the new exchange. In December 2006, Merrill de-listed itself from NYSE Arca, formerly the Pacific Exchange, saying the move would cut administrative costs and duplications following the NYSE Group's merger with Archipelago Holdings, the parent company of NYSE Arca.

Megadeals for Merrill

Merrill Lynch is taking centre stage in what is, as of press time, reportedly the largest leveraged buyout ever: Blackstone Group's $36 billion acquisition of Equity Office Properties Trust. While Blackstone has a number of financial advisors on its side, including Goldman Sachs, Bear Stearns and Bank of America, Equity Office has just one — Merrill. The deal, announced in November 2006, was followed by the notice that Merrill and JPMorgan would co-advise Freeport-McMoRan Copper & Gold in its $25.9 billion purchase of rival Phelps Dodge.

December 2006 brought more deal news, as London daily newspaper *The Telegraph* reported that financier Guy Hands' private equity vehicle, Terra Firma Capital Partners, may be preparing a £800 million IPO or sale of Infinis, one of the largest renewable energy companies in Britain. Hands hired Merrill, along with Deutsche Bank and Climate Change Capital, to serve as advisors on the potential deal.

GETTING HIRED

Choosing wisely

Merrill Lynch is a fairly selective firm, due in part to the high number of applicants it receives. One analyst says, "Merrill Lynch is looking for [candidates with] good grades, international experience and open-minded character." Another says there are "multiple rounds of interviews by various people at different levels to test the [candidate's] understanding, knowledge and communication skills." Other important aspects of each candidate taken into consideration during the interviewing process are "the personality of the individual and the way [they] carry [themselves] and express their thoughts."

Although internships are not critical to landing a job here, as with most firms, an internship at Merrill Lynch does increase the odds of getting a job offer. A first-year analyst shares, "The work is almost the same work as I am doing now [and] at the end I received the offer to join the firm full time." One contact reports that the workload mainly consisted of "data collecting, comps, profiling companies and preparing pitch books," adding, "But also, depending on the person I was working for, financial modeling." Another analyst describes the experience as "very enjoyable and rewarding. I was able to work on several desks, which enabled a more thorough understanding of the firm and all people were very helpful and approachable."

That said if you want to learn more about career opportunities at Merrill Lynch, including internships and graduate opportunities, visit the company's web site at www.ml.com and click on the "careers" link.

OUR SURVEY SAYS

Firm culture

Insiders say that Merrill Lynch compensates its staffers for its focus on hard work with a lot of recognition for that work. One source says that "although everyone is expected to contribute to the team's success, everybody is given trust-even if it makes the atmosphere seem slightly informal, such as little pressure on dress codes, ability to take a break at the gym or elsewhere if you feel that you need it, etc." Another analyst adds, "[Although it is] a competitive, hardworking, performance-based firm, it still is team-oriented, accepting and tolerant." Senior firm members contribute adequate time for the development of juniors at the desk, which one contact says is "very encouraging and helpful," adding that "responsibility comes pretty early after an [initial] period of evaluation."

Face time and money

Sources are generally satisfied with their compensation at Merrill Lynch. A first-year analyst's bonus will typically range from £8,000 to £45,000, while one third-year analyst boasts that he earned a whopping £80,000 bonus. As for benefits, an insider says, "The selection comprises a broad range of opportunities, including insurances, retail vouchers and child care schemes." Health and life insurance are also provided by the company, as well as an on-site gym with

Visit **Vault Europe's Finance Career Channel** at **www.vault.com/europe** for insider firm profiles, employee surveys of finance professionals in Europe, message boards, job listings, expert finance career advice, insider salary information and more.

VAULT CAREER LIBRARY

49

memberships from £25 per month. Car service is available after 9 p.m. and on weekends, and there are meal allowances if working through dinner or on weekends.

As with most investment banks, long days are not foreign territory at Merrill Lynch. This fact is accepted dutifully and any complaints from sources have been followed quickly with the qualifying statement, "That's how the industry works." One first-year analyst adds, "It's not entirely accepted to leave early as a junior when tasks are completed. There is also a weak face time culture, though I could imagine it [being] much worse."

Love your boss

Management is highly regarded at the firm, which no doubt stems from the company's positive culture, as described earlier. As one analyst puts it, "I feel that everyone is given the due respect, regardless of their age or rank in the hierarchy. There is little notice of titles or rank in the team and everyone works as a team." Another says, "The treatment by my superiors has been very encouraging and friendly. There was a lot of work in the initial phase, but also accompanied by patient explanations and help. Once they sensed my comfort level with the day-to-day work, there was a lot of responsibility given to me with very little supervision."

Dressed for success

The firm's London office is described as a modern building with great facilities and lots of light. One analyst proclaims it's "the best office in the city." Perhaps that's not an exaggerated claim, considering the premises boast a subsidised on-site gym, a restaurant, four onsite cafes and two snack bars that provide subsidised food. There is also an on-site medical centre. As for the dress code, it's determined largely by where you work in the firm and can fluctuate between formal and business casual. An analyst reports, "No ties are required unless there is client interaction."

Training and diversity

Training is given a high priority at Merrill Lynch, but many say they have a hard time finding the hours to dedicate. Still, many point to the "attractive" six-week training programme for recent graduates, held in New York City and Princeton, New Jersey, as a great learning opportunity. While sources at Merrill Lynch say diversity is a company priority, talent prevails and as one insider says, "Regardless of sex, if you are capable and smart, the firm will give you a chance to be hired. The hierarchies are pretty straightforward and there are women on all levels." Another insider notes: "Looking at the most senior management teams in our company, it is obvious that [the firm] pays no regard whatsoever to people's country of origin or ethnicity." The contact further adds, "Professional interaction prevails so much that I don't think sexual orientation is much of an issue.".

Little bumps

If you're interested in globe-trotting with the firm, bear in mind that this may not be the best company for you. According to some sources, Merrill Lynch is "not really known for being a firm that transfers its employees easily to other locations and countries." As for bureaucracy, while some contacts say the firm's size does work to its advantage at times, there are times when things aren't as efficiently handled as they perhaps could be. "(It's) such a large organisation; things aren't always moving as fast as they should," a contact says.

Happy campers

In general, satisfaction with the firm is high. A first-year analyst says, "My satisfaction at the firm is high relative to my peers' experience elsewhere." Another analyst adds, "I am very much enjoying the work here. And if you like what you do, there is plenty of opportunity to grow."

Sources say they enjoy the office environment, which one analyst describes as "working with exceptional individuals who, despite the competitive and tough environment, have a sense of humour and lack self-importance." The proud insider adds that everyone is "treated with respect and gratitude and given a great opportunity to learn."

Clearly the company's outstanding reputation is a source of pride among staffers, too, and insiders point to Merrill Lynch as "a great brand [with] international clout and a lot of opportunity." That idea of recognition is important at the firm as well. As one analyst puts it, "The team works as one unit and you can be sure that the effort that you put in will be recognised in due course of time."

Visit **Vault Europe's Finance Career Channel** at **www.vault.com/europe** for insider firm profiles, employee surveys of finance professionals in Europe, message boards, job listings, expert finance career advice, insider salary information and more.

VAULT CAREER LIBRARY 51

Lehman Brothers

25 Bank Street
London E14 5LE
United Kingdom
Phone: +44 (0) 20 7102 1000
Fax: +44 (0) 20 7067 8107
www.lehman.com

EUROPEAN LOCATIONS

London (Europe HQ)
Amsterdam • Frankfurt •
Luxembourg • Madrid • Milan •
Paris • Rome • Stockholm • Zurich

DEPARTMENTS

Capital Markets Prime Services
Corporate Division (Including
Corporate Advisory, Information
Technology, Finance, Operations,
Risk Management)
Equities
Fixed Income
Investment Banking
Investment Management
Private Equity

THE STATS

Employer Type: Public Company
Ticker Symbol: LEH (NYSE)
Chairman & CEO: Richard S. Fuld Jr.
2006 Revenue: $17.6 billion
(FYE 11/06)
2005 Revenue: $14.6 billion
(FYE 11/05)
2006 Employees: 25,900 (11/06)
No. of Offices: 55 principal
(Worldwide)

KEY COMPETITORS

Goldman Sachs
Merrill Lynch
Morgan Stanley

PLUSES

• Accessible managers
• "Arrogance is generally abhorred"

MINUSES

• Highly competitive
• "Long, long hours"

EMPLOYMENT CONTACT

www.lehman.com/careers

THE BUZZ
WHAT EMPLOYEES AT OTHER FIRMS ARE SAYING

• "Strong culture"
• "Too tough"
• "Doing very well at the moment"
• "Unexciting"

THE SCOOP

All in the family

The three Lehman brothers — Henry, Emmanuel and Mayer — opened a commodities brokerage and trading firm in Montgomery, Alabama, in 1850. Eight years later, they opened an office in New York and, in 1887 Lehman Brothers gained a seat on the New York Stock Exchange. More than a century later, in 1984, Lehman was bought by American Express and was subsequently spun off in 1994, becoming an independent operation again. Today, Lehman Brothers is a full-service global investment bank providing fixed income and equity underwriting, sales, trading, research, M&A advisory, public finance, private investment management, asset management and private equity.

Lehman's first international office was inaugurated in Paris in 1960. Today, the firm's European headquarters are in London while its global headquarters are in New York City. The firm also has major offices in Madrid, Rome, Amsterdam, Milan, Frankfurt, Paris and Zurich. Meanwhile, from its Asian headquarters in Tokyo, Lehman Brothers has also been building out its Asian business over the last five years. The company now employs more than 25,000 people globally but still strives to maintain the family culture feel.

Record results

Lehman continues to focus on a "one firm" approach, coordinating and integrating its global businesses. The bank reported record earnings for 2006. According to Lehman's CFO Chris O'Meara, this was driven primarily by gains in the corporate bond and credit derivatives sectors. He singled out the derivatives business, saying it had "a terrific performance across the board". For fiscal 2006, Lehman reported $17.6 billion in revenue — a $3 billion increase from 2005 — which included record net revenue across all business segments and regions for the year. Lehman Brothers has now reported record results for the past five years, an impressive accomplishment.

Excellence in equities

Lehman and the London Stock Exchange (LSE) have a longstanding relationship. In 2005, Lehman helped mount the LSE's successful defence against a £1.5 billion hostile takeover attempt by a consortium led by Macquarie Bank. Through summer 2006, Lehman set records for monthly equity volumes traded electronically on the LSE — in both June and July 2006, the firm executed more than two million transactions each month. As of November 2006, Lehman had been ranked as the No. 1 dealer on the LSE for 16 consecutive months. In addition, with Lehman's help, in December 2006, the LSE rebuffed yet another undesired takeover bid — $5.3 billion offered by Nasdaq.

Visit **Vault Europe's Finance Career Channel** at www.vault.com/europe for insider firm profiles, employee surveys of finance professionals in Europe, message boards, job listings, expert finance career advice, insider salary information and more.

VAULT CAREER LIBRARY 53

Winning streak in Europe

Gradual increases in European hiring throughout 2006 brought Lehman's total headcount in the region to almost 5,500 employees. The firm certainly has led plenty of big-name M&A advisory roles including two of Europe's biggest M&A deals: Endesa's defence following Gas Natural's €38.8 billion hostile takeover offer and E.ON's €56.2 billion hostile takeover offer. In February 2007, the firm emerged as an advisor on the €33.3 billion Gaz de France merger with Suez, the world's No. 2 water company, which would create the world's second-largest utility.

In addition to its M&A activity, at the end of 2006, Lehman reported that it had led one of the top leveraged buyout financing transactions in the European market every year since 2001. The bank also serves as a corporate broker to FTSE 100 household-name clients like Lloyds TSB, the London Stock Exchange, Tesco and 3i.

New chiefs

Ken Brown and Scott Ferguson were named co-heads of European equity capital markets in August 2006, based in London. Both are equity veterans — Brown was a specialist in the UK, Benelux and Nordic regions and structured equity, and Ferguson was formerly the head of the European financial institutions group within the equity capital markets division. Lehman said their appointments underscore the firm's commitment to building its capital markets business in coming years.

In November 2006, Lehman announced the appointment of Roberto Vedovotto as managing director and chairman of European luxury goods, a newly-created position based in Milan. Vedovotto, former CEO of the Safilo Group, reports to Perry Hoffmeister and Christian Meissner, co-heads of Lehman's investment banking business in Europe. One month later, the bank created another new role, CEO Italy, and appointed Riccardo Banchetti to fill the position. Banchetti, former head of European fixed income sales, is fully responsible for all of Lehman's activities in Italy. He will report to Benoit Savoret, the bank's chief operating officer for Europe. Soon thereafter, David Bizer, a 13-year veteran of the firm in Europe and the US and most recently head of North American equity sales, was shifted to the position of head of European fixed income sales. Lehman appointed Roger Nagioff, previously COO of Europe, as the firm's global head of fixed income, based in London in May 2007. This is the first time a global head of a business division has been based in London, reflecting the truly global nature of Lehman's business.

Taking top honours

The firm itself had reason to boast at the end of 2006, as it was No. 1 in the Barron's 500 Annual Survey of Corporate Performance for the year. CEO Dick Fuld was named to Barron's The World's Most Respected CEOs list as well — one of 13 CEOs in the world who has been named to the list every year since its inception.

The publication *Euromoney* handed Lehman a pile of 2006 awards, including Best M&A House in Western Europe, Best M&A House in the Netherlands, Best M&A House in Italy, Best Global Asset Backed Securities House and Best Debt House in Italy. According to Financial News Lehman was Most Improved Bank of the Decade, celebrating "a decade of excellence in Europe, 1996-2006." The firm also picked up four awards for its credit derivatives business from IFR, Risk, Asia Risk and The Banker magazines; IFR also awarded the firm its global securitization house of the year award.

Lehman also picked up a pair of Great Place to Work Institute awards in the UK in 2007, being dubbed one of the 50 Best Workplaces in the UK for the third year in a row and receiving a Special Award for Disability Excellence for the second year in a row.

GETTING HIRED

A treasured job

As far as accessibility is concerned, many insiders rank Lehman Brothers as akin to being behind "a moated castle with armed guards." As one insider puts it, "The firm has enjoyed tremendous success in the past few years, leading it to be considered among candidates, and rightly so, as one of the world's most preeminent investment banks." He adds, "Accordingly, interest in working here [at Lehman] has increased substantially."

Another associate says his strategy for landing a coveted position involved attending "months of networking events at business school in order to get the interview for the summer position." Then, he says, he "excelled over the summer, and got the job". As one analyst points out, "The number of applications Lehman receives has soared to record highs. It is a highly competitive process, but if you're the right candidate, Lehman will filter you out."

The firm's interview process is described as entailing "Two rounds with a particular focus on diversity, academic achievement, leadership potential and high personal values." An associate shares, "Aside from quantitative factors, such as grades and even past professional experience, the firm culture is truly very important and one must pass many levels of screening to ensure a good fit."

Feet in the door

A good number of sources have worked previously as Lehman interns. Internship work is described as "challenging" and "Lehman invests a lot of effort in training and creating opportunities for you to get to know various teams." The importance of landing a full-time position is high for interns as internships are the primary source for hiring full-time analyst and associates.

Visit **Vault Europe's Finance Career Channel** at www.vault.com/europe for insider firm profiles, employee surveys of finance professionals in Europe, message boards, job listings, expert finance career advice, insider salary information and more.

VAULT CAREER LIBRARY

55

As an associate reports, "One has to excel at the internship, be motivated, show initiative and be self-driven" to receive a full-time offer. Another insider adds that the hiring of interns as full-time employees is "based on the individual performance [not] quotas [and there is] no cutthroat competition across the class." Overall, an internship at the firm is said to provide applicants as well as Lehman Brothers with a premium opportunity "to get to know each other and assess whether it's the right fit". A contact says simply, "You should view it as a prolonged interview process."

OUR SURVEY SAYS

Just be yourself

This is a company that takes its slogan "one firm" very seriously. Survey respondents emphatically describe the culture as "open" and "collaborative" where "people are smart and work hard but are also entirely willing to train the newcomers." An insider says it's "a culture [that] allows different people to be different and be themselves, [with] no pressure to conform to an investment banker stereotype."

An associate explains, "The culture is one of the secrets to Lehman's success — it's extremely flat, meaning that even the most junior employees feel very comfortable discussing concerns with the most senior employees. Lehman stresses humility — there's no superstar culture here — and arrogance is generally abhorred. People like to have fun at work and most candidates will find it to be an extremely cordial place."

Time is money

The work hours at the firm are described as being "normal for investment banking" and, as one source points out, "The good thing about Lehman is that 'face time' absolutely doesn't exist." This lack of face time — which one colleague defines as "when we are finished with work, we leave"— is a popular source of happiness among employees. He adds that a typical day at the office would begin at 8 a.m. and end at 7 p.m. — or much later for some divisions, e.g. investment banking, during "certain periods" of the year. For those divisions, despite the sometimes long hours, one senior employee points out that "the long hours I've put in have been rewarding and looking back, it's the only way to advance even though it's very demanding at times. Getting to know the basics and learn what the analysts have to go through will make you a better senior banker who is able to manage people."

So although expected in this industry, indeed some staffers bemoan the "long, long hours we have to put in and still stay motivated." Another source isn't thrilled with the "impact on a social life" of the long hours, which limits one's "ability to combine job with a family." And yet another source grumbles that in this industry there are "sometimes needless long hours that are expected when they are not really necessary."

It is important to point out, however, that working these "long hours" is mostly an investment banking division phenomenon. Within capital markets, for example, working hours mirror the hours the markets are open — this means starting earlier but also ending earlier and not working on weekends. However, onsite opportunities to wind down abound and Lehman has a discounted "gym, health centre and restaurant" within the office in London, meals are free after 8 p.m. and there is a free car service available after 9 p.m. and on the weekends.

Access your bosses

The firm's managerial style is highly regarded. One insider admits, "In comparison to my previous jobs in the finance industry, I have been positively surprised about the genuine interest of my superiors in my career progress and job (satisfaction)." Another points out, "Management is very accessible here and [is] also very interested in the general welfare of employees."

Firm managers are said to regularly provide "understanding, support and extra guidance." An associate points to the benefits of such a culture, relating that "managers are very respectful of their teams and morale is very high from what I have seen."

Dressed to impress

Respondents at the firm's Canary Wharf office in London are very comfortable with office space, describing it as "spacious and comfortable" and in a "great, brand new building". An insider says it's great to have "a gym, doctor, dentist, dry cleaning services and restaurant" all within the office. While an abundance of amenities at work might sound like fun, co-workers say the dress code at Lehman Brothers is business formal at all times, with some casual Friday exceptions during the summer months. Clearly, the formal dress code is not a high priority among most insiders, but there are indeed some who say they "would really like to see more casual Fridays and don't quite enjoy having to wear formal attire if [they are] not meeting with clients".

Tenacious training

Lehman Brothers puts a "significant effort towards people development" with an emphasis on training more within the first year of employment. However, the firm offers ongoing continuing education classes too. A source says that "training is great — both online modules

Visit **Vault Europe's Finance Career Channel** at www.vault.com/europe for insider firm profiles, employee surveys of finance professionals in Europe, message boards, job listings, expert finance career advice, insider salary information and more.

VAULT CAREER LIBRARY   **57**

and also seminars and meetings. The only thing we need to improve is making it better advertised internally."

The firm's capital markets training program also offers a "rotation and group placement process". Analysts hired as "generalists" attend a four-week training program in which they go through "various business presentations and events before rotating through desks in the equities, fixed income and capital markets prime services divisions." This rotation process enables analysts to learn how different desks operate in the capital markets division. According to Lehman Brothers, "Upon completing these intensive, interactive rotations, placement decisions are made by the heads of the equities, fixed income and capital markets prime services divisions based on overall business needs, appropriate fit and your preferences." Investment management analysts go through a similar rotation process.

Investment banking analysts do not go through a rotation but are placed in a group through a matching process taking into account preferences, business needs and skill sets. Analysts also attend "a series of group presentations and networking events" during the initial training program to enable them to learn about each group and meet bankers from the different areas.

Definite diversity

The firm is proactive when it comes to gender diversity and supporting its women on staff. One female associate says, "There is a women's network at Lehman, the capital market intake from London Business School was 50 per cent female and there are flexible working arrangements, which is particularly attractive to women with children or with other needs."

Another insider notes, "Senior management is very active in promoting diversity and a good working environment. I have never felt discriminated [against] for being a woman — in fact, quite the opposite; [there are] lots of women in senior positions to look up to, including my boss."

The firm is also described as an "ethnically diverse environment." An associate says, "My associate group consisted of over a dozen different nationalities — 25 associates!" In terms of sexual orientation, the same accepting attitudes exist, as one source points out, "I regularly receive information around gay, lesbian, bisexual and transgender programmes and support groups and it's definitely not a taboo area within the firm."

Oh, that wonderful feeling

Lehman Brothers staffers boast of their satisfaction with their jobs. An insider says, "I love this place and think its culture is very unique." An analyst shares, "Lehman is a great place to start your career. The firm has a lot of momentum and the people you work with are highly competent and motivated. That combination makes it an enjoyable place to work even though you will suffer in the early years of your career. But the rewards are there if you make it through."

Clearly Lehman's proactive approach to diversity issues and promoting humility among staff has created a strong and positive culture at the firm. An associate says, "Lehman's culture is amazing — very down to earth and hardworking with no arrogance. There is an air of 'we're all in this together.'" An insider says, "The work you do is fairly similar at all the bulge bracket investment banks. The key difference is the people you interact with on a daily basis and with how much respect they treat you. Un that regard, I think Lehman is the place to be."

They got your back

Graduates need not worry about being left in the dark. According to an associate, the firm offers "lots of support for graduates. Within a few weeks I had met several of the managing directors on the floor for a chat or a coffee. People are very approachable and willing to help."

Lehman's helping hands extend far beyond its own staff, as philanthropy is a priority at the firm. One contact describes Lehman Brothers' philanthropic efforts as "a step above the rest", saying the firm is "an investment bank that does the right thing, encourages diversity, embraces individuals for their own identity and provides a comfortable place to work while being oneself." He adds, "Philanthropy is key and opportunities to be involved in the community are presented, helping to keep focus on the real world and not in some financial bubble."

Visit **Vault Europe's Finance Career Channel** at **www.vault.com/europe** for insider firm profiles, employee surveys of finance professionals in Europe, message boards, job listings, expert finance career advice, insider salary information and more.

VAULT CAREER LIBRARY 59

8 Deutsche Bank AG

Taunusanlage 12
Frankfurt am Main, 60325
Germany
Phone: +49 69 910 38080
Fax: +49 69 910 34225
www.db.com

EUROPEAN LOCATIONS

Germany (HQ)
Austria • Belgium • Hungary •
Italy • Luxembourg • Netherlands
• Portugal • Russia • Spain •
Switzerland • Turkey • UK

DEPARTMENTS

Corporate & Investment Bank
Corporate Investments
Private Clients & Asset
Management

THE STATS

Employer Type: Public Company
Ticker Symbol: DB (NYSE)
Chairman, Management Board: Josef
Ackermann
2006 Net Income: €5,986 million
(FYE 2/07)
2005 Net Income: €3,529 million
2007 Employees: 67, 474
No. of Offices: 1,609 (Worldwide)

PLUSES

Prestigious; one of the heavy-hitters

MINUSES

Ongoing transition

EMPLOYMENT CONTACT

www.db.com/careers

THE BUZZ
WHAT EMPLOYEES AT OTHER FIRMS ARE SAYING

• Top European investment bank"
• "High pressure"
• "Supportive and ambitious"
• "Lots of changes in IB"

THE SCOOP

A banking empire

Founded in Berlin in 1870, Deutsche Bank branches spread rapidly across Germany and arrived in London in 1873. The bank survived World War II and emerged as Deutsche Bank AG, an amalgamation of German banks, and ventured into retail banking. From the 1960s through the 1990s Deutsche Bank snapped up several European banks and financial services firms, opened offices in Asia and North America and went public on the New York Stock Exchange in 2001. In 2002 CEO Josef Ackermann took his post and embarked on a three-part management agenda designed to cut costs, streamline the bank and focus on its core businesses.

Today, the global banking giant Deutsche Bank is headquartered in Frankfurt, with more than 1,600 offices and 67,000 employees worldwide. Close to 40 per cent of its workforce is based in Germany and another 29 per cent work throughout the rest of Europe, with the remaining 31 per cent divided between Asia and the Americas. Deutsche Bank is the largest bank in Germany and one of the largest in the world. Its three core business areas are corporate and investment banking (CIB), private clients and asset management, and corporate investments. CIB is further divided into corporate banking and securities and global transaction banking.

Fantastic profits

Full year group revenue at Deutsche Bank in 2006 rose 11 per cent from the previous year to €28.3 billion, indicating strong growth. For the CIB division, revenue for the full year 2006 was €18.7 billion, up 18 per cent, or €2.8 billion from the previous year. Income before income taxes was €5.8 billion, up 33 per cent while pre-tax profit was €5.9 billion for the full year, an increase of 24 per cent, or €1.1 billion, compared to 2005. In its private clients and asset management (PCAM) business, revenue climbed 5 per cent to an impressive €2.4 billion. In asset and wealth management, revenue reached €1.1 billion. DB says the revenue was "driven in large part by strong performance fees in real estate asset management." The firm's private and business clients (PBC) revenue was also impressive at €1.3 billion, a 7 per cent increase versus the same period the year before.

Organic growth

In May 2007, Deutsche Bank announced its interest in complementary acquisitions in the wealth management and retail banking areas, though it does not see any specific targets at the moment. At perhaps the height of the biggest potential merger in banking history, between ABN Amro and Barclays plc, Deutsche Bank's chief executive, Josef Ackermann, stated he is more interested in organic growth for the firm, as opposed to pursuing a large merger. The chief indicated that while there are clearly many potential partners who may be interested in a deal with Deutsche Bank, the firm is more focused on boosting its share price at the moment.

Visit **Vault Europe's Finance Career Channel** at **www.vault.com/europe** for insider firm profiles, employee surveys of finance professionals in Europe, message boards, job listings, expert finance career advice, insider salary information and more.

VAULT CAREER LIBRARY 61

Environmentally friendly

Also in May 2007, Deutsche Bank announced it has partnered with the Clinton Climate Initiative, championed by the former US President Bill Clinton, and a coalition of municipal governments and private firms to launch a programme committed to reducing overall energy consumption in 15 major cities around the world: Bangkok, Berlin, Chicago, Houston, Johannesburg, Karachi, London, Melbourne, Mexico City, New York, Rome, São Paulo, Seoul, Tokyo and Toronto. As part of the programme which seeks to reduce energy consumption and greenhouse gas emissions in these large cities, DB has committed to arrange $1 billion in financing for "energy efficiency retrofitting projects for buildings" in the identified cities."Climate change is arguably the most important issue of our time," said Seth Waugh, the chief executive of Deutsche Bank in the Americas, in a statement, adding, "We welcome the opportunity to leverage our expertise in the global financial markets to help find sustainable, market-based solutions, rather than band-aids for the problems."

The programme is to offer financing that will allow cities and private building owners "to conduct energy audits and retrofit their buildings with no initial capital outlay." The loans are to be repaid with interest from the energy savings generated by the retrofit projects. Other top banks that have also agreed to arrange $1 billion financing for the programme are ABN AMRO, Citigroup, JPMorgan and UBS. Through Deutsche Bank's Urban Age initiative, done in partnership with the London School of Economics, the firm says it is "helping to define a new understanding of the critical role of cities in affecting social, economic and environmental success during an era of rapid globalisation." The firm adds that the initiative is part of its broader commitment to sustainability, certified according to ISO 14001, and to maintaining its leading position in the financial services industry in this area.

Significant sale

Deutsche Bank also made the headlines in May 2007 when it agreed to sell its 1.6-million-square-foot tower at 60 Wall Street, the bank's North American headquarters in New York City, to Otto Group, owned by the billionaire German mail-order retailer Michael Otto. The selling price was a whopping $1.18 billion or $732 a square foot — a record for the lower Manhattan area. The bank said it intends to remain in the building for the at least the next 15 years under a lease agreement that has been reached with the owners.

Some recent hurdles

Deutsche Bank experienced some legal troubles in 2006. In November 2006 the anticipated conclusion of a case brought against Chief Executive Ackermann was a relief. The case included charges that Ackermann had defrauded shareholders of telecommunications firm Mannesmann after a takeover by Britain's Vodafone — Ackermann and other board members had awarded massive bonuses to former

Mannesmann execs. While Ackermann admitted no wrongdoing, he had said he would step down if convicted. Instead, courts agreed to let him off with a €3.2 million fine.

In December 2006 the firm paid $208 million to settle investigations into improper mutual fund trading. American regulators and the US Securities and Exchange Commission (SEC) had accused the firm of allowing certain investors to conduct late and short-term trades. Also in 2006, Deutsche Bank got dragged into what may be the largest criminal tax case ever — the ongoing investigation of international accounting firm KPMG, which worked with it on a number of tax shelters. While the bank had no comment, federal prosecutors in the US have been investigating Deutsche Bank's internal documents in conjunction with the case, which includes separate charges against the bank itself.

We have a winner

The Finance New Europe 2006 Achievement Awards, announced in December 2006, held the spotlight on Deutsche Bank as it swept up a number of impressive awards. The bank was named Best M&A House and won awards for Top Deal/Croatia, as it represented pharmaceutical company Pliva in a major deal; Best M&A Deal, for its work in the OAO Udmurtneft — Sinopec merger; and Best Sovereign Bond Deal, for its work in the Ukraine, a $1 billion bond deal. *The Banker* magazine dubbed Deutsche EMEA Investment Bank of the Year, and gave it top honours for risk advisory, prime brokerage services, leveraged finance and high yield bonds. Also, at the IFR Awards 2006 in December, Deutsche Bank took home Covered Bond House of 2006, European CDO House of the Year, Investment-Grade Corporate Bond House of the Year and, for the third year in a row, Best Derivatives House.

GETTING HIRED

For more information about careers, the various recruiting divisions or graduate opportunities at Deutsche Bank, visit the company's web site at www.db.com/careers.

Visit **Vault Europe's Finance Career Channel** at **www.vault.com/europe** for insider firm profiles, employee surveys of finance professionals in Europe, message boards, job listings, expert finance career advice, insider salary information and more.

VAULT CAREER LIBRARY   63

VAULT
9 Citi
PRESTIGE
RANKING

Citi Centre
33 Canada Square
Canary Wharf
London, E14 5LB
United Kingdom
Phone: +44 (0) 20 7986 4000
Fax: +44 (0) 20 7986 2266
www.citigroup.com

EUROPEAN LOCATIONS

London (HQ) • Belgium • Bulgaria
• Czech Republic • France •
Germany • Greece • Hungary •
Ireland • Italy • Luxembourg •
Netherlands • Poland • Romania •
Serbia • Slovakia • Spain •
Sweden • Switzerland • Turkey •
United Kingdom

DEPARTMENTS

Citi Alternative Investments
Global Consumer Group
Global Wealth Management
Markets & Banking

THE STATS

Employer Type: Public Company
Ticker Symbol: C (NYSE)
Director & CEO: Charles O. Prince III
2006 Net Income: $21.5 billion
(FYE 12/06)
2005 Net Income: $24.6 billion
(FYE 12/05)
2006 Employees: 300,000
No. of Offices: 7,500 (Worldwide)

PLUSES

Global footprint
Lots of opportunity

MINUSES

Promotion policies unclear
Retail banking reputation is better than
IB reputation

EMPLOYMENT CONTACT

careers.citigroup.com

THE BUZZ
WHAT EMPLOYEES AT OTHER FIRMS ARE SAYING

- "Good competitor and all-rounder"
- "No attention to the individual"
- "Strong across all regions and products"
- "Could do better given size, reach and footprint"

Around the World

International banking powerhouse Citi traces its European roots to the 19th century, when J. Henry Schröder & Co. was established in London in 1818. And while Mr. Schröder is long gone, the firm that he founded was subsumed — along with dozens of others, including Citibank and Salomon Brothers — by the conglomerate now known as Citi.

The bank offers corporate and investment banking, transaction services, consumer and private banking, credit cards and personal finance to customers in 49 countries. One of the first Western banks to establish a presence in post-Communist Eastern Europe, Citi (as Citi Handlowy) now controls 8 per cent of Poland's corporate banking market and 4 per cent of Polish consumer banking.

Citi's three main business areas are the global consumer group, markets and banking, and global wealth management. Its fourth arm, Citi Alternative Investments, is a stand-alone business. The global consumer group includes retail banking, US consumer banking, credit cards, loans and insurance. CMB includes global banking services such as M&A advisory, debt, equity, restructuring and underwriting, global capital markets services and transaction services. Global wealth management encompasses the Citi Private Bank, Smith Barney American private wealth management and investment research.

Banking on Eastern Europe

Citi opened its first Serbian representative office in 2006. The bank already operates in other parts of South Central Europe (Greece, Romania and Bulgaria), and its new office in Belgrade will provide corporate and investment banking products to Serbian corporations, institutions and public sector entities. It will also offer global transaction services, corporate finance and advisory services. William J. Mills, chairman and CEO of Citi's CIB EMEA division, noted that Serbia had become attractive "due to its growth potential, geopolitical position ... and pace of development." Other Citi executives indicated the bank was committed to establishing itself in the Balkan region — which may be poised to become a global growth hot spot.

Lean, mean banking machine

Citi's CEO, Charles O. Prince III, took his post in 2003 amidst some shareholder frustration that Citi's stock prices weren't matching those of its peers. After several years without much fluctuation, Citi stock climbed in the third quarter of 2006 when Prince appointed a new chief operating officer, Robert Druskin. Prince instructed Druskin to start looking for ways to trim expenses, then announced the appointment as a sign that a "leaner, thinner Citi" was on the way. This sent the bank's stocks to a record high as investors anticipated cost-cutting measures to begin in 2007.

Visit **Vault Europe's Finance Career Channel** at **www.vault.com/europe** for insider firm profiles, employee surveys of finance professionals in Europe, message boards, job listings, expert finance career advice, insider salary information and more.

VAULT CAREER LIBRARY

65

GETTING HIRED

Akin to a marathon

Clearly working for a firm as international and, well, as huge as Citi means that opportunities for young professionals and graduates are aplenty. Information about careers and graduate opportunities at Citi can be found on the company's web site at www.careers.citibank.com.

Similar to any top investment bank, the hiring process at Citi can be a long and arduous process for applicants. The company recruits at top business schools and universities around Europe. Applying for a position begins with online registration and an online application form. If you make the initial selection, applicants go through first-round interviews. Most current employees say they went through two or three rounds of initial interviews. One analyst in the Frankfurt office says he endured a whopping total of 13 interviews.

If you get an interview, expect to be asked questions such as, "Why do you want to work for Citi?", or "What is the most difficult situation you have ever faced?" And be prepared to offer some riveting examples of leadership. "I had seven interviews with senior members of my M&A team," says an analyst in the London office. "Two interviews were technical and the rest were more casual, to get an impression of my personality and fit within the team."

"I know a lot of people who failed at the interview stage," says an insider in the sales department. Those who are lucky, or brilliant enough to make it through the first round of interviews go to an assessment centre for additional interviews and a battery of competency tests, which include a group discussion, an essay and a case study. "I was asked the expected questions about my motives in joining an investment bank, what attracted me to Citi and M&A in particular, etc.," says another insider. "There were also 'competency questions' along the lines of 'When have you received negative feedback and how did you deal with it?'"

Interviewing for a position at an investment bank isn't simply testing quantitative and analytical skills. Citi, like other banks, is interested in how you deal with real-life situations and what makes you stand out from the crowd. Be prepared to answer questions about your degree and your extracurricular activities.

Summer in the City

Without a doubt, former interns say that completing the 10-week internship increases your chances of getting hired. Citi regularly hires full-time analysts from the company's popular paid summer internship programme. One former intern who now works for the firm's mergers and acquisitions division explains, "For the internship, I had two 20- to 30-minute first-round interviews, then an assessment centre [interview] for the final round. The most junior interviewer was an associate and the most senior was the head of German/Austrian investment banking." The assessment day agenda usually entails interviews with management, a maths test, a group exercise and a presentation.

A former intern who is now a trading analyst says, "Overall, I found it relatively easy to get hired after completing the internship, not only because of the experience that you can use to your advantage, but also because you understand the business much better." He adds, "During my 10-week summer internship in 2005, I spent the majority of my time shadowing traders and working on quantitative projects such as financial instrument pricing and analysis."

Another former intern, now in the sales department, describes the internship as really being a "10-week interview." He says that during the internship he worked on the sales desk, "did lots of administrative work," and spent time moving around the floor to find out what everyone did and how things worked. And 10 weeks of anticipation is greeted with an answer: "On the last day they told us if we'd been hired or not."

But remember, there's no guarantee that an internship will lead to an offer. "Internship gets your foot into the door, but whether you make it in depends on performance in [the] summer," explains one analyst. "As far as I am aware, only 50 per cent got an offer."

The cream of the crop

Sources say it can be tough to land a job with Citi. Most investment bankers in the firm's London office are graduates of top universities such as Oxford, Cambridge or the London School of Economics. It's also interesting to note that in the era of the MBA, most Citi staffers surveyed don't have one — although a large percentage do hold other advanced degrees.

To work in corporate finance for Citi's corporate and investment banking division, applicants need strong grades from a "good" university. And like most other firms, Citi also looks at skills, experience and commitment. A successful applicant doesn't need to have a background in economics and finance, but the firm definitely wants employees who possess strong quantitative skills, a superior academic background and good communications skills.

Unless you are exceptionally brainy and have some way to prove this in the application process, an internship and work experience become rather necessary. That said, although getting hired at Citi isn't easy, it isn't impossible either. "It is a huge firm so there is always demand for staff," says one recent hire. "The selection criteria and application process are no harder or easier than any other bank."

Visit **Vault Europe's Finance Career Channel** at **www.vault.com/europe** for insider firm profiles, employee surveys of finance professionals in Europe, message boards, job listings, expert finance career advice, insider salary information and more.

VAULT CAREER LIBRARY

67

OUR SURVEY SAYS

It's not all just "face time"

Obviously investment banking isn't known for being a relaxed profession. "If you want to work 9 to 5, then don't become an investment banker," says an insider. For would-be investment bankers, it's important to understand how dynamic such a position can be, but it doesn't come without great perks. When employees work late, perks include allowances for meals after 7:30 p.m. and taxis past 9 p.m.

"Hours, hours, hours," grumbles a member of the corporate finance team. "There are very early starts and very late nights in the week, but not many weekends." Another insider says that while he works a few hours on weekends, often this can be done from home. "The sole reason people leave and give up are the hours," moans a respondent. The hours can be long, depending on the department. Whereas the majority of sources seem to work between 50 and 60 hours a week, others log between 70 and 80 hours per week — sometimes more.

"The hours are among the worst in the industry," says one second-year analyst in London, who adds that he frequently works from 9 a.m. to 3 a.m. "The hours do get better the longer you work at Citi, but they're still grueling." An associate says that, four years in, he typically works from 10 a.m. to 10 p.m. with one weekend day per month. Although the main complaint is the "horrendous hours," another downer is the company's large size and the bureaucracy that accompanies it. One member of the technology group observes that Citi is "restrictive in terms of legislation and bureaucracy — and being so large means everything we do is scrutinised even more."

"I love my boss"

Overall, employees of Citi have a positive view of management at the firm. Most insiders say communication with managers is good, and one third-year analyst says, "From day one, I was encouraged to discuss my thoughts with people at all levels — and I have never felt that what I have to say has been dismissed without consideration." An associate in London explains: "People treat each other with respect regardless of level. There is no barrier to talking to seniors. Whatever level you are at, people above you are demanding and subordinates are keen and helpful."

But there's always room for improvement. One first-year analyst in London says, "In some instances, a better understanding by superiors of how the work is divided and supervised on a junior level would make life easier for many analysts. I am quite happy with my team and it usually doesn't affect me, but I have heard from many of my colleagues on my level that they tend to be given too much work that should be divided up better among the juniors." The insider adds that managers should avoid staffing two analysts on the same project. "This has affected me in the past and what tends to happen is that the work is either pushed thoroughly to the lower end of the chain or the more senior analyst takes over the project and the junior analysts ends up being kicked out of it, which is not very motivating."

As at any company, there are good managers and bad managers. One IT analyst in the Belfast office says his manager is excellent, but says some people have had poor managers and have switched teams because of this. A London insider notes that sometimes managers seem indifferent and that they haven't always been good at motivating him. He says, "As in any firm, you also find associates who like to leave work with the analysts over the weekend, but not that many. Most operate as a team."

Some insiders have a gripe with the firm's promotion policies. Several feel that people should be able to move up in the ranks faster. One management associate in London notes that promotion policies are unclear and are not communicated well to employees. And a junior analyst in London says, "I don't find the system very motivating as there seem to be a lot of politics involved in the system that do not directly relate to individual performance. It is also not very transparent." An analyst in Zurich says Citi should "have a more merit-based promotion policy" and that promotions "currently seem quite rigid and based on time served."

Money talks

As at other European investment banks, salaries vary depending on department and office. Graduates also get annual and joining bonuses. A second-year analyst in London says "no one really moans about being underpaid." However, several members of the corporate finance and investment banking groups say they want more competitive pay and a member of the technology group feels that compensation is "below market average". One London analyst says: "Citi should have a better pay scale."

In addition to salary, employees have a pension plan after the age of 25, as well as a health plan. The London office has a cafeteria. There's also a discounted gym in London, but exercise fanatics beware: a second-year associate describes the gym as being "low quality" and a member of the sales department says it is "expensive for a not-very-good gym."

Dressed to the nines

Although most investment bankers may dress in suits every day, this isn't always the case at Citi. Sure, some analysts say they always dress formally, but others will say attire is business casual. "In practise, this means shirts but no jackets or ties, but also no jeans or trainers," explains a first-year analyst in London. Those who dress down say that they wear more formal clothing, such as a suit and tie, if they have meetings with clients. One source in London excitedly adds that sometimes there are "event days" where people wear certain colours.

Visit **Vault Europe's Finance Career Channel** at **www.vault.com/europe** for insider firm profiles, employee surveys of finance professionals in Europe, message boards, job listings, expert finance career advice, insider salary information and more.

VΛULT CAREER LIBRARY

69

Stars and gripes

As with any extremely large company, the culture at Citi varies by department and office. In Belfast, where the company is new, "people usually like to help each other along." One London associate sums up his Citi experience, saying that if you work for the firm, you get to "work with extremely diverse and smart professionals."

Several Citi respondents say the firm is more relaxed than other investment banks where they've worked. While some insiders describe Citi's office culture in its European offices as being quite "international," other European sources describe it as being rather "American." One corporate finance insider adds that the London office culture is a "good blend of American and British culture", mainly because there's a noticeable presence of American staff at the firm's London office. Many contacts note there is a strong sense of team spirit at the firm. Other adjectives insiders use to describe Citi are "open", "meritocratic", "competitive" and "fast-paced".

Diversity in the workplace

Citi says it is committed to diversity and that its workforce is approximately 98 per cent locally hired across the more than 100 countries in which it operates. That said, insiders say the firm is open to everyone in the recruitment process. "I believe that Citi is already very diverse and very open in the recruitment process," says an analyst in the London office. However, another analyst in the Zurich office notes that while Citi does a lot to promote diversity in New York and London, the company needs to work on it in smaller offices. Some female Citi sources also note that, especially in departments such as technology and finance, the firm is very male-dominated. One associate explains, "I suspect the investment banking hours culture is inherently difficult for mothers with young children. That said maternity leave and return to work are handled very well, including finding roles with more stable hours if the person wants." A few respondents observe that on-site child care would be helpful for working parents.

Although insiders say there are few openly gay employees at Citi, there is a Citi society for gay, lesbian and bisexual bankers. One openly gay analyst says nobody treats him any differently because of his sexual orientation. As one associate notes, "As long as you do your job, nobody cares what your sexual preferences are."

Opportunities to learn

Many analysts say that the firm has excellent training programmes. Analysts receive training sessions, led by outside consultants and internal Citi instructors, when they join the company. During six weeks of intensive classroom learning, new analysts learn how to build financial models, become familiar with standard Citi financial models and get an overview of financial products. A few of them report that, although initial training for new employees is good, there are not enough courses afterwards. As one insider notes, "The training they give is good, there's just not enough." A member of the technology group in London adds, "More training and professional support is needed if they want to hold onto the top staff."

Others say they have learned more on the job than in courses. "Formal training was not too bad," says an analyst, "but I have received some informal training that was very useful." The company also pays for work-related courses outside of office hours. For example, one London analyst says Citi is paying for her to take a course for a professional accountancy exam through a prominent test preparation school in the city.

The ladder of success

Perhaps the greatest benefit to working for a large multinational firm is that the opportunities to grow your career are limitless. New roles are always emerging and people are always moving around. That said, most contacts at Citi agree that they have friendly, supportive colleagues. Several people also say they were given lots of responsibility quickly. Sources praise the opportunities for career growth within the company.

While the company's large size may entail bureaucracy, there are also chances to rotate to other teams. One analyst notes that working for Citi allows you to make good contacts around the world very quickly. Due to the company's global presence, international travel and work opportunities abound. As another London analyst explains, "Citi is the world's biggest bank with a huge global footprint, unparallel to any financial institution. You can move to any department within the bank if you feel you are not working to your potential."

Visit **Vault Europe's Finance Career Channel** at **www.vault.com/europe** for insider firm profiles, employee surveys of finance professionals in Europe, message boards, job listings, expert finance career advice, insider salary information and more.

VAULT CAREER LIBRARY 71

10 Lazard

Principle European Executive Offices
Financial Advisory and Asset
Management – London
50 Stratton Street
London W1J 8LL, United Kingdom
Phone: +44 (0) 20 7187 2000

Financial Advisory – Paris
121, Boulevard Haussmann
75382 Paris, France
Phone: +33 (0) 1 44 13 01 11

Asset Management – Paris
Lazard Freres Gestion
11, rue d'Argenson
75008 Paris, France
Phone: +33 (0) 1 44 13 01 11

Financial Advisory and Asset
Management - Milan
via Dell'Orso 2
20121 Milan, Italy
Phone: +39 (0) 2 723 121

EUROPEAN LOCATIONS

Amsterdam • Berlin • Bordeaux •
Frankfurt • Hamburg • London •
Lyon • Madrid • Milan • Paris •
Rome • Stockholm

THE BUZZ
WHAT EMPLOYEES AT OTHER FIRMS ARE SAYING

- "Trusted and traditional"
- "Suave, but small-time"
- "Very elegant, great culture"
- "Elitist"

DEPARTMENTS

Asset Management
Financial Advisory

THE STATS

Employer Type: Public Company
Ticker Symbol: LAZ (NYSE)
Chairman and CEO: Bruce Wasserstein
Chief Executive, Europe: Georges Ralli
Deputy Chief Executive, Europe: William Rucker
2005 Revenue: $1.36 billion (FYE 12/05)
2006 Revenue: $1.57 billion (FYE 12/06)
2006 Employees: 2,200
No. of Offices: 29 (Worldwide)

KEY COMPETITORS

Goldman Sachs
Merrill Lynch
Morgan Stanley
Rothschild

PLUSES

Good reputation; prestigious

MINUSES

Europe-centric revenue base

EMPLOYMENT CONTACT

www.lazard.com/Careers/careers.html

THE SCOOP

Gold rush

In 1848 the Lazard brothers opened Lazard Frères & Company, a dry goods business in New Orleans, but that didn't last long. The Lazards moved west with American gold prospectors and settled in San Francisco where they sold imported goods to the growing city and exported gold bullion. As demand for retail and commercial financial services grew, the Lazards expanded into financial transactions, including banking and foreign exchange.

An office in Paris followed in 1852 and one in London in 1870. By 1880 the Lazards' business consisted entirely of financial services, with the three "Houses" in New York, Paris and London operating independently under overall control of Alexander Weill, a Lazard cousin. Under former Chairman Michel David-Weill, the Houses of Lazard were unified in 2000, in a merger that created Lazard LLC. Current Chief Executive Bruce Wasserstein became the head of Lazard in 2002 and led the firm, after 157 years of private ownership, through its grand debut on the New York Stock Exchange in May 2005.

Modern times

From its inception, Lazard has focused on what it does best: financial advisory services, particularly for M&A and asset management. The new, public Lazard has continued along the same lines. Its European principle offices are in the former "Houses" of Paris and London, as well as Milan, with additional European offices in Germany, France, Italy, the Netherlands, Sweden and Spain. Lazard serves corporate, partnership, institutional, government and individual clients around the world, advising on strategic and financial issues.

Lazard divides its business into financial advisory and asset management services. Within financial advisory, Lazard's renowned and busy M&A practice is organised into industry groups, including consumer goods, financial institutions, financial sponsors, health care and life sciences, industrial, power and energy, real estate and technology, media and telecommunications. Asset management provides equity, fixed income and cash management, alternative investment strategies, as well as merchant banking to institutional clients, financial intermediaries, private clients and investment vehicles.

Year in review

Recently closing out its first full year as a public company, Lazard is at the top of its game. In February 2007, the firm reported stellar annual results — operating revenue for 2006 was $1.57 billion, up 16 per cent on 2005, and M&A operating revenue was $793 million,

Visit **Vault Europe's Finance Career Channel** at www.vault.com/europe for insider firm profiles, employee surveys of finance professionals in Europe, message boards, job listings, expert finance career advice, insider salary information and more.

V/\ULT CAREER LIBRARY   73

a 17 per cent increase over 2005. In asset management, Lazard now manages more than $110 billion on behalf of its clients (as of December 31, 2006), with some 84 per cent invested in equities, 10 per cent in fixed income investments and the rest in cash, alternative investments and merchant banking funds.

In the financial advisory business, 81 per cent of revenue comes from M&A, 7 per cent is derived from financial restructuring assignments, with the rest coming from other financial advisory work. Geographically, 54 per cent of revenue comes from Europe, 45 per cent from the US and only 1 per cent from the rest of the world. Lazard prides itself on a shrewd geographical spread, and while other competitors are weighted towards one side of the Atlantic or the other, Lazard is well placed to take advantage of booms in Europe or in North America.

Return of the sale

Only 18 months after the firm floated on the NYSE, a second sale of Lazard shares went on the market in November 2006 and netted approximately $632 million for the firm. The bank said it would use about $262 million of the sale proceeds to fund growth in both financial advisory and asset management businesses. Upon the completion of the November sale, public shareholders owned 46.9 per cent of the firm.

From many "Houses" to one firm

Post-IPO, Lazard did some reorganising of its European investment banking business. Soon after the public float, the firm created a committee to make recommendations on European policy. The reorganisation continued into 2006. In September, Georges Ralli, the head of the Paris office, was named to the newly created position of chief executive for European investment banking. London head William Rucker was named his deputy chief executive (both men retained their top posts in Paris and London). Three Paris-based bankers, Erik Maris, Matthieu Pigasse and Antonio Weiss, were promoted to vice chairmen of the European unit. Firm CEO Wasserstein said the moves were meant to fully integrate European investment banking and create "the next generation of management" for a new "one firm" model of Lazard banking.

Behind the big deals

Lazard again proved itself as a financial advisor in 2006, participating in a number of high-volume transactions in Europe. These included advising Gaz de France on its $55 billion offer for Suez, BAA on its $27 billion sale to Grupo Ferrovial, and the $10.8 billion reorganisation and share sale between Caisse des Dépôts et Consignations and Caisse d'Epargne (Lazard advised Caisse d'Epargne on that deal, and again on its $30 billion merger negotiations with Groupe Banque Populaire to create NatIxis).

Lazard also advised Eurotunnel as it contemplated a $12.6 billion restructuring agreement with a consortium including Goldman Sachs, Barclays and Macquarie, and represented Eutelstat Communications in a major ownership restructuring that included the sale of more than half its share capital. Still, competition was stiff, and Lazard just cracked the top-10 in banking league tables for worldwide completed M&A, coming in at No. 10. For European announced M&A, Lazard came in at No. 12.

Significant hires in Europe

Gerd Häusler, one of the top executives at the International Monetary Fund (IMF), joined the firm in October as a managing director and a vice chairman of Lazard International. Mr. Häusler is now a senior member of Lazard's global government advisory business and works in a senior capacity with the firm's corporate relationships in Germany and the rest of Europe, and with financial institutions worldwide.

Also in October 2006 Lazard announced that it would add to its investment banking team in Germany, appointing Andreas Schreiber as managing director of the German financial institutions group (FIG). Schreiber had been the head of investment banking business for financial institutions in UBS' German operations. It also named Dr. Sven Helmer as director of Lazard's real estate investment banking group in Frankfurt. Helmer came to Lazard from Sal. Oppenheim where he led its real estate investment banking group.

In November, the firm hired Giorgio Frasca, also as a vice chairman of Lazard International. Frasca was previously head of the international operations of Fiat SpA and chairman and CEO of Fiat France. His focus is European cross-border transactions. Lazard also hired Jean-Louis Girodolle as a managing director in the investment banking team in Paris. Girodolle joined from the French government's treasury department, where he focused on transportation and infrastructure.

GETTING HIRED

For more information about careers and graduate opportunities at Lazard, see the "careers" section of the company's web site at www.lazard.com/Careers/careers.html.

Visit **Vault Europe's Finance Career Channel** at **www.vault.com/europe** for insider firm profiles, employee surveys of finance professionals in Europe, message boards, job listings, expert finance career advice, insider salary information and more.

VAULT CAREER LIBRARY   75

Credit Suisse Investment Banking

One Cabot Square
London, E14 4QJ
UK
Phone: +44 (0)20 7888 8888
Fax: +44 (0)20 7888 1600
www.credit-suisse.com/ib

EUROPEAN LOCATIONS

(Not limited to IB locations)
Switzerland (Global HQ)
Locations in Austria • Czech
Republic • Denmark • Egypt •
France • Germany • Gibraltar •
Greece • Guernsey • Hungary •
Italy • Jersey • Liechtenstein •
Luxembourg • Monaco • The
Netherlands • Poland • Portugal •
Russia • Slovakia • Spain • Sweden
• Turkey • Ukraine and the UK.

DEPARTMENTS

Brokerage Services
Debt & Equity
Mergers & Acquisitions
Research
Sales & Trading

THE STATS

Employer Type: Public Company
Ticker Symbol: CSGN (SWX), CS
(NYSE)
CEO, Credit Suisse Group: Brady W.
Dougan
2006 Net Revenue: $38,603 million
(FYE 12/06)
2005 Net Revenue: $30,409 million
(FYE 12/05)
2007 Employees: 45,000 worldwide
No. of Offices: 50 (locations
worldwide)

PLUSES

• "Strongly encourages a meritocracy"
• "Diversity is taken very seriously"

MINUSES

• Long hours
• Not best "name recognition" in the
industry

EMPLOYMENT CONTACT

www.credit-suisse.com/careers/en
/emea/index.html

THE BUZZ
WHAT EMPLOYEES AT OTHER FIRMS ARE SAYING

• "Solid. Rebranding worked"
• "Everyone still not on the same
page"
• "Strong brand and franchise"
• "Very hit and miss"

THE SCOOP

The big (Swiss) cheese

Credit Suisse is peaceful Switzerland's second-largest bank (after UBS), and its three core businesses are investment banking, private banking and asset management. Credit Suisse operates in 57 offices in 26 countries and provides securities and financial advisory services to corporations, governments and institutional investors.

The bank's institutional services include equities, fixed income, prime services and research. Corporate client services include mergers and acquisitions, equity capital markets, debt capital markets, private placement, leveraged finance, industry-specific expertise and regional market issues. Formerly known as Credit Suisse First Boston, the bank has more than 150 years of history, most recently culminating in a unified Credit Suisse brand that was launched at the start of 2006. Paul Calello, CEO of the investment banking division, reports to Credit Suisse Group CEO Brady Dougan. More than 45,000 people work for Credit Suisse around the world.

Holiday sales

For Credit Suisse, December 2006 meant a big sale. As part of the bank's strategy to focus on its three core businesses — investment banking, private banking and asset management — Credit Suisse announced in June 2006 that it would sell its insurance arm, Winterthur, to AXA. The sale was completed in late 2006. Under the terms of the deal, Credit Suisse received a cash payment of CHF12.3 billion and AXA agreed to redeem CHF1.1 billion inter-company debt that remained outstanding between Credit Suisse and Winterthur.

Awards, honours and accolades

Credit Suisse picked up a number of awards in 2006, including Best Bank of the Year for IPOs by *The Banker* magazine and Emerging Market Debt House of the Year by *Euromoney* magazine, among others. It also won several of *Euromoney*'s 2006 Awards for Excellence, including Best Equity House in Western Europe, Best Investment Bank in Emerging Europe, Best M&A House in Hungary and Best Bank, Best Debt House and Best Equity House in Switzerland, and European IPO House of the Year by *Financial News*.

In the first half of 2006 alone, Credit Suisse executed five of the 15-largest IPOs in Europe and five of the 20-largest IPOs in the world. *The Banker* noted that Credit Suisse doesn't just do big deals — it does them well, Credit Suisse's former European ECM head, Paul Raphael (now head of IBD Asia/Pacific) told the magazine that in 2007, the bank anticipates increased involvement in the emerging markets of Eastern Europe and the former Soviet republics.

Visit **Vault Europe's Finance Career Channel** at www.vault.com/europe for insider firm profiles, employee surveys of finance professionals in Europe, message boards, job listings, expert finance career advice, insider salary information and more.

VAULT CAREER LIBRARY

77

GETTING HIRED

Name of the game

Credit Suisse is widely regarded as being a highly selective firm, although a high level of motivation is the key. One analyst said that finding a job there is "less difficult in current market conditions, but [is] generally still very tough competition." Another insider says that in his experience, getting hired by the Swiss giant was "not quite as tough as Goldman but just as difficult as any other bulge bracket."

The firm has a reputation for selectivity, but a number of sources highlight the fact that ability alone is often not enough to impress. "Credit Suisse hires very carefully to ensure a good personality fit with the existing team, as well as looking for ability," says one vice president. He adds, "This can lead to a longish interview process, but the results are visible on the trading floor." Another source says the firm "aims to hire the best" and "strongly encourages a meritocracy." In line with the importance of merit and hard work, a fellow insider adds that "the firm is very conscious that new hires are not only skilled and qualified, but it is also very important to come through as being highly motivated."

Finding the right fit

Due to the emphasis put on personality and the ability to work in a team, the interview process at Credit Suisse is described as lengthy and in-depth. One vice president warns candidates to "be ready for lots of interviews, numerical and written English tests as well as case studies. Hiring a candidate is consensus-driven and team fit is an important factor for success." An associate adds, "There are so many very well-qualified people in the market for an entry-level position, that a very good fit becomes increasingly essential."

Internships are key

Sources agree that the odds of landing a full-time job at Credit Suisse improve considerably after the completion of an internship. They also say the pay for an intern is comparable to that of a first-year associate. One female associate was encouraged by certain initiatives, "including events where female students can meet with female employees of the firm."

In terms of the actual work, most describe it as varied and fairly challenging. One associate says, "I had to analyse the coal industry and make recommendations to actual portfolio managers at a large institution," while another former intern adds, "From the first week (I worked) with a team involved in a live deal, helping out with everything from preparing memos to modeling to doing comps. It was a tremendous learning experience and I think it was good that I had to hit the ground running."

That said if you know you've got what it takes and you want to find out more about careers and graduate opportunities at Credit Suisse, then visit the company's web site at www.credit-suisse.com/careers/en/emea/index.html.

OUR SURVEY SAYS

They've got your back

Virtually every source surveyed used the same three phrases to describe the working environment at Credit Suisse — entrepreneurial, encouraging and highly motivated. One vice president says, "I find the environment very busy and very supportive. Everyone is focused on getting the job done rather than [saying] 'that's not my job'. I've learned so much from interactions all across the firm and continue to learn more every day." Another vice president says, "Having worked at various companies, I have had quite a bit of experience with other corporate cultures. For me, Credit Suisse is the best in every aspect."

Money talks

Respondents rate their pay to be on par with or above the industry average. Bonuses for first-year analysts and associates are generally in the £40K to £60K range, while employees in sales and vice presidents report bonus amounts ranging from £200K to £700K. One vice-president says, "Associates and above are offered shares, and vice presidents and above have the possibility to make leveraged investment in Credit Suisse's alternative investments." Perks include "[an] amazing gym at the London office, meal allowances and car services for after-hours work and an 'excellent' pension."

Eight days a week

Satisfaction with salaries doesn't necessarily translate to work hours, as most report working between 60 and 80 hours per week, with many saying a few more hours are often required on the weekend. A vice president points out that "as with other banks, the hours are not great but it goes with the job and, at least, it is interesting."

However, a first-year analyst is somewhat cheery: "It is very difficult to find a balance between life and work, especially at the very early stage of your career. The platform and resources provided by the firm assure you [of] an amazingly steep learning curve and a rapid career development throughout which I am expecting to find more balance." One director shares his perspective on the long hours, saying, "You need to see it as marathon rather than a sprint. You don't notice that you work very hard — you arrive in the morning and next thing you look at your watch and its 9 p.m."

Visit Vault Europe's Finance Career Channel at www.vault.com/europe for insider firm profiles, employee surveys of finance professionals in Europe, message boards, job listings, expert finance career advice, insider salary information and more.

VAULT CAREER LIBRARY

79

Mind the bosses

Managerial relations are highly rated by insiders, with many employees encouraged by the inclusive and encouraging nature of the firm's management. A vice president says, "My manager has a very good approach to guiding his team — he gives us our strategic direction and is on hand to touch base with if needed, but leaves the day-to-day running to the team, allowing us to respond effectively to issues as they crop up." An analyst describes the environment as being "very supportive and stimulating," adding that "they smooth, rather than increase, the overall pressure of such a competitive environment."

Office and attire

Respondents rate their homes away from home right down the middle — not too bad, but not all that good. A vice president said, "The office is good, not flashy or uber-cool. The facilities are good though." While those in corporate finance say formal dress is required at all times, the majority of employees report that the dress code is somewhere between casual and smart casual — depending on the level of contact with clients. One analyst joyfully says, "I love the dress code — very relaxed, shirt and trousers unless going to see a client."

Top training and definite diversity

Overall, the training at Credit Suisse is highly rated by those surveyed. A vice president says the firm provides "first-rate training, both when you join and on an ongoing basis." Another insider's training involved going to New York for 10 weeks, "which was a great networking experience, although most of the lecture material had been covered in my MBA."

One analyst says, "The industry still lacks the ability to attract and retain as many women as men," but the firm rates well in terms of its diversity with respect to women. Indeed, while diversity is an increasingly important issue in the finance industry, Credit Suisse managers are proud of the firm's achievement in the area. A vice president says, "Great efforts have been made in past years to create a very diverse and open working environment."

While the importance of being a team player was mentioned by several respondents, one associate points out that "diversity is taken very seriously" and the firm makes "all efforts possible to recruit and retain women and minorities." Credit Suisse was also given high marks for fostering an accepting and welcome environment for gays and lesbians. In terms of ethnic diversity, the firm is also lauded for its efforts. One associate notes Credit Suisse has "several networking forums and management committees focused on ethnic minorities."

Blips and bumps

Sources point to performance stress as a major concern, but insiders also emphasise this is more industry-related than firm-specific. As one vice president put it, "The job is very involving, so there is naturally a healthy amount of stress and pressure." Perception is a more noteworthy concern, as a number of insiders noted that the good work done by Credit Suisse often goes unnoticed. As one vice president puts it, "We don't have the same name recognition of some other banks," while another insider says, "I wish the press would do a better job of understanding the leading franchise we have built."

Getting some satisfaction

Contacts at Credit Suisse are quite satisfied with the firm and its reputation for both demanding and rewarding hard work. One analyst notes, "I'm very happy with my current role. The pay, culture, people I work with and the actual work I do are all great." Similarly, one vice president says, "I love the variety of the work and the range of people/roles I get to interact with day-to-day. I'm always learning and that's always a buzz."

Insiders express contentment with their co-workers. An associate refers to those around him as being "great colleagues," adding that "the bank is very much on the up with senior management working to create a global integrated firm." Sources are encouraged by the firm's "entrepreneurial culture," and one analyst says there is "No glass ceiling, with very bright and fun people around me that want to win." Another says staffers "are given huge responsibilities [at] an early stage and a world-class platform to deliver results. Last but not least, [the] weekends are safe."

Visit **Vault Europe's Finance Career Channel** at **www.vault.com/europe** for insider firm profiles, employee surveys of finance professionals in Europe, message boards, job listings, expert finance career advice, insider salary information and more.

V∧ULT CAREER LIBRARY

81

NM Rothschild & Sons

NM Rothschild & Sons Limited
New Court, St. Swithin's Lane
London EC4P 4DU
United Kingdom
Phone: +44 (0) 20 7280 5000
Fax: +44 (0) 20 7929 1643
www.rothschild.com

EUROPEAN LOCATIONS

London (European HQ)
Belgium • Channel Islands (Britain)
• France • Germany • Italy •
Russia • Spain • Switzerland and
the United Kingdom.

DEPARTMENTS

Asset Management
Banking & Treasury
Investment Banking
Private Banking & Trust

THE STATS

Employer Type: Private Company
Chairman: Baron David de Rothschild
Finance Director: Isobel Baxter
No. of Employees: 921
No. of Offices: 65

KEY COMPETITORS

Credit Suisse
Deutsche Bank
ING

PLUSES

Big name; a global force

MINUSES

Not always easy to maintain
independence

EMPLOYMENT CONTACT

www.rothschild.com/careers

THE BUZZ
WHAT EMPLOYEES AT OTHER FIRMS ARE SAYING

• "Strong regional presence in
  corporate finance"
• "Long hours"

THE SCOOP

Literally financing history

Rothschild & Sons is the investment banking arm of the London-based, family-owned N.M. Rothschild Group (NMR), the world's largest independent merchant and investment bank. Rothschilds Continuation Holdings of Switzerland controls the Rothschild's empire. The firm specialises in M&A, restructurings and privatisations and, in a joint venture with ABN AMRO formed in 1996, provides equity underwriting services via the entity ABN AMRO Rothschild.

The Rothschild name is synonymous with art, culture, some of the most famous (and expensive) wines in the world — and, of course, finance. In 1769, Mayer Amschel Rothschild founded the eponymous firm in Frankfurt and soon after enlisted his five sons to expand it throughout Europe. In 1814, the brothers would bankroll the Duke of Wellington's battle against Napoleon, purchasing gold coins throughout Europe, secretly sending them to Holland and then shipping them into Britain. The deal established Rothschild as one of the premier banks in Europe, and led to other monumental deals including bailing out the country's banking system in 1825.

In 1875, Rothschild offered expertise to the British government during its acquisition of a large stake in the Suez Canal. In 1926, the firm helped finance London's underground tube transportation system. Like the British Empire it helped build, the firm's influence reached its apex in the 19th century. NMR never established a strong presence in the US market, but after the Cold War assisted several companies in Eastern Europe in going private. Rothschild has offices in more than 22 countries all over the world, from Toronto to Tokyo, and headquarters in both London and New York.

The fiscal year that ended in March 2006 was one of the best in the firm's history. Rothschild reported record operating income of £370 million, up from £250 million at the fiscal year ending in March 2005, as well as a record pre-tax profit of £83.2 million, up from £41.6 million in 2005. The firm had £5.5 billion in assets as of March 2006. Underscoring its success, Rothschild was named the Bank of the Year by Thomson Financial's *Acquisitions Monthly* magazine in 2005.

A real M&A player

Since the days of smuggling and subway construction, Rothschild has become a quiet force in the world of M&A advising. For the first six months of 2006, Rothschild ranked No. 11 in global announced M&A, No. 2 in European announced M&A, No. 2 in Latin American announced M&A and No. 1 in UK announced M&A. Rothschild's recent transactions include advising BNFL on the $5.4 billion sale of its Westinghouse unit to Toshiba

Visit **Vault Europe's Finance Career Channel** at www.vault.com/europe for insider firm profiles, employee surveys of finance professionals in Europe, message boards, job listings, expert finance career advice, insider salary information and more.

VAULT CAREER LIBRARY 83

Corporation, National Grid on the $575 million purchase of Southern Union Gas' Rhode Island assets, and Yell Group on its $1.6 billion acquisition of TransWestern Holdings from Thomas H. Lee Partners, CIVC Partners LLC and TransWestern management.

All in the family

The family has always strived to keep the business in the family, even arranging marriages in the early days. In April 2004, Sir Evelyn de Rothschild stepped aside as chairman of the firm to make room for his cousin, Baron David de Rothschild. Baron David had been running Rothschild's Paris-based bank and had chaired the firm's global investment bank, run jointly out of London, Paris and New York. Along with the handover came the unification of the N.M. Rothschild and the French side of the bank under one roof — a holding company called Concordia, which Baron David also chairs.

A balance of powers

The firm has struggled to remain independent and keep up with larger banks. The Socialist government of Francois Mitterrand nationalised and renamed the Paris branch in 1982, but Baron David stayed in France and rebuilt the business. After taking control of the London business he pulled the plug on its weak-performing commodities-trading unit after 200 years. Interestingly, Rothschild had hosted the twice-daily ritual of waving small Union Jack flags to signal the price of gold.

Even before the announcement of the succession, the Rothschild empire went through recent consolidation and reorganising. In September 2002, N.M. Rothschild Group combined 13 separate private banking units into a single worldwide private banking business. And, in December 2002, the group sold the retail and institutional asset management businesses of Rothschild Asset Management to Insight Investment Management, the fund arm of British bank HBOS. The redistribution of power meant that the English and French sides of the family would have an equal stake in the company, likely mitigating family friction in the complex network of clan-run private companies that control Rothschild.

Going Dutch

In 1996, Rothschild partnered with Dutch bank ABN AMRO in launching a global equity capital markets joint venture. Benefiting from the $633 billion assets and 800 equity research and trading personnel of ABN AMRO, and the advisory strength and strong global reach of Rothschild, the partnership has been a successful one.

In the first half of 2006, ABN AMRO Rothschild ranked No. 10 in global equity underwriter volume and No. 10 in EMEA underwriting volume. Recent ABN AMRO

Rothschild transactions include advising AngloGold Ashanti on its $1.5 billion secondary offering, acting as joint lead manager and joint bookrunner on Praktiker's $595.5 million secondary offering, and serving as sole coordinator and bookrunner on Univar's $305.9 million offering, all of which were completed in April 2006.

GETTING HIRED

For information on internship and full-time career opportunities throughout Europe, visit www.rothschild.com/careers.

Visit **Vault Europe's Finance Career Channel** at **www.vault.com/europe** for insider firm profiles, employee surveys of finance professionals in Europe, message boards, job listings, expert finance career advice, insider salary information and more.

VAULT CAREER LIBRARY 85

Barclays PLC

1 Churchill Place
Canary Wharf
London E14 5HP
United Kingdom
Phone: +44 (0) 20 7116 1000
Fax: +44 (0) 20 7116 7665
www.barclays.com

Barclays Capital
5 The North Colonnade
Canary Wharf
London E14 4BB
United Kingdom
Phone: +44 (0) 20 7623 2323
Fax: +44 (0) 20 7116 7665
www.barcap.com

EUROPEAN LOCATIONS

London (HQ)
France • Germany • Ireland • Italy
• Netherlands • Portugal • Spain •
Switzerland • United Kingdom

DEPARTMENTS

Credit Cards • Investment Banking
(Barclays Capital) • Investment
Management Services (Barclays
Global Investors) • Retail and
commercial banking • Wealth
Management

THE BUZZ
WHAT EMPLOYEES AT OTHER FIRMS ARE SAYING

- "Impressive growth, good
  name"
- "Strong momentum and British
  elegance"
- "A fairly closed club"
- "Over promise, under deliver"

THE STATS

Employer Type: Public Company
Ticker Symbol: BARC (LSE), BCS
(NYSE). TYO (8642)
Chairman: Marcus Agius
Group Chief Executive: John S. Varley
President: Robert Edward "Bob"
Diamond Jr.
2006 Revenue: £21,595 million
(FYE 12/06)
2006 Net Income: £7,136 million
(FYE 12/06)
No. of Employees: 123,000
No. of Offices: Locations in more
than 50 countries worldwide

KEY COMPETITORS

HBOS
HSBC Holdings
Lloyds TSB
Citigroup

PLUSES

Huge and prestigious

MINUSES

A lot of change going on

EMPLOYMENT CONTACT

Barclays plc:
www.barclays.co.uk/careers
Barclays Capital:
www.barcap.com/campusrecruitment

THE SCOOP

Global domination

Boasting more than 2,000 branches in the UK, a presence in over 60 countries and more than five million customers and clients worldwide, Barclays plc is the fourth largest financial services provider in the world, by Tier 1 capital. The bank's operations include personal financial services, corporate banking, asset management, mortgage lending through its mortgage brand Woolwich and credit card services through Barclaycard, one of Europe's leading credit card issuers. Add to that the fact that Barclays, one of Britain's oldest banks, also runs one of the UK's largest online banks with nearly four million registered users, and what emerges is literally a global banking giant.

In January 2007, British financier and businessman Marcus Agius — whose wife is a daughter of the Rothschild banking family of England — succeeded Matthew Barrett as chairman of Barclays plc after his retirement.

Under the umbrella

Barclays plc has six major businesses. UK banking delivers banking products and services to over 14 million retail customers and 780,000 businesses in the UK. Barclaycard is one of the leading credit card businesses in Europe, and has 9.8 million UK customers and 6.4 million international cards in issue. Barclays Capital, the investment banking division, provides corporate, institutional and government clients with solutions to their financing and risk management needs. Barclays Global Investors is one of the world's largest asset managers and a leading provider of investment management products and services. Total assets under management on December 31, 2006 were $1.8 trillion.

Barclays Wealth serves affluent, high-net-worth and intermediary clients worldwide, providing private banking, asset management, stock-broking, offshore banking, wealth structuring and financial planning services. As of 31st December 2006, total client assets were £93 billion.

Some European history

Barclays was founded in 1690 by John Freame and Thomas Gould on Lombard Street in London's financial district. The name Barclay became associated with the company in 1736, when Freame's son-in-law, James Barclay, became a partner. In 1896, 20 men formed a new joint-stock bank named Barclay and Company, which became known as the Quaker Bank. With a network of 182 branches located mainly in the east and southeast of England, Quaker Bank held deposits of £26 million. It expanded its branch network rapidly by taking over other banks, including Bolithos in 1905 and United Counties Bank in 1916.

Visit **Vault Europe's Finance Career Channel** at **www.vault.com/europe** for insider firm profiles, employee surveys of finance professionals in Europe, message boards, job listings, expert finance career advice, insider salary information and more.

VAULT CAREER LIBRARY

87

Barclays' global expansion continued with the creation of an investment banking operation in 1986, which developed into Barclays Capital, a major division of the bank that now manages larger corporate and institutional business. In 1995, Barclays purchased the fund manager Wells Fargo Nikko Investment Advisers and integrated it with BZW Investment Management to form Barclays Global Investors. Then, in July 2003, Barclays completed the acquisition of Banco Zaragozano, one of Spain's largest private sector banking groups. The bank sold its UK and German vendor-financing businesses to CIT group in October 2006 for an undisclosed sum.

Barclays Capital

Barclays Capital is the investment banking division of Barclays Bank PLC which has an AA long-term credit rating and a balance sheet of over £996 billion (US$1.9 trillion*). With a distinctive business model, Barclays Capital provides large corporate, government and institutional clients with solutions to their financing and risk management needs. Barclays Capital has offices in 26 countries, employs over 13,200 people, and has the global reach and distribution power to meet the needs of issuers and investors worldwide.

The bank's investment banking division, Barclays Capital (Barcap), has a balance sheet of over $1 trillion, making it one of the largest multinational financial services groups in the world. The unit is enjoying double-digit earnings gains and reduces Barclays' exposure to the UK economy because of its global business.

In recent years, Barclays Capital has increased the range of its investment banking activities, now booking significant income from mortgage-backed securities, equity products, commodities and derivative products across all asset classes.

American Bob Diamond, who is the president of Barclays plc, is the chief executive for the investment banking and investment management businesses that comprise Barclays Capital, Barclays Global Investors and Barclays Wealth. Only 20 years after Barclays plc created its focused investment banking operation, and also became the first British bank to float on both the NYSE and the Tokyo Stock Exchange, Barclays Capital can parade countless honours, awards and accolades. And 2006 was no exception to this — in February, it was named International Arranger of the Year by International Securitisation Report (ISR).

ISR described Barclays as "having it all". The report said that Barclays Capital had an incredible year in Europe and Asia in 2005, stating, "Its (Barcap's) name seemed to be attached to all the landmark deals in Europe, where it also made impressive progress in newer sectors such as CMBS and CDOs. In Asia, the bank grabbed the top spot for MBS in Asia, thanks to a stellar year in Australia."

Barcap's other 2006 awards include: *Financial News* naming Barclays European Bond House of the Decade; *Risk* magazine's Inflation Derivatives House of the Year and

Structured Products House of the Year and Derivatives Week named it US Equity Derivatives House of the Year. *Euromoney* named it Best Foreign Exchange house in July; and *AsiaRisk* named it Currency Derivatives House of the Year in September. In November, *Global Finance* named it Best Foreign Exchange Bank, UK and Derivatives Week named it US Equity Derivatives House of the Year.

Headline of the year?

On April 23, 2007 it emerged that British banking giant, Barclays was interested in taking over ABN AMRO to create the world's biggest bank, which would be headquartered in Amsterdam. Although, at press time talks are still in progress, the potential takeover has stimulated an unrivalled amount of global interest. According to initial reports in April 2007 in London daily newspaper *The Times*, Barclays was willing to pay up to €35 per share for ABN AMRO. The paper reported that mega banking groups including Bank of America are "waiting in the wings to pick up unwanted ABN AMRO assets should Barclays be successful in its attempt to buy the £40 billion Dutch banking group."

Initially, ABN AMRO agreed to an all-shares deal with Barclays plc. That day, Barclays' chief executive said, "It's the largest transaction ever in the history of the global financial services industry," as he proudly announced details of the whopping €140 billion merger proposal. The day following the announcement of the merger, *The Times* wrote, "The deal would be immediately earnings-enhancing for ABN AMRO shareholders and would boost profits per share for Barclays shareholders, too — by 5 per cent in 2010. Sweetening the deal was the promise of a €12 billion return of cash to shareholders via share buybacks, financed by the $21 billion (£10.5 billion) sale of LaSalle, ABN AMRO's American banking unit [to Bank of America]."

While the spotlight was initially on Barclays for the potential takeover of ABN AMRO, attention quickly turned to the consortium competing with the British bank and independently pursuing the Dutch giant, who, it was reported within days of Barclays' initial bid, was willing to pay €40 per share for ABN AMRO. The competing trio is a flavourful European medley comprised of Belgo-Dutch mega banking house Fortis, Spanish banking powerhouse Santander and the prestigious Royal Bank of Scotland. In early May ABN AMRO rejected the consortium's offer of $24.5 billion for its American banking arm LaSalle, and a Dutch court ruled that ABN AMRO should not have sold LaSalle without consulting shareholders first. This prompted BoA to file a lawsuit against ABN AMRO in New York. Business magazine Forbes reported on the move, that BoA was "claiming that the Dutch bank is in breach of its contract to sell LaSalle to BoA."

However, the deal hasn't been so easy to close as more players enter the arena and in the weeks following the announcement, the bidding war triggered by rival suitors has unravelled and updates on the potential sale have made headlines virtually every day. On

Visit **Vault Europe's Finance Career Channel** at www.vault.com/europe for insider firm profiles, employee surveys of finance professionals in Europe, message boards, job listings, expert finance career advice, insider salary information and more.

VAULT CAREER LIBRARY 89

7th May, 2007 the firm announced it intended to hold an EGM for shareholders, in order to stimulate a discourse about the options and "alternatives available to them at that time." Two days later, on 9th May, 2007, the bank announced that it "will lodge an appeal with the Supreme Court of The Netherlands against the provisional ruling of the Enterprise Chamber of the Amsterdam Appellate Court that the agreement to sell LaSalle to Bank of America may not complete without a shareholder vote. That ruling has created ambiguity for shareholders and has led to Bank of America filing a lawsuit against ABN AMRO in the US courts. ABN AMRO must appeal the Enterprise Chamber's ruling and endeavour to provide clarity and remove any legal threat."

Forbes reported that if the sale to Bank of America was rejected, the situation could "raise the risk" that the earlier proposed €67 billion merger between ABN AMRO and Barclays plc might also fall through." The business news source added, "Under the terms of the initial ABN AMRO and Barclays deal, both banks will put the proposed merger to a shareholder vote in August." The bidding continues.

Reigning in Spain

Barclays' most significant market in continental Europe has been Spain, where it has half a million customers and more than 500 branches. The bank opened its first branch office in Spain in 1914. By focusing on key cities and coastal resorts, it had developed a network of about 165 branches by 2003, when the business was given a boost with the purchase of Banco Zaragozano, Spain's 11th-largest privately owned banking group. The purchase tripled Barclays' branch network and customer base in Spain. In Portugal, Barclays launched its OpenPlan product, and doubled the size of its Portuguese network by the end of 2006, increasing its number of branches to more than 130. The bank is targeting British nationals buying property in the Algarve, where at any one time there are between 40,000 to 70,000 Britons. In Italy, Barclays operates through Banca Woolwich, the sixth-largest mortgage lender in Italy, and is currently growing a Barclays branded network. The bank aims to have 50 branches open by the end of 2007.

As part of its effort to offer its credit card products internationally, in December 2004 Barclays completed the purchase of US-based full-service credit card issuer Juniper Financial Corporation for $293 million from CIBC. Juniper specialises in issuing cards for other companies, including Frontier Airlines and Caesars Entertainment. The all-cash deal brought Barclays $1.4 billion in assets and 700,000 customers, nearly doubling the bank's international business. The bank says it aims to expand its international credit card business until it is as robust as its UK operations. Analysts say the expansion has proceeded slowly because many European customers aren't used to paying with plastic.

Barclays' Barclaycard unit celebrated its 40th birthday in June 2006, which also marked the birth of Britain's first credit card. Barclaycard began with seven employees in a converted Northampton shoe factory in 1966. At the end of 2006, the company boasted 9.8 million UK cardholders as well as 6.4 million around the world.

More growth in Britain

Barclays announced an 18-month restructuring plan in June 2006 for its UK-based retail banking arm, resulting in the merging of Barclays and Woolwich branches and the streamlining of back-office operations as part of an effort to boost its Woolwich mortgage brand -- the firm it bought in 2000. As a result, the bank is expected to close two IT and processing sites, one at the end of 2007 and one by mid-2008.

GETTING HIRED

For more information about careers and graduate opportunities at Barclays group, visit the Barclays plc web site at www.barclays.co.uk/careers. To learn more about opportunities at Barclays Capital, visit www.barcap.com/campusrecruitment.

Visit **Vault Europe's Finance Career Channel** at **www.vault.com/europe** for insider firm profiles, employee surveys of finance professionals in Europe, message boards, job listings, expert finance career advice, insider salary information and more.

VAULT CAREER LIBRARY 91

Macquarie Bank Limited ABN

CityPoint, Level 35
1 Ropemaker Street
London EC2Y 9HD
United Kingdom
Phone: +44 (0) 20 7065 2000
Fax: +44 (0) 20 7065 2191
www.macquarie.com/eu

EUROPEAN LOCATIONS

London (HQ)
Austria • France • Germany •
Ireland • Italy • Switzerland

DEPARTMENTS

Banking & Property
Equity Markets
Financial Services
Funds Management
Investment Banking
Treasury & Commodities

THE STATS

Employer Type: Public Company
Ticker Symbol: MBL (ASE)
Managing Director & CEO: Allen E. Moss
Executive Director & Head of
Macquarie Bank Group in Europe:
Jim Craig
2006 Income: $3,460 million
(FYE 03/06)
2005 Income: $2,956 million
(FYE 03/05)
2006 Employees: 10,000
No. of Offices: More than 50 locations in 24 countries

PLUSES

Growing extremely fast

MINUSES

Ongoing restructuring

EMPLOYMENT CONTACT

www.macquarie.com.eu/careers

THE BUZZ
WHAT EMPLOYEES AT OTHER FIRMS ARE SAYING

- "Very good reputation"
- "Turbulent in many fields"

THE SCOOP

G'day mate

Like most things in Australia, Macquarie Bank's roots lie in England. In 1969 a London merchant bank called Hill Samuel & Co. established a subsidiary branch, Hill Samuel Australia (HSA), in Sydney. Following deregulation of the financial markets in 1980s, HSA gained a banking license in 1985, and chose a new name in honour of Governor Lachlan Macquarie, the man credited with transforming Australia from a penal colony to a burgeoning nation. The bank's logo, a ring with a hole in the middle, represents the "holey dollar" — Governor Macquarie's solution to the colony's currency shortage in 1813 — he purchased Spanish silver dollars and punched out the centre, creating two coins, increasing the value by 25 per cent.

Macquarie has grown from an Australian investment bank to an international banking presence listed on the Australian Stock Exchange. Based in Sydney, its European headquarters is in London, while it has offices in Austria, Germany, Ireland, Italy and Switzerland, and global offices in New Zealand, Asia, Africa and the Americas.

Although Macquarie is a diversified investment bank and financial services provider in Asia, Australia and New Zealand, its focus in Europe and the Americas is more selective, but growing rapidly. As of early 2007, approximately 44 per cent of the bank's revenue is generated from business outside Australia. To support its international business, Macquarie expanded its workforce by nearly 25 per cent in 2006.

Bounded freedom

Macquarie divides its business into six operating groups, with a unique non-hierarchical management system that allows each business group to operate freely (within defined risk limits, of course). The bank calls this strategy "freedom within boundaries." Its operating groups include investment banking, equity markets, treasury and commodities, banking and property, funds management and financial services.

The investment banking group includes Macquarie's wholesale structuring, stock broking, underwriting and advisory capabilities. Its services include project financing, M&A and restructuring advisory, equity capital management, specialised infrastructure and fund management, specialised leasing and asset financing, institutional and corporate stock broking, and equities research.

Macquarie goes shopping

Macquarie startled the industry in early 2006 when it made a $1.5 billion takeover bid for the London Stock Exchange. Thwarted by LSE stockholders' demands for a higher price,

Visit **Vault Europe's Finance Career Channel** at **www.vault.com/europe** for insider firm profiles, employee surveys of finance professionals in Europe, message boards, job listings, expert finance career advice, insider salary information and more.

VAULT CAREER LIBRARY

93

Macquarie was undeterred and continued its focus on other deals in Europe. In 2006 it was the co-adviser to the takeover of BAA by Ferrovial, and in August 2006 it bought Corona Energy, one of the United Kingdom's largest suppliers of energy to industrial and commercial customers. Macquarie said the move would expand its presence in the European energy markets business.

Two months later, advised by Macquarie's utilities corporate advisory team, Kemble Water — a consortium led Macquarie's European Infrastructure Funds — won the bid to acquire Thames Water. In March 2007, Macquarie announced it would acquire Giuliani Capital Advisers — the boutique investment bank headed by New York's famous former mayor. In April 2007, Macquarie and its managed funds were involved in a series of deals in the UK, including the acquisition of the off-street car parking business of National Car Parks, the digital transmission networks of National Grid Wireless and the emergency communication provider Airwave. And the acquisitions are set to continue - in May 2007 Macquarie announced it had raised €7.5 billion in two new infrastructure funds that will focus on investments in Europe and North America.

Get INSEAD

In the fall of 2006 Macquarie announced it was teaming with INSEAD, the international business school, to launch a global Master of Finance program for Macquarie's investment banking managers. Starting in 2007, the new degree will be available to Macquarie staff around the world. The banks expects hundreds of employees to take advantage of the degree program and plans to make the INSEAD Master of Finance (Investment Banking) the centre piece of its professional development activities.

It's getting better all the time

The 2006 banking league tables showed Macquarie making gains. At year's end it ranked No. 17 in worldwide completed mergers and acquisitions, up from No. 31 in 2005. In 2006 Macquarie advised on 103 deals worth $98.5 billion. In European announced M&A, Macquarie ranked No. 20, up from its previous spot at No. 25 and, in the United Kingdom it came in at No. 11 and No. 10 for announced and completed deals, respectively. The bank was also strong in Germany, landing at No. 15 and No. 13 for announced and completed M&A. It also made a leap onto the Spanish M&A tables. While Macquarie didn't crack the top 25 in announced M&A in Spain in 2005, in 2006 it was No. 12. It was also No. 8 in completed Spanish M&A, up from No. 31 in 2005.

Diversification-synergy

Macquarie's real estate trusts and joint ventures are also gaining headway in Europe. Macquarie Real Estate Europe established a management agreement with self-storage operator Storage King. Its joint venture, Macquarie Global Property Advisors, has recently opened offices in France and Germany and made significant investments in Poland, France and Germany.

Sourcing out to slim down

About one per cent of Macquarie administrative jobs, including positions from payroll departments in Australia and London, are slated to be outsourced to India in 2007, Bloomberg reported at the beginning of that year. According to a spokesman for the bank, Macquarie has plans to consolidate its global human resources activities as part of a "strategic review." Macquarie's recent hiring sprees — the bank tripled its staff between 1999 and 2006 — meant related increases in labour costs. The bank has hired Accenture to consult on its streamlining plans.

GETTING HIRED

For more information about careers and graduate opportunities at Macquarie, visit the company's website at: www.macquarie.com.eu/careers.

Visit **Vault Europe's Finance Career Channel** at **www.vault.com/europe** for insider firm profiles, employee surveys of finance professionals in Europe, message boards, job listings, expert finance career advice, insider salary information and more.

VAULT CAREER LIBRARY   95

VAULT
15 Bear Stearns & Co.
PRESTIGE
RANKING

One Canada Square
London, E14 5AD
United Kingdom
Phone: +44 (0) 20 7516 6000
Fax: +44 (0) 20 7516 6030
www.bearstearns.com

EUROPEAN LOCATIONS

London (European HQ)
Dublin
Lugano
Milan

DEPARTMENTS

Capital Markets
Global Clearing Services
Wealth Management

THE STATS

Employer Type: Public Company
Ticker Symbol: BSC (NYSE)
Chairman & CEO: James E. Cayne
2006 Revenue: $9.2 billion (FYE 11/06)
2006 Net Income: $2.05 billion
2005 Revenue: $7.4 billion (FYE 11/05)
2005 Net Income: $1.46 billion
No. of Employees: 13,000
No. of Offices: 30 (Worldwide)

KEY COMPETITORS

ABN Amro
Citigroup
Goldman Sachs
JPMorgan Chase
Lehman Brothers
Merrill Lynch
Société Générale

PLUSES

Record profits for the past five
consecutive years

MINUSES

Not yet a top-tier name in Europe

EMPLOYMENT CONTACT

www.bearstearns.com
(Click on "Careers")

THE BUZZ
WHAT EMPLOYEES AT OTHER FIRMS ARE SAYING

- "Small but strong player"
- "Not much tradition in Europe"
- "Ambitious"
- "Arrogant"

THE SCOOP

Not a red year in sight

One of the largest global investment banks and securities trading and brokerage firms in the world, Bear Stearns has turned a profit for the past 80 years. Known as "Bear" on Wall Street, the firm operates in three main business areas: capital markets, wealth management and clearing. Bear Stearns' international headquarters is in New York City, but the head of its growing European operations is based in London. Through an extensive list of subsidiaries, the company provides asset management, clearing and custody, securities lending, trust, and mergers and acquisitions advisory services to individuals, institutions, corporations and governments around the world.

Breaking it down

Bear Stearns' capital markets business handles all equity and fixed income sales, trading, research and investment banking businesses. Wealth management serves the needs of the firm's private and asset management clients. Clearing, the third major services group, offers prime broker, broker-dealer and independent advisory services.

As a holding company, Bear Stearns Companies Inc. contains a web of subsidiaries and affiliates, which include Bear, Stearns & Co. Inc., Bear Stearns Bank PLC, Custodial Trust Company and Bear Stearns International Trading Limited. Bear, Stearns International Limited (BSIL) is the headquarters for all European operations. BSIL employs more than 1,100 staff in London, who provide investment banking, institutional equities and fixed income sales, trading and research, derivatives, financial futures, foreign exchange and global clearing services to clients in the UK, Europe and the Middle East.

Other Bear Stearns subsidiaries include EMC Mortgage Corporation, Bear Stearns Capital Markets, Bear Stearns Credit Products Inc., Bear Stearns Financial Products Inc, Bear Stearns Forex Inc., Bear Stearns Global Lending Limited, Bear Stearns Commercial Mortgage, Inc. and Bear Hunter Holdings LLC.

Bear Stearns also owns a majority stake in Bear Wagner Specialists, a specialist firm that handles the flow of trading for 372 companies listed on the New York Stock Exchange. Bear Wagner's clients account for over 15 per cent of the share and dollar volume of all stocks on the NYSE. They include Dow Jones Industrial Average components Alcoa, Citigroup, Honeywell International and Procter & Gamble.

Eight decades of growth

Joseph Bear, Robert Stearns and Harold Mayer founded Bear Stearns & Co. in 1923. A partnership focusing on brokerage services, the firm initially operated with a small staff out

Visit **Vault** Europe's Finance Career Channel at www.vault.com/europe for insider firm profiles, employee surveys of finance professionals in Europe, message boards, job listings, expert finance career advice, insider salary information and more.

V/\ULT CAREER LIBRARY

97

of a single office at 100 Broadway in New York City. A decade later, the firm established its institutional bond department, the forerunner to today's fixed income division. Investment banking operations began in 1943 and an international department was created in 1948. Over the next 30 years, offices opened up in major cities, including London, San Francisco and Dallas.

Bear Stearns went public in October 1985, continuing to increase its service capabilities as it headed into the 1990s. The firm launched its derivatives department in February 1993 and, in 1996, it co-managed the Lucent Technologies IPO, which was then the largest IPO in U.S. history. Bear also served as an advisor in the mega-merger of telecom giants Bell Atlantic and NYNEX, which became Verizon Communications. Today, the firm has more than 13,000 employees operating out of 30 offices in major cities in the US, China, Ireland, Switzerland, Italy, Brazil, Singapore and Japan.

Conquering Europe

Bear Stearns has made growing its European operations a priority, focusing on expanding its London office, BSIL, which recently added a new European capital markets group, in order to integrate debt and equity transactions for European and Middle Eastern clients. As part of the European expansion, Bear Stearns has shuffled the heads of top posts in Europe, promoting Michel Péretié to chief executive officer for Europe — in addition to his role as chairman of Bear Stearns International Limited. Other European appointments in 2006 include the installation of new heads of equity, fixed income, fixed income sales, commercial mortgage-backed securities and strategic finance expansion.

Breaking records

Bear Stearns is notably one of the few investment banks that has remained independent — it has never merged with another bank. For this reason the bank is smaller than competitors like Citigroup and JP Morgan. However, Bear Stearns has had the fiscal advantage of consistently reporting profits for the past 80 years straight. Moreover, the firm took in record profits for the past five consecutive years. In 2006, the firm had a net revenue of $9.2 billion, a 25 per cent increase over the previous year. Bear Stearns reported a soaring $2.1 billion in net income for the 2006 fiscal year, an increase of 40 per cent over 2005. Like peers Goldman Sachs and Morgan Stanley, Bear Stearns has also broken new records with executive pay. To reward performance in 2006, the company gave Chief Executive James E. Cayne a bonus of $14.8 million in stock. The company also gave out a total of $12 million in end-of-the-year bonuses to its staff.

Honours, awards and accolades

With 57 deals in 2006 for a total value of $151.2 billion, Bear Stearns currently ranks 17th on the list of the top-25 mergers and acquisitions advisory firms in the world. In July 2006, *Euromoney* recognized the firm as Best Investment Bank and Best in Risk Management, while *Fortune* named it the Most Admired Securities Firm in 2005. *Institutional Investor* awarded the Bear Stearns equity research department second place in its 2006 Alpha All-America Research Team survey of hedge funds, based on votes from more than 250 hedge funds.

GETTING HIRED

Fore more information about job opportunities or graduate positions at Bear Stearns, see the Careers section of the company's web site at www.bearstearns.com.

Visit **Vault Europe's Finance Career Channel** at **www.vault.com/europe** for insider firm profiles, employee surveys of finance professionals in Europe, message boards, job listings, expert finance career advice, insider salary information and more.

V/\ULT CAREER LIBRARY   **99**

Global Headquarters
16, Boulevard des Italiens
75009 Paris
France
Phone: +33 1 401 445 46
Fax: +33 1 401 469 73

Fixed Income Headquarters
10 Harewood Avenue
London
NW1 6AA
Phone: +44 207 595 4129
Fax: +44 207 595 5126
www.bnpparibas.com
www.graduates.bnpparibas.co.uk

EUROPEAN LOCATIONS

Paris (Global HQ)
United Kingdom (Fixed Income HQ)
Austria • Belgium • Bulgaria •
Cyprus • Czech Republic • Denmark
• France • Finland • Germany •
Greece • Hungary • Ireland • Italy •
Jersey • Luxembourg • Netherlands
• Norway • Poland • Portugal •
Romania • Russia • Serbia •
Slovakia • Spain • Sweden •
Switzerland • Turkey • Ukraine

DEPARTMENTS

Asset Management & Services •
BNP Paribas Capital (Private
Equity) • Corporate & Investment
Banking • Retail Banking

THE BUZZ
WHAT EMPLOYEES AT OTHER FIRMS ARE SAYING

• "Diversity of working fields"
• Occasional weekend hours

THE STATS

Employer Type: Public Company
Ticker Symbol: BNP
(Euronext Paris: BNP), 8664 (Tokyo)
President and CEO: Baudouin Prot
2006 Net Income: € 27.9 billion
2005 Net Income: € 21.9 billion
No. of Employees: 140,000
No. of Offices: 2,200 branches

KEY COMPETITORS

Credit Agricole
HSBC Holdings
Société Générale

PLUSES

Strong emphasis on training

MINUSES

Not a top-tier name outside France

EMPLOYMENT CONTACT

www.graduates.bnpparibas.co.uk

THE SCOOP

A major player

BNP Paribas is the largest European bank by total assets, the second-largest by market capitalisation and the sixteenth-largest company in the world. The bank has a foothold in 88 countries, with 2,200 branches in France, managing €54 billion of the €500 billion of assets in the French market. It divides its business into three sectors: corporate and investment banking, asset management and services, and retail banking.

BNP Paribas got its name from the phrase "Paris et Pays-Bas" (Paris and The Netherlands) — and traces its roots to the Banque de Paris et Pays-Bas, which was founded in 1872. BNP Paribas was born from a series of mergers that began in 1966, when Comptoir National d'Escompte de Paris (CNEP) and Banque Nationale pour le Commerce et l'Industrie (BNCI) joined to form Banque National de Paris (BNP). The Paribas Group formed in May 1998 after years of French banking nationalisation and reorganization, and the group included the Banque Paribas, Compagnie Financière de Paribas and Compagnie Bancaire. In 1999, with the approval of the French financial markets authorities, BNP took control of the Paribas Group. The result was one of the largest financial institutions in Europe.

A global reach

BNP Paribas dominates the French retail banking business and is aggressively expanding its services into the rest of Europe. Part of this growth is derived from its increased focus on Internet technology and online banking products, and part derives from BNP Paribas' ability to buy up other banks.

After a failed bid by Spain's BBVA and the Bank of Italy's rejection of Italian insurer Unipol's bid, in February 2006, BNP Paribas moved to take control of its biggest competitor in Italy, Banca Nazionale del Lavoro (BNL), by making an initial acquisition of 48 per cent of the company. By May, the bank had increased its ownership of BNL to 97 per cent in a gradual takeover. BNL is Italy's sixth-largest bank by deposits and loans. In a move to further boost its visibility in the region, in June 2006 BNP offered €1 billion to the Italian car company Fiat to take over half of Fidis, its finance division, but was beat out by Credit Agricole.

BNL contributed €2.23 billion to BNP's group revenue for the first nine months of 2006 — and retail banking, a key part of the business, makes up about 60 per cent of total revenue. About 25 per cent comes from corporate and investment banking and 15 per cent from asset management services. French retail banking accounts for almost half of all retail banking income, with six million customers able to access 2,200 branches and 3,400

Visit **Vault Europe's Finance Career Channel** at **www.vault.com/europe** for insider firm profiles, employee surveys of finance professionals in Europe, message boards, job listings, expert finance career advice, insider salary information and more.

VAULT CAREER LIBRARY 101

ATMs. In Paris, BNP has 15 per cent of the retail market. "We are increasing our retail activity in three key places — Italy, Ukraine and Turkey," said BNP Paribas' chief executive Baudouin Prot in January 2007. "The acquisition in 2006 of BNL has made Italy our second domestic market. Over the next three years in Italy, our plan is to exploit synergies and leverage the strong pre-existing product platform of BNP Paribas."

In December 2006, BNP acquired the Paris-based private banking arm of Franco-Belgian bank Dexia in a deal worth about €200 million. Dexia, with a staff of almost 200, had revenue of almost €19 million and net profits of €3.6 million in the first half of 2006.

Looking progressively eastward

In April 2006, BNP bought up 51 per cent of UkrSibbank, the fourth-largest bank in the Ukraine. In the same year, BNP also became one of the leading bidders in the battle to acquire 80 per cent of the Bank of Alexandria in the Egyptian government's sell-off of the state-owned institution. However, Italy's Sanpaolo was the eventual winner. Three months later, BNP arranged a $400 million, three-and-a-half year loan for Rinat Akhmetov's System Capital Management (SCM), the largest pre-export financing for the Ukraine. SCN is the Ukraine's largest financial-industrial group.

Also in April 2006, BNP acquired a 5.6 per cent stake of Shinhan Financial Group from South Korea for €800 million, boosting its stake to 9.4 per cent, making it the largest shareholder in Korea's second largest financial company. Shinhan focuses on asset management, insurance, leasing and consumer credit. Then in January 2007, BNP pulled out of its Chinese securities joint venture with Changjiang Securities after a squabble over strategy, selling its 33 per cent stake to its Chinese partner for an undisclosed sum. The venture was among the first between a foreign bank and a Chinese securities firm, as only Goldman Sachs, Morgan Stanley and UBS are involved in Chinese securities. But, at the time of press, BNP still holds a 19.2 per cent stake in Nanjing City Commercial Bank.

Taking home the gold

BNP Paribas Corporate and Invest Banking was named No. 1 in France and Top 10 in Europe in M&A by Thomson Financial, and won 2006 European M&A Deal of the Year for the Amena acquisition from *Financial News*. The bank also won Emerging Market Deal of the Year for the sale of Turk Telecom from *Acquisition Monthly*. BNP also went home with Best Deal of 2006 for its acquisition of BNL. In November 2006, BNP Paribas was awarded the Bank Deal of the Year award for its acquisition of BNL at the annual Retail Banker International Global Awards dinner in London. The deal gave BNP Paribas control of Italy's sixth-largest bank, with a national network of approximately 900 outlets and more than three million retail banking customers.

GETTING HIRED

It's a long, long list

Under the careers link at www.graduates.bnpparibas.co.uk, the bank lists internships as well as professional positions, adding that its spectrum of available openings is wide and that it's "impossible to list all of the careers available within BNP Paribas." The bank goes on to say that for most positions, "a degree is the minimum qualification required," though "many of our employees have pursued their studies at least until master's level." And in the corporate and investment banking sphere, the firm adds, "A previous internship in finance is a real advantage." Applicants are encouraged to complete an application form before the specified deadline for the programme to which they are applying. Once in the office, expect interviews with HR, group case study exercises and interviews with line managers. One candidate says he ultimately ended up interviewing with "a managing director, director, line manager and head of brokerage."

OUR SURVEY SAYS

Competitive but reasonable

The workplace culture is "competitive but fair", sources say, and managers are "very good" and "very professional." Hours range from about "50 to 60" during the week, although one insider says that he works "about once a month" on weekends. Compensation largely gets good marks from respondents, with "share plans" offered to employees. And there aren't any complaints about the casual Fridays offered, either. The firm says that training "is a priority within the group" and involves a "personalised training programme". BNP Paribas even employs a specific centre in France to "develop skills and promote knowledge" for trainees. Promoting diversity within the firm gets high marks, too, with no one noting any particular grievances.

Visit **Vault Europe's Finance Career Channel** at www.vault.com/europe for insider firm profiles, employee surveys of finance professionals in Europe, message boards, job listings, expert finance career advice, insider salary information and more.

VAULT CAREER LIBRARY   103

HSBC Holdings

8 Canada Square
London E14 5HQ
United Kingdom
Phone: +44 (0) 20 7991 8888
Fax: +44 (0)20 7992 4880
www.hsbc.com

EUROPEAN LOCATIONS

London (HQ)
Armenia • Belgium • Cyprus •
Czech Republic • France •
Germany • Greece • Guernsey •
Hungary • Ireland • Isle of Man •
Italy • Jersey • Luxembourg •
Malta • Monaco • Netherlands •
Poland • Russia • Slovakia • Spain
• Sweden • Switzerland • Turkey
• United Kingdom.

DEPARTMENTS

Asset Management
Commercial Banking
Consumer Banking
Credit Cards
Insurance
Leasing
Private Banking
Securities Trading

THE BUZZ
WHAT EMPLOYEES AT OTHER FIRMS ARE SAYING

• "Global product palette"
• "Stronger in hot emerging
  markets"
• "Culturally adaptive"
• "Weak in investment banking"

THE STATS

Employer Type: Public Company
Ticker Symbol: HSBA (LSE)
Group Chairman: Stephen K. Green
Group CEO: Michael F. Geoghegan
2006 Net income: $16, 871 million
(FYE 12/06)
2005 Net Income: $15,873 million
(FYE 12/05)
No. of Employees: 285,000
No. of Offices: 9,800

KEY COMPETITORS

Barclays
Citigroup
Lloyds TSB

PLUSES

Lots of international opportunity

MINUSES

Not yet a top-tier in IB

EMPLOYMENT CONTACT

www.hsbc.com/hsbc/careers/hsbc-in-
europe

THE SCOOP

The world's bank

HSBC Holdings is the world's largest bank by assets, overtaking Citigroup in August 2006 with assets of $1.74 trillion, up 16 per cent from the previous year. HSBC owns the Hong Kong and Shanghai Banking Corporation, France's CCF (formerly known as Credit Commercial de France) and 62 per cent of Hong Kong's Hang Seng Bank. HSBC literally has a global presence — with national branches in Europe ranging from two in Slovakia to nearly 2,000 in Great Britain. Hong Kong and Shanghai Banking Corporation has 24 outlets in mainland China.

In total, HSBC has about 10,000 offices and a presence in 76 countries, providing a full range of financial services, including consumer and business banking, asset management, investment banking, securities trading, insurance and leasing. HSBC also has almost a 20 per cent stake in the country's fifth-largest lender, Bank of Communications Co. — and an 8 per cent piece of the Bank of Shanghai.

Rising in the East

HSBC traces its history back to 1865 and the founding of the Hong Kong and Shanghai Banking Corporation Limited, which opened offices in Shanghai and London. Thomas Sutherland, Hong Kong Superintendent of the Peninsular and Oriental Stream Navigation Company, saw a need for local banking branches in Hong Kong and along the China Coast. Through the next several decades and into the 20th century, the company opened branches in China and Southeast Asia, eventually expanding into the Indian sub-continent, Europe and North America. In 1959, the Hongkong and Shanghai Banking Corp. acquired the British Bank of the Middle East (originally the Imperial Bank of Persia, which had a number of operations in the Gulf States) and the Mercantile Bank, which had operations in India and South East Asia.

Six years after that dual purchase, the company bought a controlling interest in the Hang Seng Bank which has been based in Hong Kong since 1933. Through the 1980s, the banking behemoth focused on moving into new markets, establishing the Hongkong Bank of Canada in 1981 and the Hongkong Bank of Australia five years later. In 1987, New York-based Marine Midland Bank became part of Hongkong and Shanghai Banking's holdings and part of the company's US operations. Then, in 1991, the disparate and far-flung operations were brought together under the ownership and control of a new company, HSBC Holdings.

Visit **Vault Europe's Finance Career Channel** at **www.vault.com/europe** for insider firm profiles, employee surveys of finance professionals in Europe, message boards, job listings, expert finance career advice, insider salary information and more.

V/\ULT CAREER LIBRARY **105**

Feeding frenzy

The company's acquisitive pace continued and, in 1992, HSBC bought UK-based Midland Bank and formed the HSBC Investment Bank, which tied together the company's London merchant and securities banking businesses. Throughout the 1990s, HSBC expanded into Brazil and Argentina.

In its largest and most important acquisition since the Midland deal, in March 2003, HSBC finalised its monster-sized $14.2 billion acquisition of Household International, a major provider of consumer finance and a top-10 issuer of credit cards in the US. In December 2004, Household International merged with Household Finance Corporation, the holding company for Household's US-based consumer finance operations, and subsequently changed its name to HSBC Finance. In July 2006, the firm received approval from the China Banking Regulatory Commission to proceed with plans to open a branch in Xi'an. Just weeks later, HSBC announced that it had entered into an agreement with Grupo Banistmo S.A., the leading banking group in Central America, to acquire all outstanding shares. Banistmo owns Primer Banco del Istmo, the largest bank in Panama, which will complement HSBC Bank Panama S.A.'s presence in the country.

Also in July 2006, HSBC inked a deal to buy Panama's largest bank, Grupo Banistmo, for $1.77 billion in cash, giving the bank a foothold in five Latin American countries. HSBC ended the year with some holiday shopping and returning, acquiring the mortgage loan portfolio of Champion Mortgage, a Parsippany, New Jersey-based division of Key Bank with a loan portfolio valued at about $2.5 billion and 30,000 customers. Then, in December 2006, HSBC Bank Australia inked a deal to sell its broker-originated mortgage book to FirstMac, but still retaining the majority of its Aussie residential mortgage portfolio.

Riding the tiger

In February 2005, HSBC bought a stake in China Minsheng Banking Corp., China's first listed private bank. HSBC will take advantage of its status as a Qualified Foreign Institutional Investor with a license to trade in local currency A-shares and convertible bonds to buy China Minsheng A-shares on the market. HSBC wasn't just looking to expand into the Chinese banking market, however. In May 2005, the firm spent $1 billion to double its stake in the Chinese insurer Ping An, making it the largest foreign investor in the country's financial services industry.

HSBC is just one of the banks competing for China's business, fighting over a share of the country's $1.35 trillion in household savings. China's economy is the fastest growing of the world's 20 largest economies, making it a lucrative prize for the winning banks. In April 2007, HSBC Holdings was one of four foreign banks that began accepting Yuan deposits from private Chinese citizens, marking the liberalization of China's financial sector as it was obligated to do so, after it joined the WTO

Changing of the guard

After eight years as chairman and 45 years working at HSBC, Sir John Bond retired in May 2006. Ending his career on a high note, Sir John noted the preceding three years' impressive shareholder returns, and HSBC's sustained progress in 2005. Former Chief Executive Stephen Green has taken over Sir John's position as chairman, with the position of chief executive filled by Michael Geoghegan.

Also in May, the co-head of HSBC's investment bank, John Studzinski, announced he was leaving the firm to join private equity fund The Blackstone Group. The move highlighted the challenges HSBC among other banks were having getting a foothold in the investment banking world.

Everything's gone green

In 2006, HSBC established a group sustainable development unit, to focus on "climate change, particular low carbon technology, renewable energy, water infrastructure, sustainable forestry and microfinance." The same year, HSBC became the first big company in Luxembourg to sign a delivery contract for "100 per cent green" electricity. HSBC is supplying its Luxembourg businesses with electricity produced entirely from renewable resources — at least until June 2008. The green electricity will come to HSBC Luxembourg by way of hydroelectric plants in Austria and Switzerland.

At the first ever *Financial Times* Sustainable Banking Awards in June 2006, HSBC was named the overall winner, recognised for its leadership role in merging social, environmental and business concerns. The FT Sustainable Banking Awards also commended HSBC for excellence in the Sustainable Deal of the Year category, for a project finance deal in Santiago, Chile, which will provide 1,800 low emission buses for the local transport system.

HSBC also took home an award of particular interest to young job seekers — Employer of Choice for Finance as part of *The Times* Graduate Recruitment Awards 2006. In June 2006, the company won Best Corporate Governance honours from IR magazine's UK Awards 2006. HSBC Global Transaction Banking won first place in *Euromoney*'s International Cash Management Poll in October 2006 and the next month HSBC was named Best Consumer Internet Bank-Global by *Global Finance* magazine.

GETTING HIRED

To learn more about career opportunities, internships and graduate programmes at HSBC, visit the company's European careers site at www.hsbc.com/hsbc/careers/hsbc-in-europe.

Visit **Vault Europe's Finance Career Channel** at **www.vault.com/europe** for insider firm profiles, employee surveys of finance professionals in Europe, message boards, job listings, expert finance career advice, insider salary information and more.

VAULT CAREER LIBRARY 107

RBS

The Royal Bank of Scotland Group
36 St. Andrews Square
Edinburgh EH2 2YB
United Kingdom
Phone: +44 (0) 131 556 8555
Fax: +44 (0)131 557 6140
www.makeitrbs.com

EUROPEAN LOCATIONS

Edinburgh (Global HQ)*
Frankfurt
Helsinki
London
Madrid
Milan
Munich
Oslo
Paris
Piraeus
Rome
Stockholm
*Offices throughout the UK

DEPARTMENTS

Citizens
Corporate Markets
RBS Insurance
Retail Markets
Ulster Bank Group

THE BUZZ
WHAT EMPLOYEES AT OTHER FIRMS ARE SAYING

- "Very big name"
- "Too regional"

THE STATS

Employer Type: Public Company
Ticker Symbol: RBS (London)
Chairman: Sir Thomas F.W. McKillop
Group Chief Executive & Executive Director: Sir Frederick A. Goodwin
2006 Revenue: £15,522 million (FYE 12/06)
2005 Revenue: £6,497 million (FYE 12/05)
2006 Net Income: £13,956 million
2005 Net Income: £5,558 million
No. of Employees: 137,000
No. of Offices & Global branches: 2,720

KEY COMPETITORS

Barclays
Citigroup
HSBC Holdings

PLUSES

Lots of opportunities for graduates

MINUSES

Focus unclear

EMPLOYMENT CONTACT

Graduate recruitment:
www.makeitrbs.com

Careers:
www.rbs.com/careers

THE SCOOP

Making it happen

The Royal Bank of Scotland (RBS) is the third-largest financial institution in Europe and the ninth-largest in the world. RBS, a FTSE 100 company, is also ranked No. 39 on the *Financial Times*'s FT 50. Founded in Edinburgh by royal charter in 1727, the company opened its first branch in 1783. Today its branch network blankets the British Isles. The history of the Royal Bank of Scotland has really become synonymous with the history of British banking itself. With the acquisition of National Westminster Bank (NatWest) in 2000 (the biggest takeover in the history of British banking) and the August 2004 purchase of Charter One Financial — the 40th-largest lender in the US — RBS continues to grow its businesses around the world. In January 2006, RBS joined a consortium and took a 10 per cent stake of one of China's largest banks — the Bank of China.

A failed expedition launches a financial superpower

RBS can trace its roots back to the Darien Company, which launched a disastrous expedition to establish a Scottish trading company in Panama in 1699. England compensated the Scottish creditors eight years later — because it had promised support and then pulled out, which ultimately led to the expedition's failure. The entrepreneurial creditors began lending the money they were given and eventually, in 1727, received a charter and became the Bank of Scotland. RBS opened a London branch in 1874 and almost a century later merged with the National Commercial Bank in 1968. Then, in 2000, after a long takeover fight with archrival Bank of Scotland, RBS finally bought NatWest. RBS proceeded to sell off the Gartmore Investment Management fund management division to Nationwide Mutual Insurance Co. and NatWest's Equity Partners unit, launching NatWest Private Banking to provide services to the wealthy.

For the love of Europe

RBS has offices throughout Europe. RBS' French and German offices have been open since 1998, providing global banking and markets (GBM) products. The firm's Greek branch opened in 1973 and is now the world's leading lending bank to Greece's shipping market. In Spain, RBS opened an office in 2001 and an Italian branch opened in 2002. The most recent branch, in the Nordic region, opened in 2004. RBS is comprised of five divisions that in turn are made up of 41 brands. Between its two retail banking arms, the Royal Bank of Scotland's retail banking and NatWest's retail banking, RBS operates 2,720 branches. Private banking customers have six options to choose from, including Coutts & Co., Adam & Company, The Royal Bank of Scotland International and NatWest Private Banking.

Visit **Vault Europe's Finance Career Channel** at **www.vault.com/europe** for insider firm profiles, employee surveys of finance professionals in Europe, message boards, job listings, expert finance career advice, insider salary information and more.

VAULT CAREER LIBRARY 109

The bank's GBM and UK corporate banking (UKCB) practices provide financial advisory to more than one-third of the United Kingdom's medium- and large-sized businesses. The division offers structured finance, equity finance and asset finance services to more than 75,000 clients. RBS has relationships with more than 3,000 correspondent banks and is a leader in private placements, as well as the top provider of sterling interest rate swaps, and FX and interest rate derivatives in the UK. Chairman Sir George Mathewson retired in April 2006, having presided over the bank's ascension to Scotland's first £1 billion profit company. Sir Tom McKillop, who was previously the chief executive of pharmaceuticals giant Astra Zeneca, was appointed the new chairman. McKillop has been on the board at RBS since September 2005.

Land of the rising market

RBS joined a consortium buying a 10 per cent share in the Bank of China in January 2006. The group shelled out about $3.1 billion for a stake in China's second-biggest lender, with RBS investing $1.6 billion. RBS's goal is to build on Bank of China's distribution strength and expand its credit card, wealth management, corporate banking and personal insurance business lines in China.

The two banks will co-operate in the key areas of corporate governance, risk management, financial management, human resources and information technology. Bank of China went public on the Hong Kong and Shanghai exchanges in June, diluting RBS' stake from 10 per cent to 4.26 per cent. The Chinese government holds a 67 per cent stake. In June 2006, RBS also launched a US dollar swap, trading via Bloomberg during Asian business hours. The launch is a step toward providing a fully global electronic offering for interest rate derivatives. The firm is a leader in USD IRD electronic liquidity, providing trading functionality during European, US and Asia-Pacific trading hours.

Movers and shakers

In February 2006 Guy Whittaker was appointed group finance director, and Enrico Cantarelli as managing director, head of public sector Italy. Cantarelli was previously with the Italian Ministry of Economy and Finance. Sandra Wong was named head of CDO structuring, structured credit and equity products group in March 2006. Four months later, in July, the firm strengthened its financial institutional FX sales team by hiring Michael Kiehl, based in London, and Jeff Robertson, based at RBS Greenwich Capital in New York. In December 2006, RBS named Mark Parry head of Europe and Infrastructure Finance Group, which is part of the project and export finance business.

A particularly good year

In the first half of 2006, RBS headed the league table for US mortgage-backed securities, with 65 deals totaling $64.2 billion. The firm also ranked No. 6 on the US asset-backed securities table, with $39 billion on seven issues. In global mortgage-backed securities, the bank posted $75.1 billion in proceeds in the first half of the year. RBS jumped up one spot to No. 4 on the global syndicated loans table, with 171 issues totaling $76.5 billion in the first half of 2006.

The bank was also one of the lead arrangers for the $15 billion loan to ConocoPhillips. In European, Middle Eastern and African syndicated loans, the bank fell one spot to No. 4, with 125 issues worth $56 billion. In December 2006, Thomson's International Financing Review named RBS European Securitisation House of the Year. RBS was also named Bank of the Year for Securitisation by *The Banker*. RBS reported net income rose to £2.98 billion in the first half of 2006, up 18 per cent compared to the first half of 2005. The company said its 2006 results would exceed analysts' expectations due to organic growth, but its US business faced some challenges.

A helping hand

In June 2006, the firm launched a pilot work-learning programme for youth in Manchester, England. Through Wythenshawe Education Action Zones (WyEAZs), students aged 15 to 16 years spend one day per week in work placements at the bank, working toward an NVQ in business administration. After completing the programme, students are granted an interview for a permanent position.

In addition, RBS Group is the largest corporate donor to the Money Advice Trust, which offers free and confidential advice through support for organisations such as Citizens Advice Bureau. The trust assists people struggling with debt by placing them with personal financial advisors. The RBS Innovate Fund, which is administered by Transact, the national forum for financial inclusion, works with more than 550 charities. Some of the charities the fund works with are The ARIE Centre, which provides legal advice and services to migrants, and the Salvation Army.

GETTING HIRED

Applications for all of the graduate programmes open at the beginning of September. Deadlines vary, with the corporate markets programme closing in early November and the remaining graduate programmes closing from the end of January onwards. Check the graduate recruitment web site at www.makeitrbs.com, for further information.

Visit **Vault Europe's Finance Career Channel** at **www.vault.com/europe** for insider firm profiles, employee surveys of finance professionals in Europe, message boards, job listings, expert finance career advice, insider salary information and more.

VAULT CAREER LIBRARY   111

To find out how to work for RBS, visit www.rbs.com and click on the Careers link where you can search and apply for jobs, find information about internships and graduate opportunities and also learn about RBS' interesting "Fast Track relationship management programme", which the firm describes as an "Intensive trainee programme designed to suit people from a broad range of diverse backgrounds."

"The history of the Royal Bank of Scotland has really become synonymous with the history of British banking itself"

Dresdner Kleinwort IB

30 Gresham Street
London EC2P 2XY
United Kingdom
Phone: +44 (0) 20 7623 8000
Fax: +44 (0) 20 7623 4069

Theodor-Heuss-Alle 44-46
60486 Frankfurt
Germany
Phone: +49 (0) 69 713 0
www.dresdnerkleinwort.com

EUROPEAN LOCATIONS

Amsterdam • Athens • Berlin •
Brussels • Budapest • Dortmund •
Dusseldorf • Frankfurt • Hamburg
• Istanbul • Kiev • London •
Luxembourg • Madrid • Milan •
Moscow • Munich • Paris • Riga •
St Petersburg • Stuttgart • Vienna
• Warsaw • Zurich

DEPARTMENTS

Capital Markets • Global Banking
(including Strategic Advisory,
M&A, Global Finance, Global
Loans & Transaction Services) •
Research

THE BUZZ
WHAT EMPLOYEES AT OTHER FIRMS ARE SAYING

- "Doing better"
- "Not really getting there"
- "Strong name"
- "Robotic"

THE STATS

Employer Type: IB arm of Dresdner
Bank AG
Dresdner Bank Frankfurt: DRB
Chairman: Herbert Walter
CEO: Stefan Jentzsch
No. of Employees: 5,500 (Globally)
No. of Offices: 50

KEY COMPETITORS

Citigroup
Credit Suisse
Deutsche
Goldman Sachs
HSBC
JP Morgan
Lazard
Morgan Stanley

PLUSES

Recent high-profile deals

MINUSES

Management recently in transition

EMPLOYMENT CONTACT

www.dresdnerkleinwort.com/eng/care
ersp

THE SCOOP

New name, same bank

Dresdner Kleinwort (DKIB) is the investment banking arm of Dresdner Bank AG, a member of financial service provider, Allianz Group. The bank provides a range of services to corporate, institutional and government clients worldwide and maintains European headquarters in both Frankfurt and London, as well as branches in other financial centres, including New York, Tokyo and Hong Kong.

DKIB is focused on deals in Germany and the UK, but also has offices in France, Italy, Luxembourg, Poland, Russia, Spain and Switzerland, as well as Brazil, China, Malaysia, Singapore and South Africa. As a member of the Allianz Group, Dresdner Kleinwort's corporate family includes thousands of offices around the world.

The bank was created through many mergers and acquisitions, beginning in 1961 with the merger of two small family-owned banks: Robert Benson & Lonsdale and Kleinwort and Sons. The new entity, named Kleinwort Benson, became a major player in the privatisation of British industries (including British Telecom and British Gas) in the 1980s. In 1995 Kleinwort Benson was acquired by the Germany-based Dresdner Bank AG. Dresdner Kleinwort Wasserstein dropped the "Wasserstein" to become, simply, "Dresdner Kleinwort" on June 29, 2006. As part of a corporate restructure, the firm now has two divisions: global banking and capital markets.

Building a giant

The foundation for the bank was laid in January 2001, when Dresdner Bank paid $1.4 billion to purchase the American investment banking boutique Wasserstein Perella. A mergers and acquisitions specialist, Wasserstein Perella was led by star rainmaker Bruce Wasserstein, who built the M&A department at Credit Suisse First Boston before leaving to start his own shop with Joseph Perella.

Dresdner combined Wasserstein Perella with its European investment banking operations, Dresdner Kleinwort Benson, to form Dresdner Kleinwort Wasserstein, providing a platform with substantial resources in both Europe and North America. That same year, the Allianz Group acquired Dresdner Bank AG, thereby creating one of the Eurozone's largest and most powerful integrated financial services providers.

Changing of the old guard

A week before being acquired by Allianz, Steve Berger, head of corporate finance and origination at Dresdner Kleinwort, resigned. Berger left the firm after only two years, and amid frustration with Allianz's alleged lack of strategic clarity regarding Dresdner

Visit Vault Europe's Finance Career Channel at www.vault.com/europe for insider firm profiles, employee surveys of finance professionals in Europe, message boards, job listings, expert finance career advice, insider salary information and more.

VAULT CAREER LIBRARY 115

Kleinwort's future. Another big upheaval came in November 2005, when Andrew Pisker resigned as CEO of the bank after losing his leadership role to Stefan Jentzsch, who took over as head of Dresdner's combined corporate and investment bank.

In March 2006, Steve Bellotti resigned as head of capital markets and was replaced by Jens-Peter Neumann, who worked with Jentzsch at HVB and Goldman Sachs. All three of DKIB's co-heads of capital markets under Bellotti also jumped ship. Don Meltzer, former co-head of corporate finance and origination with Dryer, left in May and became an advisor. The exodus of Pisker's team continued, Joe Dyer, who left BNP Paribas with Pisker to join DKIB, resigned in September 2006 as co-head of advisory. He was replaced by Bert Piedra, former head of European investment banking at Bank of America.

Staying the course

The bank seems to be weathering its changes well and has recently had significant roles in some impressive deals. As sole corporate broker on behalf of NASDAQ, Dresdner Kleinwort successfully executed the crucial purchase of a series of stakes in the London Stock Exchange (LSE), receiving acclaim for catching the market unaware. In July 2006, the bank was one of the joint global coordinators of Rosneft's IPO, said to be the fifth-largest such opening ever, the largest IPO to date on the LSE and Russia's largest ever flotation. Also in July 2006, Dresdner Kleinwort won Inchcape plc as a corporate broking client. The bank claims more than 60 FTSE corporate broking mandates, including seven in the FTSE 100. In October 2006, DKIB teamed up with Barclays Capital to launch a syndicated $1.25 billion in loans with about 25 banks to back Macquarie Infrastructure Partners and Diversified Utility and Energy Trusts in a buyout of Duquesne Light Holdings.

As of July 2006, Dealogic ranked the bank third in German M&A, a position partly attributable to its role as adviser to German pharmaceutical company Schering AG during its €16.5 billion merger with Bayer. Dresdner Kleinwort first advised Schering during a hostile bid by Merck (originally the largest ever German hostile takeover attempt), and eventually negotiated Bayer's white knight bid.

Going green

In January 2007, DKIB teamed up with the Russian energy conglomerate Gazprom in a carbon trading joint venture to invest in mainly Russian and Eastern European projects that create "carbon credits" as per the Kyoto Protocol. Under the UN agreement, companies that invest in projects in Eastern Europe that cut emissions get credits for each ton of carbon dioxide that they eliminate. The credits can then be sold to EU states and other countries that emit more than they were allotted from 2008 to 2012. The venture could generate up to one billion tons of credit that could be worth €15 billion.

Bringing home the gold

DKIB didn't fail to win some rather notable awards in 2006 — it was named Best International M&A Arranger Bank in Russia by *Global Finance Magazine*, Best Arranger of German Loans Best Arranger of Russian Loans in the *EuroWeek* Syndicated Loans & Leveraged Finance Awards, and Emissions Trading House of the Year in *The Banker*, Investment Banking Awards. The bank's deals have also garnered recognition, as it won Corporate Bond of the Year from *Financial News* magazine for Linde's €1.06 billion hybrid bond and IPO of the Year from Financial News for Rosneft's $10.8 billion flotation.

GETTING HIRED

In addition to strategic advisory, M&A, global finance, global loans and transaction services, capital markets and research, Dresdner Kleinwort also recruit graduates into IT and risk management. For more information about careers and graduate opportunities at DKIB, visit the company's web site at www.dresdnerkleinwort.com.

Visit **Vault Europe's Finance Career Channel** at **www.vault.com/europe** for insider firm profiles, employee surveys of finance professionals in Europe, message boards, job listings, expert finance career advice, insider salary information and more.

VAULT CAREER LIBRARY 117

20 Bank of America (Europe)

5 Canada Square
London E14 5AQ
United Kingdom
Phone: +44 (0) 20 7174 4000
Fax: +44 (0) 20 7174 6400
www.bankofamerica.com

EUROPEAN LOCATIONS

Amsterdam
Antwerp
Athens
Dublin
Frankfurt
London
Madrid
Milan
Paris

DEPARTMENTS

Capital Markets
Corporate & Investment Banking
Global Markets
Global Middle Office
MBNA Europe
Risk
Technology & Operations
Treasury Services

THE STATS

Employer Type: Public Company
Ticker Symbol: BAC (NYSE)
Chairman, CEO and President:
Kenneth D. Lewis
2006 Revenue: $74,247 million
(FYE 12/06)
2006 Employees: 200,000
2005 Employees: 176,638
No. of Offices: 6,000 (Worldwide)

PLUSES

Big European ambitions

MINUSES

Relatively new to Europe

EMPLOYMENT CONTACT

www.bankofamerica.com/careers

THE BUZZ
WHAT EMPLOYEES AT OTHER FIRMS ARE SAYING

- "Big, expanding, acquiring"
- "Good, friendly people"
- "Underdog"
- "Trying to get a foothold in Europe"

THE SCOOP

Start at the beginning

The banks that eventually became Bank of America were the first banks in the new nation, back in the late 18th Century. In 1784 the Massachusetts Bank was chartered, followed in 1791 by the Providence Bank in Rhode Island. These banks grew with the country, undergoing decades of expansion and M&A. Fast-forward to two centuries later and the modern roots of Bank of America can be found in the 1960s, when North Carolina National Bank (NCNB) began an aggressive plan of expansion based on a "hometown bank" model that would allow each branch to be fully shaped by the needs of its community.

In 1991 NCNB merged with C&S/Sovran Corporation to form NationsBank. Then in 1998, NationsBank acquired BankAmerica to become Bank of America, creating a bank whose business reached across the country. The next major step of the banking giant's growth came in 2004, when Bank of America acquired with FleetBoston Financial for $47 billion. The following year, Bank of America acquired MBNA, a commercial bank with operations in the US, England, Scotland, Ireland and Canada, for $35 billion. Today Bank of America is ranked among the world's largest financial institutions, serving individual clients, small and middle-market businesses and large corporations in over 175 countries. It can also boast business relationships with 80 per cent of the Global Fortune 500.

A peek inside

Bank of America has had a presence in the European region since 1922. As of the first financial quarter 2007, the company employed more than 8,350 people in Europe. Of this, approximately 2,850 are legacy Bank of America businesses based offices in the UK, Belgium, France, Germany, Greece, Italy, The Netherlands, The Republic of Ireland and Spain. Close to 5,500 work for Bank of America's Europe Card Services division (i.e. legacy MBNA).

Bank of America's global corporate and investment banking group (GCIB) focuses on companies with an annual revenue of more than $2.5 million, middle-market and large corporations, institutional investors, financial institutions and government entities. GCIB provides innovative services in M&A, equity and debt capital raising, lending, trading, risk management, treasury management and research.

Many of the company's services to corporate and institutional clients are provided through its US and UK subsidiaries, Banc of America Securities LLC and Banc of America Securities Limited. The company's GCIB division covers a range of industries, including consumer and retail, financial institutions, financial sponsors, global industrial, health care, media and telecommunications, natural resources and real estate, and gaming. Building on

Visit **Vault Europe's Finance Career Channel** at **www.vault.com/europe** for insider firm profiles, employee surveys of finance professionals in Europe, message boards, job listings, expert finance career advice, insider salary information and more.

VAULT CAREER LIBRARY **119**

its global strengths, the bank has particularly strong financial institutions and financial sponsors client coverage groups in place that are rapidly gaining market share.

A representative from Bank of America says, "Our focus in Europe is on building long-term relationships with our clients and providing them with integrated business solutions. The bank does this by capitalising on its strong debt and equity product expertise, capturing leveraged finance opportunities, expanding its M&A capabilities and leveraging its strengths. Bank of America is committed to methodically building its businesses into positions of leadership."

The firm's growth strategy is to expand the universal bank model, with global markets as a core competency. This expansion is centred on a systematic build of market presence and profitability through close global coordination of the major markets presences in New York, Charlotte, London, Hong Kong and Tokyo. In addition, the bank believes that close linkages to the other major client facing businesses including investment banking, corporate banking and global treasury services are key to providing its clients with a fully integrated banking service. Bank of America's global treasury services group is a leading global provider of integrated working capital management solutions, focused on relationships with targeted clients, including multinational corporations, US businesses, financial institutions and the US government.

Off to London

Several US-based executives have recently moved from the US to London, including Mike Meyer, EMEA/Asia head of global credit products; Jeff Pagano, EMEA/Asia head of global liquid products and Joel Van Dusen, EMEA head of global investment banking. In the beginning of 2006, Bank of America significantly boosted its European equity financial products (EFP) business with the transfer of Ben Wilkinson from New York. In his position as global head of equity derivative products, Wilkinson's establishment of the London-based group is a significant achievement in Bank of America's strategy to extend a number of its US-based product competencies into a cohesive European platform that balances market presence and profitability.

In the US, Bank of America EFP is one of the largest equity derivatives dealers in terms of revenue and capital commitment to client activities and is a top-five player in US prime brokerage. In Europe, the team is leveraging this leading equity derivatives business, risk management infrastructure and US client franchise and is making a concerted push into the Europe.

Growing, growing

Bank of America made two significant acquisitions in the second half of 2006, fueling its growth worldwide. First it agreed to exchange its BankBoston operations in Chile and Uruguay for $650 million in stock in Banco Itau Holding Financeira S.A. (Itau). This came in August, after a similar BankBoston/Itau deal, in which Itau bought Bank of America's Brazilian operations for $720 million, was struck in May 2006. Bank of America now owns approximately 7.4 per cent of Itau's equity. Then in November, Bank of America acquired US Trust Corporation, an American firm focused exclusively on wealth management for high-net-worth and ultra-high-net-worth individuals and families. The purchase, from The Charles Schwab Corporation, is set to close in the third financial quarter 2007. The deal is valued at $3.3 billion.

In December 2006 Chief Financial Officer Alvaro G. de Molina announced his retirement from the company. Joe Price, a risk management executive for global corporate and investment banking, was named as his successor. Price, a 23-year veteran of the bank, joined Bank of America from Price Waterhouse's financial institutions national industry group.

Where they stand

The 2006 banking league tables showed Bank of America doing well, though its biggest lead wasn't in flashy mergers and acquisitions. For both worldwide announced and completed M&A the bank placed No. 14, with 121 deals worth $233.8 billion and 92 deals worth $188.6 billion, respectively. But in global loans for 2006, Bank of America ranked third, making 1,074 issues worth just over $330 billion. Also, it placed sixth in global high-yield debt, with 72 transactions for the year and ninth for global debt, global asset-backed securities and global convertibles.

GETTING HIRED

To find out more about careers and graduate opportunities at Bank of America, see the careers section of the company's web site at www.bankofamerica.com/careers.

Visit **Vault Europe's Finance Career Channel** at **www.vault.com/europe** for insider firm profiles, employee surveys of finance professionals in Europe, message boards, job listings, expert finance career advice, insider salary information and more.

VAULT CAREER LIBRARY   121

Greenhill & Co.

Lansdowne House
57 Berkeley Square
London W1J 6ER
United Kingdom
Phone: +44 20 7198 7400
Fax: +44 20 7198 7500
www.greenhill.com

EUROPEAN LOCATIONS

London (HQ)
Frankfurt

DEPARTMENTS

Financial Advisory
Merchant Banking
Mergers & Acquisitions

THE STATS

Employer Type: Public Company
Chairman & CEO: Robert F. Greenhill
Ticker Symbol: GHL (NYSE)
2006 Net Income: $75.7 million
(FYE 12/06)
2006 Revenue: $290.6 million
(FYE 12/06)
2005 Net Income: $55.5 (FYE 12/05)
2005 Revenue: $221.2 million
(FYE 12/05)
No. of Employees: 201
No. of Offices: 5

KEY COMPETITORS

Goldman Sachs
Lazard
Merrill Lynch
Morgan Stanley
Rothschild

PLUSES

Great reputation
Growing fast

MINUSES

Small fish in big sea
Only two divisions can limit
opportunities

THE BUZZ
WHAT EMPLOYEES AT OTHER FIRMS ARE SAYING

- "Prestigious boutique, pays well"
- "Very demanding work environment"
- "Good place to work"
- "Niche place"

EMPLOYMENT CONTACT

www.greenhill.com
(See "Careers" section)

THE SCOOP

Unique in size, not results

Greenhill is a small fish in the world of finance — and it hopes to stay that way. In contrast to its many-sided competitors, Greenhill is divided into just two divisions: financial advisory services and merchant banking. The firm prides itself on its independence from large institutions and its focus — both of which have enabled it to excel in merger, acquisition and restructuring advice for a growing list of large international clients. As part of its merchant banking division, Greenhill's private equity funds are sparking interest by participating in an increasing number of high stakes deals around the globe.

The history of one man

Greenhill was founded just over 10 years ago by current Chairman and CEO Robert F. Greenhill. Prior to launching the firm, Greenhill was chairman and CEO of Smith Barney — and before that, he had spent more than three decades at Morgan Stanley, where amongst other things, the firm explains Greenhill "founded the M&A group and overran the establishment of Morgan Stanley's private equity group". An energetic banker now in his 70s, Greenhill's involvement in, ah, Greenhill, is impressive for any age. In addition to holding the top spot, he serves on the firm's management committee and on Greenhill Capital Partners' investment committee.

Just two years after the opening of its first office in New York, Greenhill opened a second office in London to serve European clients and to engage in transatlantic business. Greenhill Capital Partners, the private equity arm, was launched in early 2000, and subsequently raised $423 million in investment capital. Later the same year, Greenhill opened a second European office, this time in Frankfurt, Germany. A financial restructuring practice was added in January of 2001, expanding the firm's advisory practice. Greenhill opened offices in Dallas, Texas and Toronto in 2005 and 2006, bringing its total number of offices to five, firmly establishing the firm's global presence.

More M&A means more business

Greenhill is primarily an advisory firm, with financial advisory services contributing approximately 72 per cent of total revenue. Its mergers and acquisitions practice offers sell-side and buy-side advisory, merger advisory and cross-border advisory, leveraging the firm's international network of offices. With M&A activity heating up around the globe, Greenhill has reaped the rewards in increased revenue from advisory services. Recent transactions advised by Greenhill include the $25 billion proposed sale of SLM Corporation (Sallie Mae) to a consortium led by J.C. Flowers and including Bank of

Visit **Vault Europe's Finance Career Channel** at www.vault.com/europe for insider firm profiles, employee surveys of finance professionals in Europe, message boards, job listings, expert finance career advice, insider salary information and more.

VAULT CAREER LIBRARY   123

America and JP Morgan Chase, the pending $19.1 billion sale of Gallaher Group plc to Japan Tobacco, and the pending $225 billion sale of Alliance Boots plc to KKR.

Greenhill's restructuring advisory division guides debtors, creditors and acquirers, both inside and outside of formal bankruptcy, through a range of restructuring activities. These can include reorganisation proceedings, the identification of targets or buyers, sales or court proceedings, or recapitalisations. Greenhill's restructuring clients, like its M&A clients, come from a range of industries. Advised restructurings include the Chapter 11 proceedings of General Motors suppliers Delphi and the restructuring of Delta Air Lines, specifically in connection with strategic and labour issues relating to its Chapter 11 proceedings.

The Greenhill angle

Greenhill's private equity arm, Greenhill Capital Partners, currently manages two private equity funds. Together these two funds have raised $1.3 billion in capital, approximately 25 per cent of which comes from Greenhill & Co. and its employees. GCP aims for long-term growth in middle-market companies, focusing primarily on the financial services, energy and telecommunications industries.

The fund's strategy is to invest in companies with strong managerial staff holding equity stakes in their businesses, allowing management teams to drive financial success. The company also strives to avoid direct conflict with Greenhill's advisory clients in its investments. Recent GCP investments include the newly formed global insurance company Ironshore Insurance Ltd. and the recapitalisation of credit card issuer First Equity Card.

In 2006, the company reported increased revenue from financial advisory services, which it attributed to high levels of M&A volume. Merchant banking revenue also increased, mostly due to investment gains and higher asset management fees. Earlier that year, the firm closed its first venture capital fund, Greenhill SAVP, after raising $101.5 million in committed capital.

European appointments

In 2006, Greenhill recruited Brian Phillips from Legal & General Ventures to lead the establishment of a European primary merchant banking business, to be based in London. The new business acts as the European equivalent of Greenhill Capital Partners and focuses on small and mid-cap opportunities in Europe. Prior to this, Greenhill was only in advisory services for Europe, where major clients included UK retailer Tesco plc, German commercial vehicles and industrial equipment group MAN AG, and the international pharmaceuticals group Bayer AG.

Also in 2006, Greenhill named former lawyer Jan Werner as a managing director in the London office to lead advisory projects in the Nordic region. Werner came to Greenhill with plenty of Nordic experience; he had spent two decades as a Nordic corporate advisor and had directed Nordic investment banking teams at Merrill Lynch and Citigroup. Meanwhile, in the Frankfurt office, Philip Meyer-Horn was named a managing director and tasked with expanding the bank's advisory activities throughout Germany. Before joining Greenhill, Meyer-Horn had led BNP Paribas' German corporate finance division.

GETTING HIRED

To learn more about analyst and associate positions at Greenhill & Co., or to find out how to apply, visit www.greenhill.com. Greenhill offers internships and a summer analyst programme at its London and Frankfurt offices. To find out more about Greenhill's investment banking analyst and intern programme, visit www.oxbridgelife.com/greenhill.

Visit **Vault Europe's Finance Career Channel** at **www.vault.com/europe** for insider firm profiles, employee surveys of finance professionals in Europe, message boards, job listings, expert finance career advice, insider salary information and more.

VAULT CAREER LIBRARY 125

29 Blvd. Haussman
Paris 75009
France
Phone: +33 (0) 1 42 14 20 00
Fax: +33 (0) 1 42 14 54 51
www.socgen.com

EUROPEAN LOCATIONS

Paris (Global HQ)
Austria • Belgium • Croatia • Czech
Republic • Germany • Greece •
Hungary • Italy • Luxembourg •
Netherlands • Norway • Poland •
Portugal • Republic of Macedonia •
Romania • Russia • Slovakia •
Slovenia • Spain • Sweden •
Switzerland • Ukraine • UK

DEPARTMENTS

Corporate & Investment Banking
Global Investment Management &
Services
Retail Banking & Financial Services

THE STATS

Employer Type: Public Company
Ticker Symbol: GLE (Euronext Paris)
Chairman & CEO: Daniel Bouton
2006 Net income: € 5,221 million
(FYE 12/06)
2005 Net income: € 4,402 million
(FYE 12/05)
No. of Employees: 120,000
No. of Offices: Global offices in 77
countries.

PLUSES

• "Reasonable working hours"
• "Job security"

MINUSES

• "No clear corporate strategy"
• "More transparency needed"

KEY COMPETITORS

BNP Paribas
Crédit Agricole
Natixis

EMPLOYMENT CONTACT

www.socgen.com
(Click on "Careers" link on site)

THE BUZZ
WHAT EMPLOYEES AT OTHER FIRMS ARE SAYING

• "Powerhouse"
• "Arrogant"

THE SCOOP

A French giant with global arms

Société Générale, is often referred to as "SocGen" in the banking world, and perhaps for obvious reasons is seldom referred to what it was originally called: Société Générale pour favoriser le développement du commerce et de l'industrie en France — translated in English as "General Company for the support of developing commerce and industry in France". Nevertheless, Société Générale is one of the leading European financial services companies and a major player in the global market. The group is the fifth-largest French company by capitalisation, as of April 2007. It is also a powerhouse in financial services for the Eurozone, employing more than 120,000 people around the world. As a bank, SocGen operates over 2,900 branches in France and more than 2,300 branches throughout the rest of the world. SocGen most recently reported a net income of €1.18 billion for the fourth quarter of 2006, an increase of 6.3 per cent over the comparable quarter in 2005.

Treble distinction

The Société Générale Group handles Europe's money through three distinct businesses: retail banking and financial services, global investment management and services, and corporate and investment banking. The retail banking and specialised financial services business has a total of 13.3 million customers around the world.

In France, Société Générale has two distribution networks: Société Générale and Credit du Nord, which was acquired in 1997. Together these brands have 9.15 million individual customers in France alone, making Société Générale the leading non-mutual bank in the country. Outside of France, the bank has retail operations in 32 countries. Société Générale's specialised financial services businesses, which include corporate financing and vehicle leasing, consumer credit, insurance and life insurance, have significantly expanded in recent years to service 42 countries around the world.

The firm's corporate and investment banking business is the third-largest of its kind in the Eurozone by net banking income. Société Générale's corporate and investment banking services corporations, financial institutions, and investors in more than 45 countries in Europe, the Americas and Asia. The business is divided into three specialist areas: euro capital markets, derivatives and structured finance. SG CIB is a world leader in equity derivatives, export, project and commodity finance and a top-five player in euro debt capital markets.

Société Générale's global investment management and services business segment is an umbrella business set up in January 2004 to include Société Générale Asset Management, SG Private Banking, Société Générale Securities Services and Boursorama, the French

Visit **Vault Europe's Finance Career Channel** at www.vault.com/europe for insider firm profiles, employee surveys of finance professionals in Europe, message boards, job listings, expert finance career advice, insider salary information and more.

VAULT CAREER LIBRARY 127

online banking and brokerage portal. The combined businesses employ approximately 8,900 people. With €354 billion in assets under management (as of December 31, 2006), Société Générale Asset Management is the fourth-largest bank in the euro zone, and the third-largest bank according to assets under custody, which amount to €2,262 billion (also as of December 31, 2006).

Napoleon's social project

On May 4, 1864, Emperor Napoleon III signed the decree founding Société Générale in order to "foster the development of trade and industry in France". Société Générale began its international expansion in 1871, with a branch in London. By 1913, Société Générale had established 1,400 branches and distinguished itself as a network bank. It remained private until 1945, when the bank's capital stock passed into the hands of the French government. In 1970, Société Générale stepped up its development outside of France, concentrating on Asia and Eastern Europe and within 10 years, by 1980, the bank had branches in 54 countries.

In 1987, Société Générale created its capital markets subdivision and was privatised in late July of that year. In 1998, following the lead of many commercial banks, the firm acquired an investment banking arm by purchasing New York-based Cowen & Company (now called SG Cowen). The following year, it set up retail banking outside France, expanding into Romania, Bulgaria and Madagascar. These operations in Central Europe, along with acquisitions in Africa, have led the bank's external growth. Today the company continues to expand its Central and Eastern European operations, most recently acquiring 70 per cent of a leading bank in Moldova for €18.4 million, as well as banks in the Republic of Macedonia and Albania, in early 2007.

Distinguished leadership

Serving as chairman and CEO since 1997 is Daniel Bouton, a native Frenchman with a long history in finance. Prior to joining Société Générale in 1991, Bouton worked for the French government in the Ministry of Finance, spending many years in the budget department. He also served as chief of staff for former Prime Minister of France Alain Juppé, during his time as Minister of Budget. Société Générale's director and co-chief executive is Philippe Citerne, also formerly of the Ministry of Finance. Citerne joined Société Générale in 1979 and spent several years directing economic research and financial management.

A new face in private banking

In early 2007, Société Générale appointed Daniel Truchi as the global head of SG Private Banking. One of Truchi's primary objectives will be to continue the development of private banking operations in the Asia-Pacific, a key growth region for the company.

Private banking is an increasingly important business for Société Générale, having averaged growth in assets under management of 35 per cent per year since its creation in 1998. As of end-December 2006, private banking held €67.8 billion under management and employed close to 2,400 people. The business is a market leader in France and holds a top-10 position in the UK, Luxembourg, Switzerland, Belgium and Asia. The business is recognised within the industry as well: in 2006 it was named Best Private Bank in Europe by *Private Banker International* magazine.

GETTING HIRED

Name drop

"Staff recommendations" and "networking" are two big ways to land a possible job at the bank. But the firm also recruits through its web site, "headhunting agencies," and "various specialised and general newspapers," insiders say. And the difficulty of getting hired "depends on the position," one source adds. Another notes that the firm is "not very selective," adding that "a bachelors degree is the minimum requirement." There are also reports of "people who are placed in the wrong department and position" and "employees who are not competent in their field of operations."

Getting trickier

One source says that "Since 2002, it has become more difficult to get hired by the bank" because "the number of interviews has since increased, and candidates now have to pass an economic test." An insider says his interview process was "straightforward" with "no tricky questions" and involved "an initial interview with HR and later with the head of department." During an interview, be prepared to speak about your "past positions" as well as take a "test on general banking knowledge", which a contact says should be rather "easy for those coming out of college".

Visit **Vault Europe's Finance Career Channel** at **www.vault.com/europe** for insider firm profiles, employee surveys of finance professionals in Europe, message boards, job listings, expert finance career advice, insider salary information and more.

VAULT CAREER LIBRARY   129

OUR SURVEY SAYS

Needs a little work

The company culture could stand to be improved, insiders say. "The group values of professionalism, team spirit and innovation are not reflected at all in the corporate culture," a contact notes. Another complains that "the corporate culture is unhealthy." Others add that while there's a "very nice team" of workers that makes for a "good atmosphere and interesting job," "a better place will come about through a positive and open culture."

On the bright side, sources offer few complaints about amenities. Those who have been on staff "at least six months" can buy SG shares "at a 20 percent discount," and the "food is excellent" and "cheap — about three to four euros for lunch." Plus, "dinner is free after 8:30 p.m." and "there is a taxi available after 9 p.m." There is also "a discount of about 25 per cent available for the gym."

Mixed management

One respondent reports, "It seems that the SG head office does not pay attention to the small Banque Hors France Metropolitaine subsidiaries," and adds that "The appointment of non-local general managers on a short-term basis is detrimental to the bank as their objectives are often not congruent with the bank's overall objectives." Another insider adds, "A lack of communication and rivalry among managers is the norm" and "there is overall poor management and a lack of fundamental knowledge in lending, motivating and communicating with people."

Still, a first-year analyst praises managers, calling them "excellent" and adding "they already take me to client meetings." But largely, sources seem less-than-pleased with their experiences. One says that "management had a personal attitude that was noted by the whole team," adding that "there were several harassment cases, which had been reported to the head office because no actions had been taken on this matter, so people had nothing else to do but leave the company."

Training gets mixed marks from survey respondents as well. "Formal and informal training is minimal." One insider says he received "mostly on-the-job training." Co-workers say they "had only one official professional training session" and "while some of my colleagues applied for additional training, they were declined due to budget optimisation reasons."

Time to boost diversity?

The bank's diversity efforts could use a shot in the arm, say insiders. "Women are not treated any differently than men, but their extra contribution is often unnoticed and taken for granted." A source working in Paris says that the staffers there are "mainly French people," but adds, "I think the portion of non-French people will increase in the future." Sensitivity training may be in order for some, says one contact — "discriminatory and even racist remarks from the French executives are common."

Pretty good looking

Dress is "formal always for men and women" but "casual Fridays" are offered. "Officially it is formal always, but the female staff dresses smart casual every day." One insider confides that "I always have a tie in my drawer just in case, but I usually only wear it for client meetings."

Generally, hours are a little less stringent. An insider reports that staffers are "allowed to work reasonably normal working hours where we rarely work late." Another says that there is a "high volatility of working hours. Sometimes we work until 1 a.m. if there is a lot of work to do, but weekends are free." A source working in Cyprus adds: "Working hours are regulated by the Cyprus bank labour union — work starts at 8 a.m. and ends at 4.15 p.m. with a 45-minute lunch break." The contact adds that "overtime is not paid and is discouraged by senior management."

For the most part, offices are rated highly by insiders. One working in the firm's Moscow office, describes the offices as being "very comfortable" with "more than enough working space," adding that "people are generally satisfied." Another proudly boasts he has a "great corner office with a panoramic view of the city."

Visit **Vault Europe's Finance Career Channel** at **www.vault.com/europe** for insider firm profiles, employee surveys of finance professionals in Europe, message boards, job listings, expert finance career advice, insider salary information and more.

VAULT CAREER LIBRARY   131

ING Groep N.V.
ING House
Amstelveenseweg 500
Amsterdam, 1081 KL
Netherlands
Phone: +31 (0) 20 54 15 411
Fax: +31 (0) 20 541 5497
www.ing.com

EURPEAN LOCATIONS

Amsterdam (HQ)
Offices throughout Europe,
Americas and Asia Pacific

DEPARTMENTS

ING Direct
Insurance Americas
Insurance Asia/Pacific
Insurance Europe
Retail Banking
Wholesale Banking

THE STATS

Employer Type: Public Company
Ticker Symbol: ING (NYSE)
Chairman: Michel Tilmant
2006 Underlying Net Profit:
€7,750 million
2005 Underlying Net Profit:
€6,234 million
No. of Employees: 120,000

KEY COMPETITORS

ABN AMRO
Allianz SE
AXA
Citigroup Inc.
Fortis

PLUSES

Huge in Benelux

MINUSES

Better known for insurance than
banking

EMPLOYMENT CONTACT

www.ing.jobs

THE BUZZ
WHAT EMPLOYEES AT OTHER FIRMS ARE SAYING

• "Good in some niche markets"
• "Not coherent"

THE SCOOP

A force to be reckoned with

ING is a considerable force to be reckoned with. In the 2006 *Forbes* Global 2000, ING was the 11th-largest company in the world. The Dutch bank operates in insurance, banking and asset management, with clients in over 50 countries. ING is active in retail banking as well as wholesale banking. Based on market cap, ING ranks among the 20-largest financial institutions in the world, and among the top-10 in Europe.

While it holds a strong presence in the global arena, ING is the No. 1 financial services company on its own turf, in the Benelux countries. Within its home market, ING provides its clients with banking, insurance and asset management services. Outside of the Benelux market, ING provides retirement services and life insurance to the US as one of its top-five providers. In Canada, ING is the top property and casualty insurer. As a direct bank, ING has more than 15 million customers in nine large countries, and a growing customer base in Asia-Pacific, Central Europe and South America, where the company provides life insurance, wholesale, and in some countries also retail banking services. As an asset management firm, ING manages around €500 billion in assets.

Six lines of business

ING is structured into six divisions: Insurance Europe, Insurance Americas, Insurance Asia/Pacific, Wholesale Banking, Retail Banking and ING Direct. The three insurance divisions are divided by geography, with variations in products offered across each group. Insurance Europe covers all of the company's insurance activities for the Netherlands, Belgium, Spain, Greece and Central Europe.

This segment provides a significant 23 per cent of ING's total profit, mostly through sales of life insurance. Insurance Europe also offers non-life insurance to clients in the Netherlands and Belgium. Insurance Americas handles all insurance and asset management in the Americas, particularly in the US, where it offers retirement services, annuities and life insurance. This business provides roughly 20 per cent of ING's total profit. Insurance Americas also operates in Canada, Mexico, Chile, Brazil and Peru. Insurance Asia/Pacific mostly offers life insurance and asset and wealth management services. This division has positioned itself for growth, particularly in China, India and Thailand.

Wholesale Banking provided the largest chunk of ING's profit in 2006, at approximately 25 per cent. Operations are divided into five segments: clients, network, products, corporate finance and equity markets, and financial markets. Within the Benelux countries, ING provides a full range of products to corporations and institutions. Elsewhere, ING's

Visit **Vault Europe's Finance Career Channel** at www.vault.com/europe for insider firm profiles, employee surveys of finance professionals in Europe, message boards, job listings, expert finance career advice, insider salary information and more.

VAULT CAREER LIBRARY **133**

offerings vary. Retail banking is focused upon the Netherlands, Belgium, Poland, Romania and India. Private banking is also offered in the Benelux countries, Switzerland and selected countries in Asia. ING Direct is the virtual retail-banking brand for the bank, providing ATM, telephone and online banking services to private clients in Australia, Canada, France, Germany, Austria, Italy, Spain, UK, the United States and Japan. An offshoot of this segment is the ING Card, which manages a credit card portfolio within the Benelux region.

150 years of history

ING is the offspring of a 1991 merger of prominent Dutch banks Nationale-Nederlanden and NMB Postbank Group. The combination created the first Dutch banking and insurance giant and, ever since then, the group has been expanding to become the international financial services provider that ING is today. At the time of the merger, the company was known as Internationale Nederlanden Groep — but to serve the interests of the international tongue-tied, the markets swiftly abbreviated the name to "ING". The new company took the cue, rebranding straight away and changing its legal name to ING, which currently offers banking, insurance and asset management services in more than 50 countries.

Remarkably, ING has over a century of history. Dutch bank De Nederlanden was founded in 1845 and Nationale Levensverzekering-Bank was founded in 1863. The two companies came together 100 years later to form Nationale-Nederlanden, which became the largest insurer in the Netherlands. NMB Postbank Groep came about in 1986 after the merger of Rijkspostspaarbank (founded in 1881) and Postcheque-en Girodienst (founded 1918). In 1991, ING emerged as the latest in a long lineage.

Know your leaders

At the helm in ING's corporate headquarters in Amsterdam is the Belgian Michel Tilmant, who has served as chairman of the board since April 2004. The former CEO of Bank Brussels Lambert (BBL), Tilmant was appointed to the ING board after BBL's acquisition by ING in 1998. ING CFO Dutchman Cees Maas who also served as vice-chairman of the Board, retired in May 2007 and was replaced by a CFO and CRO. A well-respected academic, Maas served as CFO for ING since 1996, guiding the firm through several large purchases, such as the acquisition of BBL. He also served as chairman for the Dutch chapter of the European League of Economic Cooperation.

The China strategy

ING has been steadily building up a presence in China to take advantage of the country's persistent economic growth and development. ING is currently active in 12 cities in China, operating in life insurance, retail banking, corporate and investment banking, asset management and properties development. In March 2005, ING purchased a 19.9 per cent stake in Bank of Beijing, one of China's largest city banks.

According to ING, the deal, worth €166 million, was part of a broader strategic alliance. Founded in 1996, Bank of Beijing, which was renamed from Beijing City Commercial Bank, is now China's second-largest city commercial bank. It employs more than 3,600 people in 120 branches, and at the time of purchase had total assets of €18.9 billion. In December2006, ING received approval from China's Insurance Regulatory Commission to set up life insurance branch operations in the Henan Province in China, the largest in terms of population. ING Capital Life will partner with Beijing Capital Group to offer products to approximately 100 million people. ING offers a number of training, development and career opportunities

GETTING HIRED

For more information on vacancies and traineeships, visit the ING company web site at www.ing.jobs/careers. Also, as of April 2007, ING is extending its ING Talent Programme (ITP) — a three-year traineeship offering nine starting areas related to various business divisions at ING — to non-Dutch speaking graduates with a master's degree and no more than two years of work experience. For non-Dutch speaking graduates, there are five starting areas to enter the ING Talent Programme. To learn more about ITP, check out www.recruitment.ing.nl/non-dutch.

Visit **Vault Europe's Finance Career Channel** at **www.vault.com/europe** for insider firm profiles, employee surveys of finance professionals in Europe, message boards, job listings, expert finance career advice, insider salary information and more.

VAULT CAREER LIBRARY

135

Nomura Holdings, Inc.

Nomura House
1 St Martin's-le-Grand
London EC1A 4NP
United Kingdom
Phone: +44 (0) 20 7521 2000
Fax: +44 (0) 20 7521 2121
www.nomura.com

EUROPEAN LOCATIONS

London (European HQ)
Austria • France • Germany •
Hungary • Italy • Luxembourg •
Netherlands • Poland • Russia •
Spain • Switzerland • UK

DEPARTMENTS:

Asset Management
Global Markets
Investment Banking
Merchant Banking

THE STATS

Employer Type: Public Company
Stock Symbol: NMR (NYSE)
President & CEO: Nobuyuki Koga
2007 Total Net Revenue:
$9.28 billion (FYE 3/07)
2006 Total Net Revenue:
$9.8 billion (FYE 3/06)
2007 Employees: 16,144
No. of Offices: Japan: 150;
Worldwide: 30

KEY COMPETITORS

Daiwa Securities Group
Merrill Lynch
Nikko Cordial

PLUSES

Global ambitions

MINUSES

Not yet a top firm in Europe

EMPLOYMENT CONTACT

www.nomura.com/europe/careers

THE BUZZ
WHAT EMPLOYEES AT OTHER FIRMS ARE SAYING

- "The only Japanese player with sufficient strength to compete"
- "Internationally, always struggling"

THE SCOOP

Japanese powerhouse

Established in 1925 in Osaka, Japan, as Nomura Securities, the Nomura Holdings brand we know today resulted as a spin-off from Osaka Nomura Bank. Nomura Holdings is Japan's largest global investment banking and securities firm and was rated No. 3 on Thompson Financial's 2006 list of M&A deals of up to $50 million, inking 104 mid-market deals worth $1.3 billion.

In 1946, the head office of Nomura Securities in Osaka was moved to Tokyo. Nomura began managing investments in 1951 and continued growing throughout the late 20th century, opening up consulting practices and branching out internationally. The 1990s were a promiscuous time for the firm as it was accused of reimbursing customers for investment losses and approving payoffs to corporate extortionists.

Today, however, Nomura is on the up and up — at least as far as employees are concerned. The firm was ranked No. 5 on Here Is The City's Best Places to Work in the Global Financial Markets 2006 survey. Nomura was the runner-up to Daiwa Securities in the category for best Asia-Pacific-based firm.

A strengthening new structure

Nomura currently offers a full range of securities and investment banking services through its 16,144 employees in more than 30 countries and over 185 offices worldwide. The firm's four main departments are asset management, equities, fixed income and investment banking. It also offers a merchant-banking feature. Financial and advisory services and products are primarily dispensed to individual, institutional, corporate and government clients.

As of April 2006, the firm began operating under a new structure designed to give Nomura more flexibility to invest in new areas and amplify its business portfolio. Nomura now manages group firms as a holding company, and only has 11 executive officers.

With the exception of a few people, executive officers no longer serve concurrently in positions at Nomura Securities and Nomura Holdings. The firm has also reappointed all current business-line heads as "division CEOs" under the new structure, and Nomura Holdings formed an operating board consisting mainly of newly appointed divisional CEOs.

Coming to America

In the Americas, the firm opened its doors in 1927, when the New York City office was launched. Nomura officially operates under the Nomura Holding America Inc. brand, and works out of offices in New York, Chicago, San Francisco, Los Angeles and São Paulo, with

Visit **Vault Europe's Finance Career Channel** at www.vault.com/europe for insider firm profiles, employee surveys of finance professionals in Europe, message boards, job listings, expert finance career advice, insider salary information and more.

VAULT CAREER LIBRARY 137

more than $1 billion in capital and 1,200 employees as of May 2005. Nomura Securities International (NSI) is the official name of the firm's American broker/dealer unit. Through its four main divisions, the firm offers capital raising, corporate advisory, sales and trading, foreign exchange, derivatives, research, asset management and online services in the Americas.

The firm is vested in bringing on new talent, developing current employees and giving back to the community in the Americas. In June 2005, Jack Leventhal joined Nomura as managing director and the head of US financial institutions. Leventhal, former managing director and head of multinational financial institutions at UBS, is responsible for developing Nomura's financial advisory business to multinational financial institutions based in the US, and for the creation of a middle-market investment banking business to US financial institutions.

In June 2007, Shigesuke Kashiwagi was nominated as senior managing director and head of regional management, Americas. Kashiwagi, who is based in New York, joined Nomura Holding America, Inc. as chief operating officer in April 2006. Prior to that, he was senior managing director and head of global fixed income of Nomura Group.

Not bad looking

Nomura's M&A group in New York is responsible for structuring and executing a wide range of domestic and cross-border transactions including mergers, acquisitions, divestitures, joint ventures, corporate restructurings and leveraged buyouts across a wide range of industries. Since 1988, Nomura has conducted cross-border M&A business between the US and Japan. Over the last few years, Nomura has successfully advised leading Japanese and US companies on various strategic transactions such as Eastman Kodak's acquisition of Chinon Industries, and Seiyu's strategic alliance with Wal-Mart and Sumitomo Corporation.

After coming in at No. 15 in 2005, Nomura fell from the top 25 on Thompson Financial's 2006 ranking of worldwide-announced M&A deals. But the firm remained on top in both the Japanese announced and completed M&A categories, and also performed well on the mid-market tables, coming in at No. 3 in deals valued at up to $50 million. Nomura announced 104 deals in 2006, worth nearly $1.3 billion.

The firm's New York-based equity capital markets group covers the origination, structuring, syndication, marketing and placement of equity-related securities in North America. It provides exceptional investment opportunities in Japan and other parts of Asia for US investors through public and private placements of equity and equity-linked securities. Some of the firm's more successful transaction work in recent years includes the ¥97 billion global offering of Aeon Co., the ¥231 billion IPO of Shinsei Bank and the ¥273 billion global offering of Mitsubishi Tokyo Financial Group.

In Thomson Financial's global equity and equity-related league table, and global common stock underwriting area, Nomura held its No. 10 rankings for the fourth consecutive year.

The firm held steady at No. 2 for Japanese IPOs, leading 37 deals valued at $3.25 billion, but kept the No. 1 spot for Japanese equity and equity-related deals, leading 111 transactions valued at an impressive $20.5 billion.

Good boss

In April 2005, Yugo Ishida was named president and CEO of Nomura International. Deputy CEO for the year prior, Ishida replaced Hiromi Yamaji, who returned to the company's headquarters in Tokyo after three years in London. Ishida joined Nomura in 1979 and during his career has worked in Nomura's offices in Bahrain, Hong Kong and Italy — as well as Tokyo. In 2000, he moved from Milan to London to become managing director of European equity before becoming deputy CEO in July 2004. Ishida appears to be making quite an impression; in December 2006, he was ranked No. 3 on Here Is The City's 2006 Boss of the Year Poll.

Battling over bonuses

In September 2006, news broke that a former Nomura International trader was suing his ex-firm for withholding $14 million in unpaid bonuses. The trader, Luis Marti-Sanchez, claims that his $2.47 million (in deferred shares) 2005 bonus wasn't enough, as Nomura promised him between 20 and 25 per cent of whatever he earned, which according to Marti-Sanchez was upwards of $38 million. Nomura's response? According to a company spokesperson, "We do not believe that we breached the terms of his contract."

The case could have legs though, and not just for the trader, whose lawyer, according to Here Is The City, "has said that the case may have an impact on the ability of investment banks and other financial institutions to pay staff in deferred shares or options." By the end of September 2006, another ex-Nomura trader had come forward with similar complaints.

Global ambitions

In February 2007, Nomura Holdings paid $1.2 billion to buy electronic stockbroker Instinet Inc. At the time, The Associated Press reported the move to be "the latest sign of its revived ambitions to expand overseas." Nomura bought the New York-based company, which gets about half of its $400 million in revenue from outside the US, from majority owner Silver Lake Partners, making Instinet a unit within Nomura. The deal, initially announced in late 2006, enables Nomura to trade on more than 50 securities markets around the world.

According to the article, "The acquisition comes as Nomura begins to expand overseas again, aided by a recovery in Japan's stock market in recent years. Nomura, once a major player in financial markets in New York and London, pulled back from overseas operations in the 1990s,

Visit **Vault Europe's Finance Career Channel** at **www.vault.com/europe** for insider firm profiles, employee surveys of finance professionals in Europe, message boards, job listings, expert finance career advice, insider salary information and more.

V/\ULT CAREER LIBRARY **139**

hurt in part by the slump in the Japanese economy and markets. As its earnings and stock price have improved, Nomura has started to build back its business outside its home turf."

Nomura's interest in building its foreign business is clear. In late 2005 Nomura bought Code Securities, a "boutique investment bank" in the UK. And then in February 2006, Nomura acquired a stake in Taishin Financial Holding Co., a large Taiwan bank, for $125 million. American daily business newspaper *The Wall Street Journal* reported: "Nomura, with revenue more than double its nearest domestic competitor, typically has relied on executing trades to generate the bulk of its revenue. Market liberalisation and the growth of electronic trading have eroded commissions, forcing Nomura to look for new business."

GETTING HIRED

For more information about careers and graduate opportunities at Nomura, visit the company's web site at www.nomura.com/europe/careers.

"Today Nomura is on the up and up — at least as far employees are concerned."

9, quai du Président Paul Doumer
92920 Paris La Défense Cedex
France
Phone: +33 1 41 89 00 00
Fax: +33 1 41 89 15 22
www.calyon.com

EUROPEAN LOCATIONS

Paris (HQ)
Offices throughout Europe

DEPARTMENTS

Brokerage
Capital Markets
Corporate Banking & Cash
Management
Investment Banking
Loan Syndication
Structured Finance

THE STATS

Employer Type: Subsidiary of
Crédit Agricole
Ticker symbol: CAGR (Euronext, LSE,
Berlin, XETRA, Frankfurt, Munich,
Stuttgart, Virt-Z, Dusseldorf,
Hamburg); CRARF.PK (OTC)
Chairman: Jean Laurent
CEO: Edouard Esparbès
2006 Net income: €1.65 billion
2005 Net income: €1.63 billion
No. of Employees: 13,000
No. of Offices: 55+

KEY COMPETITORS

Citigroup Global Markets Europe
Lazard
UBS Investment Bank

PLUSES

"World leader"

MINUSES

Not yet a key bank across Europe

EMPLOYMENT CONTACT

www.calyon.com
(Click on "Human Resources" section)

THE BUZZ
WHAT EMPLOYEES AT OTHER FIRMS ARE SAYING

- "Strong in select regions"
- "Not the best managed franchise"
- "Strong in trade finance"
- "Struggling"

THE SCOOP

Investment banking, à la Française

Calyon is the corporate and investment bank of the Crédit Agricole Group, combining the businesses of Crédit Agricole Indosuez and Crédit Lyonnais' corporate and investment banking division. Calyon is a wholly owned subsidiary of France's largest financial institution, Crédit Agricole Group, which is listed on the Paris Euronext exchange as CAGR — but like many other major European investment banks, is also listed on the major German exchanges and the London Stock Exchange. Calyon is active in a broad range of capital markets, investment banking and financing activities. Calyon's activities are organised into two major divisions, capital markets, brokerage and investment banking, and the financing division. Calyon ranked first in European IPOs in 2005, notably advising the French government on the privatisation of Electricité de France, a nuclear energy giant and one of the most important European IPOs since the late 1990s.

Business by business

Each of Calyon's two divisions is divided into several subdivisions. Capital markets controls a network of 30 trading rooms around the world. Product lines include foreign exchange, commodities, interest rate derivatives, debt capital markets, credit markets and CDO, treasury, equity and fund derivatives. Investment banking is organised into global corporate finance, which is responsible for executing all merger and acquisitions transactions; global equity capital markets, or ECM, which conducts primary issues, IPOs, secondary market offerings bond issues and also global sector groups, which are linked together by industry. Calyon's other division, financing, is divided into structured finance, loan syndication, corporate banking and cash management, and acquisition finance.

Calyon announced plans in early 2007 to merge its brokerage activities with those of Société Générale. The newly formed entity, controlled equally by Société Générale and Calyon, is expected to be a world leader in the execution and clearing of listed financial futures and options. At present, Calyon carries out these activities through its subsidiaries Cheuvreux, CLSA and Calyon Financial.

Banking on history

Calyon emerged from French bank Crédit Agricole S.A. in 2004, as the new brand and corporate name for its financing and investment banking business. Assets were partially transferred from the newly acquired Crédit Lyonnais to Crédit Agricole Indosuez, the bank's international banking arm. Prior to its acquisition, Crédit Lyonnais was in business for over a century. Due to this well-established base, upon its launch Calyon had assets of approximately $380 billion — as well as offices in 60 countries around the world.

Visit **Vault Europe's Finance Career Channel** at www.vault.com/europe for insider firm profiles, employee surveys of finance professionals in Europe, message boards, job listings, expert finance career advice, insider salary information and more.

VAULT CAREER LIBRARY   **143**

Leading the European IPO set

In recent years, Calyon has established a leading role in French IPOs. In addition to the EDF deal of 2005, Calyon was a bookrunner and lead manager for Gaz de France's IPO, which was the world's largest share sale at €4.5 billion. Then in 2006, Calyon acted as co-arranger for several IPOs, including Legrand and Ansalso, and in rights issues including Vinci and Swiss Re. The Legrand IPO was a high-profile offering, due to an unexpected surge in demand for Legrand shares. Legrand SA, the world's largest manufacturer of power plugs and switches, sold off about 20 per cent of its stock in order to raise funds for takeovers. About 57.8 million shares were launched on the Paris bourse, which were sold to yield a total of €972 million.

Honours, awards and accolades

Particularly in 2005 and 2006, Calyon's increase in both the volume and number of M&A deals has garnered increased prominence in global rankings. In 2005, Calyon was ranked seventh in France for M&A advisory services and first for initial public offerings in Europe — particularly due to the firm's role in advising the French government on the long-awaited privatisation of nuclear giant Electricité de France — widely regarded as the most important European IPO since the late 1990s, according to Thomson Financial and Capital Finance. Calyon's equity brokerage unit Cheuvreux was the No. 1 French equity research company, as ranked by Institutional Investor. In financing, Calyon entered the top-10 global bookrunners, as ranked by Thomson Financial and, for the first time, was ranked by Bloomberg as No.1 bookrunner (IPOs) in France.

Likewise, 2006 was strong as well — that year Calyon advised 26 deals for a total value of $91 billion, an increase of rank value of 152 per cent. In 2006, Calyon also ranked 19th in the world for M&A advisors (rising seven spots over 2005), as listed by Thomson Financial, and second in the world for Global Project Finance Loans. In international debt, Calyon rose two spots to No.10 among Euro bond issuers.

GETTING HIRED

For more information career development, vacancies and graduate opportunities at Calyon, visit the company's website at www.calyon.com and click on the Human Resources link.

THE BEST OF THE REST

TOP 25

BANKING EMPLOYERS

Abbey National

2 Triton Square
Regent's Place
London, NW1 3AN
United Kingdom
Phone: +44 (0) 870 607 6000
www.abbeynational.com

EUROPEAN LOCATIONS

Belfast
Bradford
Glasgow
London
Milton Keynes

DEPARTMENTS

Abbey for Intermediaries
Abbey Wealth Management
Central Units (including Strategy,
Planning & Communications)
Finance & Markets
Human Resources
Legal, Secretariat & Compliance
Retail
Retail Risk
Santander Asset Management UK
Wholesale Risk

THE STATS

Employer Type: Subsidiary of a Public
Company
Ticker Symbol: STD (NYSE)
Chief Executive: António Horta-Osório
2006 Net Income: £684 million
(FYE 12/06)
2005 Net Income: £555 million
(FYE 12/05)
2006 Employees: 17,146
No. of Branches: 712

PLUSES

Efficient in cost-cutting efforts

MINUSES

Ongoing transition

EMPLOYMENT CONTACT

www.jobsatabbey.com

THE BUZZ
WHAT EMPLOYEES AT OTHER FIRMS ARE SAYING

- "Consistent"
- "Bland"

THE SCOOP

British born, Spanish bought

The venerable Abbey National dates back to 1849, when the National Freehold Land and Building Society was established in London. Nearly a century later, the Society joined with the Abbey Road Building Society to create Abbey National. In 1989 it became the first building society to gain plc status and to be floated on the London Stock Exchange. Today Abbey is one of the United Kingdom's foremost personal financial services companies, serving more than 18 million customers in the UK. It provides mortgages and savings, bank accounts, loans, credit cards, long-term investments, and offshore banking services for UK citizens living abroad.

Abbey's defining moment came in November 2004 when it was acquired by Grupo Santander, parent company of Banco Santander Central Hispano, Spain's largest financial group and one of the 10-largest financial groups in the world. With operations in 40 countries, a network of more than 10,000 branches and over 63 million customers, Grupo Santander has the third-largest consumer finance business in Europe — and the largest in Latin America. Retail banking provides roughly 85 per cent of Grupo Santander's revenue, but it also offers a broad range of financial services.

Divisions of business

Since 2004, clearly Abbey has had closer ties to Spain, but its primary offices remain in London, Milton Keynes, Bradford, Glasgow and Belfast. The bank has more than 700 branch offices throughout its home market in the UK and Ireland. Business at Abbey is divided into four major financial channels. Retail handles direct sales via branches, telephone, and internet banking. Abbey for Intermediaries oversees sales through brokers and financial advisers.

Abbey Wealth Management consists of two primary units: James Hay — focused on self-invested pension plans and intermediary markets — and specialist banking, which includes subsidiary operations Cater Allen Private Bank, Abbey International and Abbey Share-Dealing. The finance and markets division includes Abbey Financial Markets, providing finance and treasury services. These businesses are supported by operations divisions that include manufacturing, which handles IT and customer service, risk, central units (which includes internal audit, tax, regulatory and legal affairs) and human resources.

A new leader

Abbey Chief Executive António Horta-Osório moved to the top spot in August 2006, following the death of former Chief Executive Francisco Gómez-Roldán. Horta-Osório

Visit **Vault Europe's Finance Career Channel** at www.vault.com/europe for insider firm profiles, employee surveys of finance professionals in Europe, message boards, job listings, expert finance career advice, insider salary information and more.

VAULT CAREER LIBRARY

147

joined Abbey as a non-executive director in 2004 as part of Santander's takeover. He is also an executive vice president of Grupo Santander and a member of its managing board, the Comité de Dirección. He began his career at CitiBank Portugal, where he headed the capital markets division, later moving to Goldman Sachs' New York and London offices, where he worked on Portuguese corporate finance. He joined Santander in 1993 as the CEO of one of its Portuguese subsidiaries.

In September 2006 Abbey sold its life businesses, including subsidiaries Scottish Provident Limited, Scottish Mutual Assurance plc, Scottish Provident International Life Assurance Limited, Scottish Mutual International plc, and Abbey National Life plc, to UK life funds manager Resolution plc. Abbey CEO Horta-Osório described the deal as "a clean exit" that would allow his firm to focus on expanding its position in the United Kingdom's investment and pensions market through retail and intermediary channels.

Looking ahead

Abbey's 2006 year-end reports showed the bank on solid footing, meeting its revenue target and continuing on a path of cost reductions. As part of the Santander takeover in 2004, Abbey embarked on a three-year cost-cutting plan, aiming to achieve £300 million cost savings by the end of 2007. At the close of the 2006 fiscal year, the bank was able to report cost savings of £290 million, helped in part by the sale of life businesses to Resolution, a specialist fund manager of life insurance assets, among other streamlining measures. Since it seems likely that Abbey will exceed its original savings goal of £300 million in 2007, the bank says it will simply reinvest the surplus in its own business efforts.

As part of the Banco Santander group, Abbey is in the process of transitioning to Partenon, Santander's in-house banking system. Abbey's Partenon platform is being unveiled in stages — the process began in 2006 and is expected to conclude in late 2007. Santander executives say the Partenon platform lets their businesses increase profitability and productivity by providing better information and analysis. The Partenon rollout at Abbey is being supervised by Isban, a Santander IT subsidiary established specifically for that purpose. That said, on Abbey's 2007 agenda, clearly completing the Partenon rollout is key, as well as launching a new credit card line in the UK, strengthening intermediary business in retail banking, and increasing coordination between business divisions.

Asset management

One of Santander's first missions in 2007 was the realignment of Abbey's UK asset management units, which were integrated into Santander Asset Management UK. The affected Abbey companies included Abbey National Asset Management, Inscape, Abbey National Multi-Managers, and Abbey National Unit Trust Managers. The new combined asset management business will have a staff of 260 employees in the UK, joining a network of Santander's 1,100 asset management employees worldwide.

GETTING HIRED

For more information about careers, current vacancies, and graduate opportunities at Abbey, visit the company's web site at www.jobsatabbey.com. To learn more about the firm's new Talent Development Programme in its finance, audit and market risk lines of business, visit: www.abbeytdp.com.

Visit **Vault Europe's Finance Career Channel** at **www.vault.com/europe** for insider firm profiles, employee surveys of finance professionals in Europe, message boards, job listings, expert finance career advice, insider salary information and more.

VAULT CAREER LIBRARY   149

ABN Amro Holding N.V.

Gustav Mahlerlaan, 10
1082 PP Amsterdam
The Netherlands
Phone: +31 20 628 9393
Fax: +31 20 629 9111
www.abnamro.com

EUROPEAN LOCATIONS

Amsterdam (Global HQ)
Austria • Belgium • Channel
Islands • Czech Republic •
Denmark • Finland • France •
Germany • Gibraltar • Greece •
Ireland • Italy • Luxembourg •
Netherlands • Norway • Poland •
Portugal • Romania • Russia •
Slovakia • Spain • Sweden •
Switzerland • Turkey •UK

DEPARTMENTS

Asset Management
Business & Commercial Banking
Commercial & Institutional Banking
Private Banking
Retail Banking

THE STATS

Employer Type: Public Company
Ticker Symbol: AAB (Euronext
Amsterdam), ABN (NYSE)
Chairman, Supervisory Board:
Arthur C. Martinez
Chairman, Managing Board:
Rijkman W.J. Groenink
Total assets: €987.1bn (FYE 12/06)
Net Operating Profit: €4,780 million
(FYE 12/06)
Revenue: $53.96 billion (FYE 12/05)
Net Income: $3.4 billion (FYE 12/05)
No. of Employees: 107,000
No. of Offices: 4,600

KEY COMPETITORS

Deutsche Bank
ING
JPMorgan Chase

PLUSES

"International environment is a plus"
"Lots of interesting developments"

MINUSES

"Constant reorganisations cost a lot
of time and energy"
"You're constantly explaining the
basics"

THE BUZZ
WHAT EMPLOYEES AT OTHER FIRMS ARE SAYING

- "Has global footprint"
- "Good culture"
- "Always restructuring"
- "Second tier"

EMPLOYMENT CONTACT

www.abnamro.com/careers

THE SCOOP

Grown in Holland

Many banks have historical royal connections, but few are actually descendants of royalty. ABN AMRO is one of them. In 1824, King Willem I of the Netherlands issued a royal decree creating the Nederlandsche Handel-Maatschappij (fortunately shortened to NHM), a bank charged with maintaining trade between the Netherlands and its colonies, specifically the Dutch East Indies. In 1861, De Twentsche Bank was formed; NHM and De Twentsche Bank merged in 1964 to form Algemene Bank Nederland (ABN). ABN became a Dutch powerhouse in 1991 when it merged with the Amsterdam-Rotterdam (AMRO) Bank. AMRO was formed by the 1964 merger of Amsterdamsche Bank and Rotterdamsche Bank, two Dutch financial institutions with roots dating back to the 19th century.

Like the Dutch empire of old, today's ABN AMRO and its predecessors expanded across the globe. The bank now has one US subsidiary, LaSalle Bank, which was acquired in 1979. Its other 1997 US acquisition, Standard Federal Bank, was rebranded as La Salle Bank in 2005. The two American banks are major players in the Midwest and regularly account for a quarter of ABN AMRO's revenue.

ABN AMRO now has a presence in 56 countries, and provides banking products and financial services on a global basis through its 10 business units. The firm ranks eighth in Europe and 13th in the world based on total assets. While ABN AMRO has a diverse spread of clientele, the bank's strategic focus is on its consumer and commercial clients division, which caters to the needs of the mid-market segment. The bank is also ambitious, aiming for a 20 per cent average return on equity from 2005 to 2008.

Transcending borders

Within Europe, the Dutch bank has its eyes on the Italian and German markets. ABN AMRO owns Italian bank Antonveneta and has stakes in Capitalia. The firm also acquired German private bank BethmannMaffei, which was incorporated completely in 2004 along with private bank Delbruck, which has been part of ABN AMRO since 2002. ABN AMRO spent much of 2004 divesting some businesses in an effort to reallocate capital to its core services and markets. The firm sold its professional brokerage unit to Merrill Lynch in April 2004 and sold its stake (over 80 per cent) in Thailand-based Bank of Asia to United Overseas Bank. Additionally, two more deals have been completed: the sale of Standard Federal's Executive Relocation Corporation to SIRVA and ABN AMRO's trust business to Equity Trust. On February 8, 2007, ABN AMRO announced a new share buy-back programme of €1 billion, planned to be completed by June 30, 2007.

Visit **Vault Europe's Finance Career Channel** at **www.vault.com/europe** for insider firm profiles, employee surveys of finance professionals in Europe, message boards, job listings, expert finance career advice, insider salary information and more.

VAULT CAREER LIBRARY   **151**

An offer they couldn't refuse

ABN AMRO's move to break into the closed Italian market by taking over Banca Antonveneta drew a lot of attention. The bank made its bid for the Italian bank in March 2006, offering €6.3 billion. It was the next step in a new movement in Italy to allow foreign acquisition of Italian banks. Then Italian Prime Minister Silvio Berlusconi and Antonio Fazio, the head of the Bank of Italy, agreed on a maximum foreign participation of 15 per cent. ABN AMRO already held 12.7 per cent of Antonveneta, though the firm wanted total control.

In July 2005, Fazio came under fire for alleged bias against ABN AMRO's attempts to acquire the Italian bank. Recorded conversations between Fazio and Gianpiero Fiorani, chief executive of Banca Popolare Italiana, were published in international newspapers, and suggested that the central bank governor favoured a rival bid by BPI. While ABN AMRO said it had abandoned plans for a full takeover, the Italian market regulator Consob announced that it had suspended BPI's bid. Then, in a surprising twist, ABN AMRO gained control of the Antoneventa board after BPI's voting rights were suspended. In April 2006, ABN AMRO announced the definitive results of its bid to buy Banca Antonveneta. After launching the bid in February 2006, the bank owned 98.9 per cent of the target by the start of April, and then used a "squeeze out" right to buy the remaining shares. Antonveneta de-listed from the Italian stock exchange in April 2006.

Celebrity deal

On April 23, 2007 it emerged that British banking giant, Barclays plc was interested in taking over ABN AMRO to create the world's biggest bank, which would be headquartered in Amsterdam. Although, at the time of press talks are still in progress, the potential takeover has stimulated an unrivalled amount of global interest. According to initial reports in April 2007 in London daily newspaper *The Times*, Barclays was willing to pay up to €35 per share for ABN AMRO. The daily paper reported that mega banking groups including Bank of America are "waiting in the wings to pick up unwanted ABN AMRO assets should Barclays be successful in its attempt to buy the £40 billion Dutch banking group."

Initially, ABN AMRO agreed to an all-shares deal with Barclays plc. That day, Barclays' chief executive said, "It's the largest transaction ever in the history of the global financial services industry," as he proudly announced details of the whopping €140 billion merger proposal. The day following the announcement of the merger, *The Times* wrote, "The deal would be immediately earnings-enhancing for ABN AMRO shareholders and would boost profits per share for Barclays shareholders, too — by 5 per cent in 2010. Sweetening the deal was the promise of a €12 billion return of cash to shareholders via share buybacks, financed by the $21 billion (£10.5 billion) sale of LaSalle, ABN AMRO's American banking unit [to bank of America]."

Despite the spotlight initially being on Barclays plc for the potential takeover of ABN AMRO, attention quickly turned to the consortium competing with the British bank and independently pursuing the Dutch giant, who, it was reported within days of Barclays' initial bid, was willing to pay €40 per share for ABN AMRO. The rival suitors are a truly European trio comprised of Belgo-Dutch mega banking house Fortis, Spanish banking powerhouse Santander and the prestigious Royal Bank of Scotland.

In early May 2007 ABN AMRO rejected the consortium's offer of $24.5 billion for its American banking arm LaSalle, and a Dutch court ruled that ABN AMRO should not have sold LaSalle without consulting shareholders first. This prompted BoA to file a lawsuit against ABN AMRO, in New York. The US business magazine *Forbes* reported on the move, saying that BoA was "claiming that the Dutch bank is in breach of its contract to sell LaSalle to BoA."

As more players entered the arena and in the weeks following the announcement, the deal has hardly been easy to close, as the bidding war triggered by all rival suitors has unravelled and updates on the potential sale have made headlines virtually every day. On May 7, 2007 the firm announced it intended to hold an EGM for shareholders, in order to stimulate a discourse about the options and "alternatives available to them at that time." Two days later on May 9, 2007, the bank announced its intention to "lodge an appeal with the Supreme Court of The Netherlands against the provisional ruling of the Enterprise Chamber of the Amsterdam Appellate Court that the agreement to sell LaSalle to Bank of America may not complete without a shareholder vote. That ruling has created ambiguity for shareholders and has led to Bank of America filing a lawsuit against ABN AMRO in the US courts. ABN AMRO must appeal the Enterprise Chamber's ruling and endeavour to provide clarity and remove any legal threat."

Forbes magazine reported that if the sale to Bank of America was rejected, the situation could "raise the risk" that earlier proposed €67 billion merger between ABN AMRO and Barclays plc might also fall through." The US publication added, "Under the terms of the initial ABN AMRO and Barclays deal, both banks will put the proposed merger to a shareholder vote in August." The bidding continues.

The power of 10

ABN AMRO broke up its three main business units — consumer and commercial, wholesale, and private clients and asset management — into 10 units to focus on fewer midmarket corporate clients and to give its customers access to more products. The bank now has five regional client business units — the Netherlands, Europe, North America,

Visit **Vault Europe's Finance Career Channel** at www.vault.com/europe for insider firm profiles, employee surveys of finance professionals in Europe, message boards, job listings, expert finance career advice, insider salary information and more.

VAULT CAREER LIBRARY   153

Latin America and Asia; two global client business units — private clients and global clients; and three product business units — global markets, transaction banking and asset management. In April 2006, ABN AMRO announced it would cut 1,500 back-office jobs in Europe and the US, outsourcing IT contractors and consultants in a bid to save a further € 900 million. In total, the bank plans to lighten its operations staff in transaction processing, clearing and settlement by some 11 per cent over the next three years.

Getting focused

Perhaps in the lead up to the firm's headline frenzy in the spring of 2007, ABN AMRO made a number of divestments in 2006. Some that stand out include in April 2006, ABN AMRO Capital announced it had agreed to sell Rontgen Technische Dienst Holding (RTD), a provider of oil and gas testing and inspection services, to Applus Servicios for €193 million. The asset management arm sold off its mutual fund business for $38.6 million to Highbury Financial, deciding instead to focus on US institutional investment businesses. In May the bank sold its global futures business to UBS for $386 million, after a strategic review decided the business wasn't core. The sell-offs continued into the summer, with the bank shedding its Bouwfonds subsidiary to Rabobank for €845 million. The deal included Bouwfonds Asset Management, Bouwfonds Property Development, Bouwfonds Fondsenbeheer, Rijnlandse Bank and Bouwfonds holding.

Everything's gone green

In June 2006, ABN AMRO's Brazilian subsidiary was named Emerging Markets Bank of the Year at the *Financial Times* Sustainable Banking Awards, while the bank as a whole was commended in the categories of Global Excellence in Environmental and Social Risk Management Systems and for the Deal of the Year. That deal saw the world's first bank-intermediated, carbon credit transaction between private entities. In the same month, executives from ABN AMRO were part of a list of 14 senior UK business leaders who wrote to then UK Prime Minister Tony Blair demanding tougher action on climate change.

GETTING HIRED

Consider becoming a master

If you're trying to get on board at ABN AMRO, "a master's degree is a definite plus," but is not a requirement an insider says. Another says that he was selected "on the basis of my CV and the recommendation of a recruitment agency." But don't worry if you don't happen to have a contact within an agency — anyone can apply for a position with the bank through the "careers" link at www.abnamro.com.

Once you're in the door, you can expect several rounds of interviews. "My first interview was with the future line manager to see if my personality matched the team," comments one analyst, adding that his second interview with the head of the department revolved more around "my motivation to work in the banking industry." HR conducted the source's third interview, which was targeted "to test my ambition and goals."

OUR SURVEY SAYS

Saying it like it is

Clearly culture varies from firm to firm, but the company culture at ABN AMRO, says one contact, is "quite informal among different teams." However, the Dutch are admittedly direct and this insider adds that, "Those who aren't Dutch might call it blunt." The source also notes, "There is a distance between commercial departments and risk departments."

Benefits generally get high marks. In addition to offering subsidised health care, one insider says the pension plan is paid by the company. And as an added bonus, he reports that employees can get a "discount" on their mortgage once they have "a permanent contract with the company." Another employee working in Amsterdam is enthusiastic about the "free gym in the office."

Insiders give their working hours a thumbs-up as well. "On a typical day, you start at 9 a.m. and leave at 6 p.m. When you're still working after that, you're usually the last one left." And while working 36 hours comprises a typical workweek, "40 [hours] is an option, but hours worked above that are generally not paid — so it's encouraged to not exceed the 40 hours too much."

There are no major complaints with management either, although one insider notes: "My direct manager is external, which brings its own problems, such as unfamiliarity with company procedures." And while firm-provided training is "okay," ultimately, "the ball is in your court to make use of it."

As for office attire, dress is "formal always" says an insider, adding, "Although we're not seeing clients and don't have an official dress code, formal wear is the norm." Offices get average marks. One source reports that at his office, although "there's lots of light and space," the downside is that "the air conditioner is really bad."

Fine diversity

Diversity efforts receive mostly high scores among respondents. "The 36-hour work week is good if you have kids, of course," says one male employee, who adds: "Although we

Visit **Vault Europe's Finance Career Channel** at **www.vault.com/europe** for insider firm profiles, employee surveys of finance professionals in Europe, message boards, job listings, expert finance career advice, insider salary information and more.

VAULT CAREER LIBRARY 155

have many women working at the bank, I can't say how they perceive problems with promoting, etc." Ethnic diversity gets good marks as well, as does diversity with respect to gay staff — one insider notes that there's even a "gay bankers' network" within the firm.

Allied Irish Banks

Bankcenter, Ballsbridge
Dublin, 4
Ireland
Phone: +353 (0) 1 660311
Fax: +353 (0) 1 6609137
www.aibgroup.com

EUROPEAN LOCATIONS

Dublin (HQ)
Ireland • Poland • UK

DEPARTMENTS

Financing
Leasing
Life Insurance
Pension
Retail & Commercial Accounts &
Loans
Trust Services

THE STATS

Employer Type: Public Company
Ticker Symbol: ALBK (London), AIB (NYSE)
Chairman: Dermot Gleeson
Group Chief Executive and Director: Eugene J. Sheehy
2006 Revenue: €2,615 million (FYE 12/06)
2005 Revenue: €1,706 million (FYE 12/05)
No. of Employees: 23,300

KEY COMPETITORS

Bank of Ireland
HSBC Holdings
RBS

PLUSES

Still growing

MINUSES

Quite regional

EMPLOYMENT CONTACT

See "Careers" section at
www.aibgroup.com

THE BUZZ
WHAT EMPLOYEES AT OTHER FIRMS ARE SAYING

- "Specialised"
- "Low to mid-tier"

Visit the Vault Finance Career Channel at **www.vault.com/finance**—with insider firm profiles, message boards, the Vault Finance Job Board and more.

VAULT CAREER LIBRARY 157

THE SCOOP

Green giant ...

Allied Irish Banks, commonly referred to as simply AIB, is the Republic of Ireland's biggest banking and financial services organisation. In addition to its operations in Ireland, the bank operates in Britain, Poland and the US. Ranked No. 362 on the *Financial Times*'s annual FT Global 500 list, the bank offers a full range of banking services, including commercial and retail accounts and loans, financing, leasing, pension, financing and trust services. Additionally, the bank offers a range of general insurance products, including home, travel and health insurance. AIB has approximately 270 branches in Ireland and an additional 65 in Northern Ireland, where it operates First Trust Bank.

With massive arms

AIB operates through four main divisions: AIB Bank Republic of Ireland, encompassing all retail and commercial activities in the country; AIB Bank Great Britain and Northern Ireland, which provides retail and commercial banking services in those areas; AIB Capital Markets, which oversees the global treasury and international, investment banking and corporate banking activities — as well as the Allied Irish America Network. AIB's fourth segment is the Poland division, which is comprised of AIB's majority shareholding in Bank Zachodni WBK.

Allied Irish Banks was formed in 1966 from the union of three Irish Banks: Provincial Bank, Royal Bank of Ireland and Munster & Leinster Bank. The banks merged to overcome the fragmented nature of the Irish banking industry, and to strengthen their position in the global business era and compete with North American banks, which were just beginning to enter Ireland. In November 2006, Allied Irish Bank was voted Britain's Best Business Bank in a biannual survey of the business sector, commissioned by the Forum of Private Business.

Growing overseas

In order to remain competitive, AIB has looked to expand internationally. In July 1991, the merger of AIB Group's interests in Northern Ireland with those of TSB Northern Ireland created First Trust Bank. Today, AIB has a large presence in the US. In 2003, the company sold troubled Maryland-based bank Allfirst Financial (which was formed by AIG's merger of First Maryland Bancorp and Dauphin Deposit Corp.) to New York-based M&T Bank Corp. As part of the deal, AIB assumed a 22.5 per cent stake of M&T. At present, approximately one-third of the bank's assets and profits come from outside Ireland.

Aer Force

AIB has been involved in quite a few notable deals recently. AIB Capital Markets division is one of Aer Lingus' corporate advisors (with UBS). The bank is advising the government on the sale of, and thus effective privatisation of, Ireland's state-owned airline. AIB Corporate Banking Ireland arranged and acted as underwriter, security trustee, documentation and facility agent for the €1.3 billion privatisation of the Jurys Doyle Hotel Group in November 2006.

At the time of press in early summer 2007, AIB is involved in a number of "sale and leaseback" deals for its branch network, which could release approximately €421 million of equity for the bank, and thus free up capital for its banking operations and boost overall profits. In December 2006, AIB announced it had completed the sale of its 50 per cent stake in AIB/BNY Securities Services Ltd. to the Bank of New York Company.

New year, new faces

In January 2007, AIB announced three top-level appointments. Anne Maher and Dan O'Connor joined the bank as non-executive directors, and Donal Forde became executive director. Maher was previously the chief executive of the Pensions Board for Ireland until her retirement in 2006. O'Connor previously served as president and chief executive, GE Consumer Finance-Europe and a senior vice-president of GE. Forde had held the post of managing director of AIB's Republic of Ireland division.

In March of 2005, Eugene Sheehy was announced to take over the post of chief executive upon the retirement of Micahel Buckley. Sheehy was a long-term staffer who served to sort out the bank after the rogue trader scandal in February 2002, when it was discovered that John Rusnak, a rogue currency trader at subsidiary Allfirst, racked up losses of £363 million from 1996 to 2002, presumably from bogus foreign exchange transactions. Rusnak ultimately pleaded guilty to bank fraud.

GETTING HIRED

For more information about job opportunities, vacancies and graduate positions, see the Careers section of Allied Irish Bank's web site at www.aibgroup.com.

Visit **Vault Europe's Finance Career Channel** at **www.vault.com/europe** for insider firm profiles, employee surveys of finance professionals in Europe, message boards, job listings, expert finance career advice, insider salary information and more.

VAULT CAREER LIBRARY 159

Anglo Irish Bank Corporation

Stephen Ct., 18/21
St. Stephen's Green
Dublin, 2
Ireland
Phone: +353 (0) 1 6162000
Fax: +353 (0) 1 6162481
www.angloirishbank.ie

EUROPEAN LOCATIONS*

Dublin (HQ)
Austria
Ireland
Switzerland
United Kingdom

*In Europe

DEPARTMENTS

Business Banking
Retail Banking
Treasury
Wealth management

THE STATS

Employer Type: Public Company
Ticker Symbol: ANGL (London Stock Exchange)
Chairman: Sean P FitzPatrick
Group Chief Executive and Director: David Drumm
2006 Revenue: €850 million (FYE 9/06)
2006 Net Income: €658 million (FYE 9/06)
2005 Revenue: €615 million (FYE 9/05)
2005 Net Income: €477 million (FYE 9/05)
No. of Employees: 1,638

KEY COMPETITORS

Allied Irish Banks
Bank of Ireland
Close Brothers

PLUSES

Great perks and benefits
Diversity is above average

MINUSES

Training programmes could be improved
"Communication can be poor"

EMPLOYMENT CONTACT

www.angloirishbank.ie/careers

THE SCOOP

Lucky charms

Founded in 1964, in only 43 years, Dublin-based Anglo Irish Bank, has grown fast, climbing bank rankings to No. 41 in the world, based on a capitalisation of €10 billion. The bank had a capitalisation of €1 billion in 2000. Anglo Irish Bank has grown through acquisition, starting with the buy of Austrian Royal Trust Bank in 1995 from the Royal Bank of Canada. In 1996 the bank bought Ansbacher Brothers, which was established in Dublin in 1950, and two years later snapped up Credit Lyonnais, an Austrian bank it combined with its other Austrian operations. The acquisitions continued with the 1999 buy of Dublin-based Smurfit Paribas Bank, and in 2001 the bank acquired Geneva-based Banque Marcuard Cook & Cie.

The bank offers business and private banking services with operations divided into three main units: business banking, treasury and risk management. The business banking unit provides services such as loans and bonds, while the treasury unit focuses on risk management, capital markets and international finance. Its wealth management services include portfolio management and investment consulting. Anglo Irish is listed on the London and Dublin exchanges. In addition to its presence in Ireland, the UK and Isle of Man, the bank has offices in Austria, Switzerland and the USA. In the UK, Anglo Irish has locations in London, Manchester, Birmingham, Leeds, Banbury, Glasgow and Edinburgh.

The bank has continental branches in Vienna and Geneva. Additionally, Anglo Irish has a treasury relationship with a network of 350 banks located worldwide. In April 2006, the bank won three prizes at the annual Investor Relations Awards — Grand Prix for Best Overall Investor Relations, Best Investor Meetings and Roadshows, and Best Investor Relations by a chief executive in a large-cap company. The bank has also won Investor awards in 2007. In December 2004 the bank underwent something of a management shake-up after David Drumm took over as CEO from Sean FitzPatrick, who became chairman. Drumm was 35 at the time, one of the youngest CEOs of an Irish company. He had been in charge of the bank's Dublin operations, a role that was assumed by Declan Quilligan.

Pots of gold

The bank raised €416 million in January 2006 to support its growth, placing 33.6 million shares priced at €12.40 per share, the largest placing ever by an Irish-listed company. At the time, CEO Drumm said, "It further strengthens the bank's capital base and positions us well to take advantage of future organic growth opportunities in each of our core markets."

Visit **Vault Europe's Finance Career Channel** at **www.vault.com/europe** for insider firm profiles, employee surveys of finance professionals in Europe, message boards, job listings, expert finance career advice, insider salary information and more.

VAULT CAREER LIBRARY 161

In October 2006, Anglo Irish gathered up $100 million and their private bank rounded up another $49 million, to buy two Midtown Manhattan-based hotels — the Beekman Tower Hotel and Eastgate Tower Hotel. Anglo Irish bought the hotels for the Peninsula Real Estate Fund I, created by Anglo Irish Private Banking and former Tishman Hotel Corp. Executive Vice President Timothy Haskin for Irish investors looking to make commercial real estate buys in the US. Haskin will manage the renovation of the hotels over the following two years.

Seeing green

2006 was a good year for the bank. Pre-tax earnings grew 38 per cent to €850 million and net loans were up 56 per cent to €15.6 billion. Loans that have been approved but not disbursed were up 45 per cent to €8.7 billion. Exuding satisfaction, Drumm said, "2006, for the bank, can be summarised as a year of outstanding growth and investment for the future," adding, "Our strategy of consistent execution and high-quality delivery for our customers enabled us to achieve record lending growth. We are confident that the bank will continue to deliver a strong, superior performance into the future."

GETTING HIRED

If the glove fits

Jobseekers can view all of the bank's available openings at www.angloirishbank.ie/careers/index.asp, where you can peruse detailed descriptions of specific positions and, if interested, send in an application via a human resources e-mail address available on the site. Potential candidates can complete the online application form on the firm's web site. The vast majority of graduate positions are in Dublin and London, mainly offering careers in commercial lending, wealth management and treasury. Work placements and on-the-job training is strongly encouraged until the 12- or 24-month program is completed and the best permanent career placement can be evaluated. One experienced insider says, "Anglo Irish Bank is well aware of how important it is for graduates to gain a thorough grounding in how the bank and its systems work."

The interview-athon

That said, successful candidates can expect to endure a typical two-step interview process where they will need to voice their thoughts about career choice as well as attend an assessment centre before their second interview with senior management and human resource representatives. A recent recruit advises, "Expect lots of questions on performance, relative experience and why you wanted to join." During the hiring process, expect to encounter an "emphasis on finding the right fit for the bank's unique culture," notes a source. Another says to expect "two interviews with senior management and a third with human resources if terms are agreed upon."

OUR SURVEY SAYS

Look to the customer

Not unlike other top banks, the company culture at Anglo Irish Bank is a "'work hard, play hard' one with a major focus on customers." And be sure to bring your upbeat outlook into the bank — "a 'can-do' attitude is essential", and staffers "strive to be the best and put the customer first." Management gets mostly good marks, too. One insider says that the bank has an "open-door policy from management that helps keep a flat structure." Others add that communication is "good, open and frank" with a "team atmosphere", and even though "communication can be poor" at times, there's always "respect given."

And the perks aren't too shabby, either. There's a "pension, stock options and a savings plan" along with a "save-as-you-earn share purchase." The average workweek ranges from 55 to 60 hours; however, an insider notes that "while this may be slightly more than competitors, it is still not far from the industry norm." In addition, "billing pressure isn't relevant" and weekend work is rare, although "every couple of months I may do two or three hours of extra work on a Saturday to catch up during or after a busy period," says one contact. Feedback regarding the bank's training programmes vary, ranging from reports "mentoring in place at all levels" to accounts of "receiving some training, but I haven't been asked or approached much about it further."

Like a tin of sardines?

General opinions on the office conditions are not particularly enthusiastic with one Dublin banker complaining "the air conditioning and number of bodies in the area is excessive," while a slightly more optimistic co-worker adds, "The office is just OK" adding that "We are awaiting the building of a new headquarters, due to be ready for January 2009." Another notes that casual Fridays don't exist at this bank, so basically leave your trainers and jeans at home. "Dress code is always formal," the contact notes and almost touchingly adds: "apart from the occasional charity day tie-ins."

Money talks

Despite the cons, insiders give the impression that financial compensation at Anglo Irish Bank is good and they enjoy a competitive salary, pension and stock options, along with a

Visit **Vault** Europe's **Finance Career Channel** at **www.vault.com/europe** for insider firm profiles, employee surveys of finance professionals in Europe, message boards, job listings, expert finance career advice, insider salary information and more.

VAULT CAREER LIBRARY 163

save-as-you-earn share-purchase scheme. However, no mention is made of any further company perks such as car allowance, gym membership, career breaks or tuition compensation.

Dedicated to diversity

Employment diversity is well above average right across the board with healthy numbers of both sexes and minority groups in employment. One worker comments, "Although the drinking culture is a bore on the social side of things, Anglo Irish Bank is full of great people and opportunities, along with good pay and conditions."

B. Metzler seel. Sohn & Co.

Grosse Gallusstrasse 18
60311 Frankfurt/Main
Germany
Phone: +49 (0) 69 21 04 0
Fax: +49 (0) 69 28 14 29
www.metzler.com

EUROPEAN LOCATIONS

Cologne/Dusseldorf
Dublin
Frankfurt
Munich
Stuttgart

DEPARTMENTS

Asset Management
Corporate Finance
Equities
Financial Markets
Information Technology
Private Banking

THE STATS

Employer Type: Private Company
CEO: Friedrich von Metzler
No. of Employees: 700
No. of Offices: 10 (Worldwide)

KEY COMPETITORS

Berenberg
MM Warburg
Sal Oppenheim

PLUSES

"Expertise"

MINUSES

Somewhat regional

EMPLOYMENT CONTACT

www.metzler.com
(Click on "Career at Metzler" link)

E-mail: jobs@metzler.com

THE BUZZ
WHAT EMPLOYEES AT OTHER FIRMS ARE SAYING

- "Elegant, good and focused"
- "Small; regional"

Visit the Vault Finance Career Channel at **www.vault.com/finance**—with insider firm
profiles, message boards, the Vault Finance Job Board and more.

VAULT CAREER LIBRARY 165

THE SCOOP

300 years of history

Headquartered in Frankfurt and with offices around the globe, Metzler seel. Sohn & Co. has been in business for more than 330 years. Founded by Benjamin Metzler in Frankfurt am Main in 1674, it is the oldest German bank still managed by the family that created it. Today the bank is run by 11th-generation descendant Friedrich von Metzler. In 1760, B. Metzler made the transition from trading house to banking house and, in 1779, began issuing its first loan stocks.

By the end of the 19th century, B. Metzler had successfully transformed into a private bank, switching its focus from balance-effectual business tactics to individual finances. While it started as a trading company, it now functions as a merchant bank offering financial services, as a partner in securities transactions, as an asset manager for private clients and as a corporate finance consultant.

Germany entered the 20th century with roughly 2,000 independent banks, and through cunning restructures B. Metzler managed to survive two World Wars, the Great Depression and the Third Reich. Today, it is one of 55 German private banks to survive the turbulence of the 20th century. The firm has €30 billion under management, with 80 per cent coming from institutions, as its specialty is pension management and fund administration.

The bank recently opened a Tokyo office to target Japanese institutional investors. The Metzler family was struck by tragedy, which was front page news in 2002, when Friedrich von Metzler's 11-year-old son Jakob was kidnapped and murdered by a family acquaintance looking to extort a million-euro ransom from the family.

A variety of services

B. Metzler offers an extensive menu of services. Its asset management division covers all portfolio management for private and institutional clients. Brokerage services are covered by the equities division, which includes such features as equity research, advice and trading. The corporate finance arm covers mergers and acquisitions, IPO consulting, advice on privatisation of companies and structured financing. Metzler's bond and currency management, special customer advisory services and bank relations operations are combined in its core financial markets business area.

Metzler North America Corporation, Seattle, which was founded in 1976, and Metzler North America GmbH, Frankfurt am Main, act as asset managers for US and Canadian institutional real estate portfolios. In addition to managing direct investments and closed-end funds, Metzler acts as a consultant for segregated real estate funds.

Based in Los Angeles, Metzler/Payden, LLC is a 50-50 joint venture between Metzler Bank and Payden & Rygel with $2 billion in assets under management. The combination offers customers access to the expertise of the two partners: Metzler's proven knowledge of the European capital market is complemented by Payden & Rygel's expertise in North American bonds. Payden & Rygel has $54 billion in assets under management and is one of the largest independent investment managers in the US. In addition to Los Angeles, the firm has offices in London, Dublin and Frankfurt.

In April 2007, Metzler/Payden reported that its European Emerging Markets Fund (MPYMX), which invests in Eastern European and Russian publicly traded companies, produced a year-to-date return of 22.05 per cent through March 31, 2006. The firm's flagship mutual fund, the Metzler/Payden European Emerging Markets Fund (MPYMX), has a five-star Morningstar rating.

Heir apparent

At the firm's annual press conference in spring 2006, CEO Friedrich von Metzler announced his satisfaction: "2005 was a very successful year." Up 27 per cent against the previous year, B. Metzler's commission income hit €120 million, while assets under management rose by 25 per cent, from €20 billion to €24 billion. The Metzler Fund Xchange is currently managing mutual funds worth €6.6 billion and the bank's employee count is growing.

Rumour has it that the bank is already grooming von Metzler's nephew as the heir apparent. Metzler family members are expected to learn the tools of the trade; Friedrich von Metzler gained banking experience at Schroder Wagg in London, Smith Barney in New York and at Deutsche Bank in Germany. Besides experience, the next head of the family empire will need cash, since he will have to buy out the shares of another family member to replace him, as the bank is privately owned.

GETTING HIRED

For more information on current job vacancies and graduate opportunities at B. Metzler seel. Sohn and & Co, visit the company's web site at www.metzler.com, and click on the "Career at Metzler" link. Alternately, job seekers can send a query via e-mail to jobs@metzler.com.

Visit **Vault Europe's Finance Career Channel** at www.vault.com/europe for insider firm profiles, employee surveys of finance professionals in Europe, message boards, job listings, expert finance career advice, insider salary information and more.

VAULT CAREER LIBRARY 167

Banco Popular Espanol S.A.

34 Velazquez St.
28001 Madrid, Spain
Phone: +34 91 520 70 00
Fax: +34 91 577 92 08
www.bancopopular.es

EUROPEAN LOCATIONS

Madrid (Global HQ)
Locations in Belgium, Germany,
the Netherlands, Spain,
Switzerland and the UK, with
subsidiaries in France and
Portugal.)

DEPARTMENTS

Asset Management
Commercial & Retail Banking
Life Insurance
Pension & Mutual Fund
Administration
Private Banking

THE STATS

Employer Type: Public Company
Ticker Symbol: POP (Spanish/IBEX)
Chairman: Angel Ron
CEO: Francisco Fernandez Dopico
2006 Revenue: €2.06 billion
(FYE 12/06)
2006 Net Income: €1.02 billion
(FYE 12/06)
2005 Revenue: €1.88 billion
(FYE 12/05)
2005 Net Income: €877.74 million
(FYE 12/05)
2006 No. of Employees: 14,056
2006 No. of Offices: 2,200+ branches

KEY COMPETITORS

BBVA
Grupo Santander

PLUSES

Huge in Spain

MINUSES

Not a key player

EMPLOYMENT CONTACT

www.bancopopular.es

THE BUZZ
WHAT EMPLOYEES AT OTHER FIRMS ARE SAYING

- "Profitable but regional"
- "Not international"

Visit the Vault Finance Career Channel at **www.vault.com/finance**—with insider firm
profiles, message boards, the Vault Finance Job Board and more.

VAULT CAREER LIBRARY 169

THE SCOOP

Mainly in Spain

Banco Popular is the third-largest bank in Spain behind Santander Central Hispano and Banco Bilboa Vizcaya Argentaria. The bank offers commercial and retail banking services through more than 2,200 branches. Ranked No. 429 on the *Financial Times'* annual FT Global 500 list, Banco Popular is focused on its home market with an emphasis on commercial loans to small and midsized businesses. It also administers mutual funds and offers asset management, consumer credit, life insurance, factoring and securities trading.

The firm is made up of a national bank, Banco Popular Espanol; five regional banks: Banco de Andalucia, Banco de Castilla, Banco de Credito Balear, Banco de Vasconia and Banco de Galicia; and a mortgage bank — Banco Popular Hipotecario. In addition, Banco Popular has French subsidiary Banco Popular France and Portuguese subsidiary Banco Popular Portugal. Banco Popular also operates a separate internet bank, bancopopular-e.com. Besides the Iberian Peninsula, Banco Popular also has a presence in Belgium, Chile, Germany, Hong Kong, Caracas, Morocco, the Netherlands, Switzerland — in both Geneva and Zurich — and London. The bank owns a 60 per cent stake of Banca Privada.

The bank was founded in 1926, and opened its first foreign branch office in Paris in 1968. By 1991, Banco Popular Espanol offered 14 branches in France. In 1992, the firm converted its French subsidiary into a joint venture with Banco Comercial Portugues under the name Banco Popular Comercial. In 2000, Banco Popular established a network of Portuguese branches and then, two years later, Banco Popular Comercial became a wholly owned subsidiary of Banco Popular and changed its name to Banco Popular France. In Portugal, Banco Popular bought Banco Nacional de Credito Inmobiliario and in 2005 renamed it Banco Popular Portugal.

An Angel named Ron

After 47 years on the board (32 as chairman), 78-year-old Luis Valls retired in October 2004 to resolve the succession issue at an "opportune moment." Although Valls stepped down as executive chairman, he remains chairman of the general shareholders' meeting. The board named the bank's current managing director, Angel Ron, chairman to replace Valls, making him the youngest chairman in Spanish banking at 44. Ron shares chairmanship with Valls' brother Javier, who is co-chairman but has no executive responsibilities. Fernandez Dopico, who has been with the bank for 34 years, was named CEO.

A very good year

At the end of the third quarter of 2006, the bank reported on-balance sheet total assets of €87.4 billion, up 19.3 per cent from the same period in 2005. Total business for the first nine months of the year was €104.6 billion, up 19.1 per cent over the same period a year prior. The bank attributed the growth to personal loans and credits, which were up over 20 per cent; mortgage loans, up 18.6 per cent, and commercial paper discounting, up 16.9 per cent. More than 91 per cent of the business came from Spain, with the remainder coming from Portugal. Spanish assets grew 18.5 per cent, while Portuguese assets were up 29.6 per cent.

GETTING HIRED

The careers section of Banco Popular's website declares that the bank is ready to "make dreams happen" for "our people, our communities, and for our financial performance." Quite the lofty assertion, but you can apply and decide for yourself at www.bancopopularcareers.com, where the firm's "people filter" lets you sift through a list of positions based on category and keyword. After selecting a position, you can apply online, where you'll be asked the standard questions along with ones such as your preferred "maximum commute."

Visit **Vault Europe's Finance Career Channel** at **www.vault.com/europe** for insider firm profiles, employee surveys of finance professionals in Europe, message boards, job listings, expert finance career advice, insider salary information and more.

V/\ULT CAREER LIBRARY 171

Bank of Ireland

Lower Baggot Street
Dublin, 2
Ireland
Phone: +353 1 661 5933
www.bankofireland.com

DEPARTMENTS

Asset Management
Corporate Banking
Corporate Finance
First Rate
Global Markets
Securities Services

THE STATS

Employer Type: Public Company
Ticker Symbol: BKIR (LSE), IRE (NYSE)
CEO: Brian J. Goggin
2006 Revenue: €15.99 billion (FYE 3/06)
2006 Net Income: €12.96 billion (FYE 3/06)
2005 Revenue: €13.10 billion (FYE 3/05)
2006 Net Income: €10.54 billion (FYE 3/05)
2006 Employees: 16,190
No. of Offices: 250

PLUSES

"Culture is excellent"
Good perks

MINUSES

"Bureaucratic at times"
"Dress code is not very flexible"

EMPLOYMENT CONTACT

www.bankofireland.com/careers

THE BUZZ
WHAT EMPLOYEES AT OTHER FIRMS ARE SAYING

- "Traditional"
- "Regional"

THE SCOOP

Deep roots

The Bank of Ireland (BoI) opened its doors by royal charter in 1783, in an office at Mary's Abbey in Dublin. It was named official banker to the Irish government in 1922 and diversified in 1966, adding asset management and investment banking businesses. Today the bank is the largest in Ireland by total assets and is the highest-rated listed Irish financial institution. While its headquarters are in Dublin the bank's 16,000-plus employees are located in its 250 offices in eight countries.

BoI is a fully diversified financial services group, offering corporate banking, global markets services, asset management, corporate finance, securities services and first rate/foreign currency services. It also has personal and business retail banking lines. For the fiscal year 2006, 64 per cent of BoI profits came from Ireland, 22 per cent from the United Kingdom and 14 per cent from the rest of the world.

New people, new divisions

In the second half of 2006 BoI made several important appointments, naming Kevin Twomey (previously head of trading) to the position of head of markets. In September 2006 the bank hired Jamie Wood, a well-known London portfolio manager, to become a senior equity manager. Barry Glavin, HSBC's global head of industrials research, was another steal from London — he was named BoI's senior research analyst, charged with expanding the bank's young global research team.

In September 2006 BoI also created a new capital markets division, which incorporated operations from both wholesale financial services and asset management services. The division is led by Denis Donovan, who had been the head of wholesale financial services. BoI Chief Executive Brian Goggin noted that the realignment was "a logical strategic development of our ambitious international growth strategy," as it combined two of the bank's main growth businesses.

Pension problems

Pensions are a major topic for BoI researchers and analysts, whose findings are frequently discussed as the Irish government tackles the country's pension crisis. In a comprehensive survey released in late September 2006, BoI revealed that almost 71 per cent of the country's population doesn't understand the tax benefits associated with pensions and nearly half of all employed citizens don't have a pension plan in place. Surprisingly, the bank's researchers found that 60 per cent of people with no pension say they can afford one

Visit **Vault Europe's Finance Career Channel** at www.vault.com/europe for insider firm profiles, employee surveys of finance professionals in Europe, message boards, job listings, expert finance career advice, insider salary information and more.

VAULT CAREER LIBRARY   173

— meaning awareness of benefits, not affordability, is the primary barrier to pension involvement.

But BoI's own pension plans came under fire in the fall and winter of 2006 when it changed pension terms to affect all employees hired after October 1, 2006. Staff hired before that date will continue to be covered by a defined benefits pension scheme, whereas new hires will have a hybrid plan that combines elements of a defined benefit and a defined contribution plan. The Irish Bank Officials Association (IBOA), a trade union representing Ireland's banking and finance employees, launched a public criticism of the new hybrid scheme. The bank defended itself, saying that "new employees will have a very attractive pension prospect," but the IBOA called for a strike in November 2006 after talks with the Labour Relations Commission failed. Approximately 200 Bank of Ireland staffers were involved with the action. The case went to Labour Court in December 2006 and a decision is expected sometime in 2007.

Trading spaces

According to a BoI-commissioned study of Irish mortgages, the "mover purchaser" — a customer who is moving from a starter home to a bigger, better house — represented the largest segment of the market in the first half of 2006. The research also showed that over half the people surveyed described their mortgage/moving experience as "stressful," mostly because of unexpected costs of trading up — such as decorating a bigger space, moving costs and agent fees — and the overwhelming number of financial and legal organisations involved with the process. Responding to this trend, the bank launched a Trade Up mortgage programme in October 2006, specifically aimed at these customers. The programme offers personalised assistance, booklets explaining the organisations and regulations involved with mortgages and real estate, as well as step-by-step advice for transitioning to a better home.

A card of gold ...

In December 2006 BoI unveiled a new Gold Visa Business card, designed to attract on-the-go business customers. The BoI Gold Visa Business card offers unique perks, like free access to Aer Lingus's Gold Circle Lounges worldwide, priority check-in on long-distance flights and around-the-clock emergency travel assistance. Cardholders can manage their accounts via a customised online transaction management system, Gold Visa Business Online, which is meant to help companies track their employees' expenses and simplify expense reports.

... and a heart of gold

BoI has a long history of supporting educational and charitable organisations in Ireland. Established in 2000, its Millennium Scholars Trust is a relatively recent project, providing annual scholarships to qualified students who cannot otherwise continue their education because of poverty or disability. The bank is also the proprietary sponsor of the Special Olympics Network, committing funds and five full-time staff members to manage the promotion and organisation of the Special Olympics and the World Summer Games. BoI is a major supporter of the Irish Cancer Society, the Irish Rugby Football Union and many local and national charities selected by BoI staff through a staff matching fund. The bank also preserves rare 18th-century tapestries in its art collection and sponsors an annual football tournament.

GETTING HIRED

Committed to recruitment

The bank is always "actively recruiting top professionals," one insider says. Others note that in addition to its web site, the firm also recruits from "career fairs" and "advertising." Another source comments, "We have a very comprehensive graduate selection process for a very competitive programme."

The bank's site offers tips on creating a CV (a two-page CV is fine to submit, but make sure it's "definitely no longer than three pages") and invites users to submit their finished applications via e-mail to jobs@boimail.com. During interviews, one contact says to expect to "complete ability tests and assessment centres." And not to worry if you're called back multiple times — three rounds of interviews are "typical," notes an insider.

OUR SURVEY SAYS

Mostly satisfied

There's a "strong culture" at the bank, and most sources report satisfaction with their jobs. Insiders also report enjoying the "stock options", "free banking", "reduced lending rates", "gym membership", "subsidised canteen", "holiday pay" and "the option to do extra work." Indeed, hours staffers work aren't too taxing — they tend to clock around "40 to 50" per week and "rarely or never" work on the weekends, though one insider says he "would like to have more comprehensive flexible working options available." The dress

Visit **Vault Europe's Finance Career Channel** at **www.vault.com/europe** for insider firm profiles, employee surveys of finance professionals in Europe, message boards, job listings, expert finance career advice, insider salary information and more.

V/\ULT CAREER LIBRARY   **175**

code is slightly more flexible, offering casual Fridays, but one respondent rather amusingly notes that the policy is "restricted to no jeans — which I feel is extreme."

The bank's diversity could also be improved upon, insiders say. One notes, "We are an organisation that has a very large proportion of females, yet they are not represented to the same degree at the top of our organisational structure."

Bank of New York, The

One Canada Square
London E14 5AL
United Kingdom
Phone: +44 (0) 20 7570 1784
Fax: +44 (0) 20 7964 4792
www.bankofny.com

EUROPEAN LOCATIONS

London (European HQ)
Brussels
Channel Islands
Dublin
Edinburgh
Frankfurt
Luxembourg
Milan
Madrid
Paris

DEPARTMENTS

Individual & Regional Banking
Investment Management
Private Banking
Securities Servicing
Treasury Management

THE STATS

Employer Type: Public Company
Ticker Symbol: BK (NYSE)
CEO: Thomas A. Renyi
2006 Revenue: $6,821 million
(FYE 12/06)
2006 Net Income: $3,011 million
(FYE 12/06)
2005 Revenue: $6,038 million
(FYE 12/05)
2005 Net Income: $1,271 million
(FYE 12/05)
2006 Employees: 23,800
(Worldwide)
No. of Offices: 1,600 (Worldwide)

PLUSES

Good European presence; good
business

MINUSES

Lacks instant recognition in Europe

EMPLOYMENT CONTACT

www.bankofny.com/careers

THE BUZZ
WHAT EMPLOYEES AT OTHER FIRMS ARE SAYING

- "Big"
- "No investment bank footprint
  really"
- "Very strong in the US in
  commercial and retail banking"
- "Going through takeover pains"

Visit the Vault Finance Career Channel at **www.vault.com/finance**—with insider firm
profiles, message boards, the Vault Finance Job Board and more.

V/\ULT CAREER LIBRARY 177

THE SCOOP

The gentlemen's bank

Once upon a time, in 1784, a small advertisement appeared in a New York City newspaper inviting "Gentlemen in this City" to meet and discuss the establishment of a new bank formed "on liberal principles," with "stock to consist of specie only." Among the gents who attended this meeting was Alexander Hamilton, who eventually wrote the fledgling bank's constitution, and spearheaded its organisation and early development.

The Bank of New York (BNY) is America's oldest bank and opened its doors at the Walton House in lower Manhattan on June 9, 1784. The New York Stock Exchange opened eight years later and the bank's corporate stock was the first to be traded on the NYSE. As New York City's business and industrial sectors grew, the bank became an important financial partner to the city, making loans to support building costs in the area. BNY entered the trust business in 1922 when it merged with the New York Life Insurance and Trust Company. Decades later, in 1988, it acquired the Irving Bank Corporation, creating the 10th-largest bank in the United States at the time and laying the groundwork for the Bank of New York as it exists today.

In 2006 BNY was the 14th-largest bank in the United States, serving corporations and institutions, consultants and advisors, small businesses, private clients and individual consumers. Industry specialty groups include banks, health care, hedge funds, insurance, investment managers, media and technology, nonprofits and foundations, professional services, public and government entities, real estate and mortgage banking, retailing, securities and unions.

European expansion

Today, BNY's global headquarters remain in New York and its European headquarters is in London. BNY's continental European offices, with more than 2,800 employees, are located in Europe's major financial centres, including Brussels, Paris, Milan, Madrid, Frankfurt and Dublin. As of 2006, BNY managed more than 1,500 pension funds and held $106 billion in assets and $1.9 trillion on behalf of European investors. BNY's presence in the UK is bigger than its entire combined presence on the European continent. In the UK, the bank manages more than 1,500 UK pension funds and specialises in unit trusts, offshore funds and OEICs.

Swap meet

On October 1, 2006, BNY and JPMorgan Chase closed a long-awaited deal: JPMorgan Chase bought BNY's retail and regional middle-market banking businesses valued at $2.3

billion and BNY bought JPMorgan Chase's corporate trust business valued at $2.15 billion. According to BNY, this swap was part of the bank's long-run strategy to focus on its securities services, private banking and asset management business. Following the completion of the sale, BNY's corporate trust position rose significantly, with the bank reporting a combined client base with $8 trillion in total debt outstanding in 20 countries.

Converging on global business

In October 2006, BNY announced the completion of transactions resulting in the formation of BNY ConvergEx Group LLP, a wide-ranging brokerage aimed at institutional clients worldwide. The ConvergEx deal, first announced in June 2006, involved agreements between BNY, Eze Castle Software and a private equity firm called GTCR Golder Runner. BNY brought its trade execution, commission management, independent research and transition management prowess to the table, while Eze Castle offered cutting-edge trade order management and related investment technologies.

BNY's B-Trade and G-Trade businesses will be fully assimilated into BNY ConvergEx by 2008. ConvergEx is technically an "affiliate" of the bank and will be operated from offices in London, New York, Boston, San Francisco, Chicago, Dallas, Stamford, Bermuda, Tokyo, Hong Kong and Sydney. As of October 2006 ConvergEx was staffed by 635 employees.

Third time's the charm

A third and final merger deal was announced in 2006, and BNY said it was "the describing transformational event" of the bank's year. It agreed in December to merge with Mellon Financial Corporation, pending regulatory and shareholder approval. If completed, the deal would create one of the world's largest securities services and asset management firm. The combined entity would list $16.6 trillion in assets under custody and $8 trillion in assets under trusteeship. It would also be ranked among the world's top-10 asset managers with more than $1.1 trillion in assets under management.

BNY Chairman and CEO Thomas Renyi will be the new organisation's chairman and Robert P. Kelly, chairman, president and CEO of Mellon, will serve as CEO. The merger is set to close sometime in the third quarter of 2007. In its announcement of the agreement, BNY noted that the merger will involve 40,000 staff at the two firms — of whom approximately 4,000 will be laid off over the three years following the close of the deal.

Making deposits

As a global leader in securities servicing, BNY often acts as a successor depository for international companies through its American depository receipt (ADR) program. BNY is

Visit **Vault Europe's Finance Career Channel** at **www.vault.com/europe** for insider firm profiles, employee surveys of finance professionals in Europe, message boards, job listings, expert finance career advice, insider salary information and more.

VAULT CAREER LIBRARY **179**

a depository for more than 1,250 depository receipt programs worldwide, with a 64 per cent market share.

In late October 2006 BNY was chosen as successor depository by Edinburgh-based HBOS, a massive entity formed by the 2001 merger of Halifax and Bank of Scotland. HBOS boasts market capitalisation of more than £40 billion, assets of more than £540 billion and approximately 22 million customers. Each HBOS ADR represents one ordinary share in the company and the ADRs trade on the over-the-counter market.

Pats on the back

BNY picked up several awards at the end of 2006, including Best Foreign Exchange Research Worldwide as chosen by *Global Finance* magazine — the third year in a row that BNY topped the list. *Global Finance* also awarded BNY the title of "Best Custody Bank in the world" for the seventh consecutive year. *Global Custodian* magazine's 2006 Global Custodian Bank Survey named BNY the world's top securities lending provider for the third consecutive year. BNY was also awarded the title of Number One Overall Global Trustee for 2006, according to year-end data compiled across all debt segments by the industry's leading information providers.

GETTING HIRED

For more information about careers, vacancies or graduate opportunities at Bank of New York, visit the company's web site at www.bankofny.com/careers.

BBVA S.A.

Paseo de la Castellana, 81
28046 Madrid
Spain
Phone: +34 91 374 6000

Plaza San Nicolas, 4
48005 Bilbao
Spain
Phone: +34 94 487 6000
www.bbva.com

EUROPEAN LOCATIONS

Madrid (HQ)
Belgium
France
Italy
Portugal
Russia
Spain
Switzerland
United Kingdom

DEPARTMENTS

Asset Management & Private
Banking
Corporate Banking
Global Businesses
Investment Banking
Retail Banking

THE STATS

Employer Type: Public Company
Ticker Symbol: BBVA (Spain), BBV
(NYSE)
Chairman & CEO: Francisco Gonzalez
2006 Revenue: €15,701 million
(€15.7 billion)
2005 Revenue: €13,024 million
(€13 billion)
2006 Employees: 98,553
No. of Offices: 7,500 (Worldwide)

PLUSES

"Our focus on results"
"Professional development"

MINUSES

Occasional long hours
Salaries could be better

EMPLOYMENT CONTACT

www.bbva.com
(Follow the Employment at BBVA
link)

THE BUZZ
WHAT EMPLOYEES AT OTHER FIRMS ARE SAYING

- "Strong footprint in Spanish
  speaking world"
- "Regional"

Visit the Vault Finance Career Channel at **www.vault.com/finance**—with insider firm
profiles, message boards, the Vault Finance Job Board and more.

VAULT CAREER LIBRARY 181

THE SCOOP

Made in Spain

The banks that would become the global financial services group known as Spain's Banco Bilbao Vizcaya Argentaria (BBVA) date back to 1857, when the Spanish Board of Trade established a currency-issuing and discount bank called Banco de Bilbao. Several decades later, Banco de Vizcaya, a commercial bank, was created. After more than a century of mergers, growth and expansion, Banco de Bilbao and Banco de Vizcaya merged in 1988 and formed BBV. A year later BBV announced its intention to merge with Argentaria, another consortium of private Spanish banks. The deal was completed in 2001, and the new group became BBVA. Current BBVA Chairman Francisco Gonzalez was previously chairman of Argentaria.

Spectacularly, a century and a half since it was first established, today's BBVA "is the result of the merger and acquisition of 150 banks," explains the firm. Today BBVA is one of Spain's largest banks. It has approximately 7,500 offices in more than 30 countries. While most of its European operations are concentrated in Spain, Portugal, France, Italy and the UK, the bank also has offices in Belgium, Switzerland, Russia and Andorra. BBVA has also come to dominate Latin America, where it has busy subsidiary operations in 10 countries. BBVA's services include retail, corporate and institutional banking, investment banking, asset management and insurance.

Global ambitions

Like any self-respecting bank worth its own salt these days, BBVA has global aspirations. To achieve this, the bank says it "will develop a profitable growth strategy, both organic growth as well as via acquisitions".

In 2006 BBVA did a bit of internal reorganising as part of what it calls "a diverse global strategy." The bank broke its business areas into five (not three) parts. Retail banking services in Spain and Portugal include retail banking, asset management and private banking. Wholesale banking services include domestic and international corporate and institutional banking. The realignment brings the trading rooms in Spain, throughout Europe and New York under the same umbrella. Global markets, corporate and investment banking and real estate projects for large corporate clients are also part of wholesale banking.

In line with its global ambitions, BBVA admits to be "strengthening new business lines, with the financing of infrastructures or foreign trade," and is "permanently seeking its entry into these new client sectors." Well, the bank is clearly on the right track, as at the end of

2006, BBVA was one of the 40-largest banks in the world — in terms of assets managed — and was also on the list of the 20-largest banks in the Eurozone.

Looking after SMEs

BBVA has carved out a niche market by creating branches specializing in small- and medium-sized enterprises (SMEs). BBVA's SME branches provide customised services and financial products created especially for SME owners. These products and services include foreign trade, cash-flow management solutions, payment collection, tax and social security products, and transfer mechanisms. The bank also offers special discount lines, loans, advances, liability services and flotation to SMEs — and each SME client has a BBVA advisor assigned to his or her company to personally handle all service requests and questions. Much of BBVA's SME business relies on the bank's extensive online banking systems.

Eyes on the global markets

Apart from being one of the two biggest banks in Spain, BBVA has built the first international financial franchise in Latin America. The first operations took place in 1995 with the purchase of Banco Continental de Peru. A year later, operations began in Colombia and Argentina with the acquisition of Banco Ganadero and Banco Francés, respectively. Venezuela and Chile followed. The quantum leap in Latin America came in 2000, with the acquisition of a majority stake in Bancomer, Mexico's top bank. Four years later, BBVA acquired 100 per cent of its capital, strengthening its position as Latin America's top banking franchise.

Also in 2004, the BBVA Group launched another great international expansion platform by entering the US market. Since then, BBVA has purchased four banks in the world's first economy: Valley Bank, Laredo National, Texas Regional and State National. In 2007, BBVA agreed to buy 100 per cent of Compass Bancshares, the leading bank in the southern United States, taking a definite step forward in its US growth strategy.

In 2005, BBVA made the strategic decision to bolster its position in the Asia-Pacific region. As a result, BBVA Group has now opened major offices in the area's main financial hubs. This plan has reached a zenith with the signing of the Citic Group Strategic Alliance, which transforms BBVA into one of the few large international groups with a sizeable position in China. Thanks to this agreement, BBVA takes a stake in China Citic Bank, the third commercial bank in the country, and in CIFH, the international arm of the groupwith headquarters in Hong Kong. This will allow the group to make significant progress in commercial banking in China and wholesale banking in the rest of Asia.

The year of BBVA

The year 2007 marks BBVA's 150th anniversary — a year that Chairman Gonzalez has declared will be "the year of BBVA." While acknowledging the strides made in 2006, Gonzalez said "the past is history, and we must focus on the future." If Gonzalez's wishes come true, BBVA's future will involve further significant growth. Speaking at the company's year-end gathering, he told his employees that he foresaw four primary lines of action for 2007 and beyond: using technology to expand the bank's customer base and enter new markets, using research to create targeted new products, improving overall efficiency and emphasising a worldwide BBVA culture to facilitate idea exchanges between business units and groups. And with a hint of mystery, he went on to add, "We have been pushing ahead with many other innovative projects that we will reveal when the time is ripe."

GETTING HIRED

Check your aptitude

Under the Employment at BBVA link at www.bbva.com, candidates can check out job opportunities for all skill levels, from university graduates to experienced professionals and send in an electronic CV — the bank notes on the site that it no longer accepts paper applications. If the bank likes what they see and you're called in, insiders say you can anticipate taking "aptitude tests" — and coming in for at least two rounds of meetings.

OUR SURVEY SAYS

Visualise a better future

The bank "has a vision — 'we work for a better future for people'", and operates under "seven principles and 17 commitments toward our customers, shareholders, employees and society," one insider says. It sounds rather enigmatic, but sources seem to be satisfied for the most part. One adds that the firm offers a great "balance for personal and professional life." Hours spent in the office aren't particularly arduous either, insiders report, although one notes that "working with people around the world makes it necessary to be available for different time zones."

In terms of a formal business dress code, it's not button-up dress all of the time, since there are "casual Fridays," says a contact. Diversity gets mostly high marks from respondents as well and another insider says, "65 per cent of people we are currently hiring are women."

Visit **Vault Europe's Finance Career Channel** at **www.vault.com/europe** for insider firm profiles, employee surveys of finance professionals in Europe, message boards, job listings, expert finance career advice, insider salary information and more.

VAULT   CAREER LIBRARY   **185**

CIBC World Markets

European Headquarters
Cottons Centre
Cottons Lane
London SE1 2QL
United Kingdom

Phone: +44 20 7234 6000
Fax: +44 20 7407 4127
www.cibcwm.com

EUROPEAN LOCATIONS

Toronto (Global HQ)
London (European HQ)
Dublin

DEPARTMENTS

Debt Capital Markets
Equity Sales & Structured Products
European Corporate & Investment
Banking

THE STATS

Employer Type: Public Company
Chairman & CEO: Brian Shaw
Head of Bank, Europe: Peter Letley
Ticker Symbol: CM (Toronto, NYSE,
Berlin, Frankfurt, Munich)
2006 Revenue (Globally): CAD
$2,884 million
2005 Revenue (Globally): CAD
$3,575 million
2006 Revenue: CAD $2,660 million
2005 Revenue: CAD $3,384 million
2006 Net Income: CAD $646 million
2005 Net Loss: CAD $1,1671 million
No. of Employees (globally): 2,500
No. of Offices (globally): 26

KEY COMPETITORS

BMO Capital Markets
RBC Capital Markets
TD Securities

PLUSES

Well known for its breadth and
quality

MINUSES

Not yet a key player in Europe

EMPLOYMENT CONTACT

www.cibcwm.com (See "Careers"
section)

THE BUZZ
WHAT EMPLOYEES AT OTHER FIRMS ARE SAYING

- "Good performer"
- "Second-tier IB"

THE SCOOP

Oh Canada!

CIBC World Markets is the investment banking division of the Canadian Imperial Bank of Commerce. As an investment bank, CIBC World Markets helps large companies, governments and other large institutions obtain capital and credit. Professionals at CIBC World Markets provide capital solutions and advisory services across a wide range of industries, as well as merchant and commercial banking and top-ranked research. The firm's headquarters are in Toronto, with international offices located in major financial centres. The European headquarters are in London, led by Peter Letley, head of bank, Europe. In the European market, CIBC World Markets operates as both CIBC World Markets and CIBC World Markets Plc, with three core businesses: debt capital markets (DCM), European investment and corporate banking, and global equities.

Homegrown institution

CIBC World Markets was formed in 1988, when the Canadian Imperial Bank of Commerce acquired a majority interest in Wood Gundy Inc., one of Canada's leading securities dealers and the foremost Canadian dealer internationally. The combination of CIBC capital and Wood Gundy's underwriting reputation created an investment banking arm that became one of the leading investing institutions in Canada. The result, CIBC Wood Gundy Inc., formed the core of CIBC World Markets, which was created in 1997. Today the company has roughly 2,500 employees around the world.

It's all about the details

At the CIBC World Markets London office, the debt capital markets business provides clients in Europe, the Middle East and Asia with services such as advisory, origination, syndication, trading and sales. The business uses an integrated, multi-product approach, offering cash and derivative solutions in fixed income, securitisation, credit, foreign exchange, commodity and equity products. Meanwhile, the European investment and corporate banking group operates on the direct investment side, working in financial advisory services, mergers and acquisitions, leveraged finance and distribution.

Key industry sectors include gaming, lodging and leisure, infrastructure finance, mining, oil and gas, and power and utilities. The third segment, equity sales and structured products, has a targeted focus in the trading of US and Canadian cash equities, and is known as a leading distributor of North American equity products in the European market. The equity sales and structured products division also offers equity-linked notes and commodity-linked notes.

Visit **Vault Europe's Finance Career Channel** at **www.vault.com/europe** for insider firm profiles, employee surveys of finance professionals in Europe, message boards, job listings, expert finance career advice, insider salary information and more.

VAULT   CAREER
         LIBRARY   **187**

Top-notch research

CIBC World Markets has more than 200 analysts around the world conducting equity, fixed income and economics research. World Markets research is well known for its breadth and quality, with the Canadian fixed income research team ranking No. 1 in Canada. Economics is another strong point in the research department — CIBC World Markets' chief economist, Jeff Rubin, is one of Canada's foremost economists. The World Markets US equity research team also ranks high for stock-picking as noted by *The Wall Street Journal*'s All Star Analysts Survey.

The European economics research team offers products such as European Weekly Focus, which publishes weekly commentary and analysis of major economic and financial market issues affecting Europe, the United States and Asia (the latter with particular focus on Japan), and the European Monthly Outlook, a monthly update on the latest economic and financial markets issues in the Eurozone and the UK. The monthly update includes the latest monetary policy decisions and an outlook for the coming month's interest rates decisions.

When the tough gets going ... things improve

In 2005, disaster struck in the form of the aftermath from the Enron scandal, which resulted in $2.5 billion in litigation expenses and settlements. That year, CIBC World Markets reported a loss in net income of $1.67 billion. One year later, the firm was back in the black. In the fourth quarter of 2006, CIBC World Markets reported exceptionally strong earnings of $220 million, a 15 per cent rise from an already strong third quarter. Annual net income for CIBC World Markets in 2006 was $646 million. World Markets held onto its market strength in Canada, finishing the fiscal year as the leader in equity underwriting and M&A.

Fortunately, in December 2006, the US Federal Reserve terminated the enforcement action against the bank over its transactions with Enron prior to its infamous collapse in 2001. The enforcement action, which CIBC signed four years earlier in December 2003, had prohibited it from engaging in certain types of structured finance deals. Moving forward, CIBC has named business strength, productivity and balance sheet strength as its top-three priorities for 2007.

Climbing ranks

In the rankings, CIBC World Markets is No. 1 on the list of top-25 financial advisors for Canadian mergers and acquisitions. Also, the firm climbed 10 places in 2006 to rank number 25th in the world for M&A financial advisors. CIBC completed 77 M&A deals in 2006, for a total value of US$69.5 billion. A significant portion of these deals took place in Canada, where CIBC World Markets surpassed RBC Capital Markets as the No. 1

financial advisor for M&A deals. CIBC World Markets completed 56 deals in Canada in 2006, for a total rank value of US$65.94 billion. CIBC World Markets was also the top equity underwriter for companies incorporated in Canada with 51 deals and a total value of US$4.44 billion.

For the love of minerals

One of CIBC World Markets' largest deals for 2006 was the CAD$22.4 billion acquisition of Falconbridge by the Swiss mining group Xstrata. CIBC World Markets advised Falconbridge throughout the tender offer, which was completed in November 2006. CIBC World Markets acted as financial advisor to Goldcorp Inc in its $9.4 billion acquisition of Glamis Gold Ltd. CIBC World Markets was also one of the underwriters, along with BMO Capital Markets, Merrill Lynch Canada Inc. and TD Securities Inc., for Teck Cominco's $17.8 billion bid to acquire Inco Ltd., the Canadian mining company. Teck Cominco, the world's largest zinc producer, was eventually outbid by the Brazilian mining company Companhia Vale do Rio Doce, which bought Inco for $19 billion.

GETTING HIRED

For more information about career and graduate opportunities at CIBC World Markets, visit the company web site at www.cibcwm.com and click on the Careers link.

Visit **Vault Europe's Finance Career Channel** at **www.vault.com/europe** for insider firm profiles, employee surveys of finance professionals in Europe, message boards, job listings, expert finance career advice, insider salary information and more.

VAULT CAREER LIBRARY 189

Close Brothers Group plc

10 Crown Place
London EC2A 4FT
United Kingdom
Phone: +44 20 7655 3100
Fax: +44 20 7655 8916
www.closebrothers.co.uk

EUROPEAN LOCATIONS

London (HQ)
France
Germany
United Kingdom

DEPARTMENTS

Corporate Finance Advice
Deposits & Treasury Services
Investment Funds
Lending Services
Securities Trading
Wealth Management

THE STATS

Employer Type: Public Company
Ticker Symbol: CBG (LSE)
Chairman: Rod Kent
CEO: Colin Keogh
2006 Net Income: £536 million
2006 Revenue: £157 million
(FYE 7/31/06)
2005 Net Income: £447 million
2005 Revenue: £112 million
No. of Employees: 2,500 (Worldwide)

PLUSES

Strong reputation

MINUSES

No central recruiting or HR
department

EMPLOYMENT CONTACT

www.closebrothers.co.uk

THE BUZZ
WHAT EMPLOYEES AT OTHER FIRMS ARE SAYING

- "Small but good"
- "Weak"

THE SCOOP

Independent and noteworthy

Close Brothers Group is one of the UK's leading independent investment banks. While most of its competitors have been bought up by larger global banks over the years, Close Brothers has managed to hold onto its independence by providing services to the often neglected small and medium-sized business segment. The group is comprised of some 30 businesses, each with a managing team and a board of directors. The bank operates in four primary segments: asset management (including wealth management and investment funds), corporate finance, securities (market-making) and banking (including treasury services and lending).

A Close family

The modern Close Brothers Group has its origins in a banking and investment firm founded in 1878 by W.B. Close and his brothers. The Close family had over 100 years of banking in their blood, including James Close, an advisor to Neapolitan King Ferdinand II. W.B. Close and his brothers began their enterprise investing in cheap land in the American Midwest, which was sold at a remarkable profit to the growing number of settlers heading west. The partnership, based in London, thrived on exploration, buying land and financing the White Pass & Yukon railway. As the company expanded, it added banking, investment and lending as sources of income, offering these services primarily to a select group of wealthy individuals.

Following World War II, Close Brothers began investing in traditional mining, utility, property and banking projects. A major chunk of the bank was acquired by London & Western Trust in 1972, following years of slumping profits. This stake was reacquired in a management buyout in 1978. Close Brothers launched a series of acquisitions in the 1980s, which greatly expanded its areas of operations. The company capitalized on a UK recession in the early 1990s, acquiring a specialist in BES transactions (now Close Brothers Investment) and automobile financing operations (now Close Consumer Finance). One of Close Brothers's most significant additions was Winterflood Securities, which it acquired for £19 million in 1993. Winterflood specialises in small company stocks, and as a market-maker, positioned Close Brothers to capitalise on the emerging high-technology stock bubble of the late 1990s. In 2000, profits from the Winterflood operations comprised almost 60 per cent of Close Brothers' entire operating profits.

Visit **Vault Europe's Finance Career Channel** at **www.vault.com/europe** for insider firm profiles, employee surveys of finance professionals in Europe, message boards, job listings, expert finance career advice, insider salary information and more.

VAULT CAREER LIBRARY 191

Fattening up

In 2006, Close Brothers Group reported a profit before tax and goodwill of £157 million, an increase of over 21 per cent from the previous year. The firm experienced growth across all segments — asset management profit rose 21 per cent to £38 million. Funds under management increased 16 per cent, to £8.2 billion. Securities profit increased 34 per cent to £48 million, while both banking and corporate finance reported record profits of £74 million and £17 million, respectively. Most recently, Close Brothers announced in December 2006 that it was able to raise a total of £445 million in loans for refinancing from debt markets — a record for the company.

Corporate Finance

Close Brothers's corporate finance business offers advisory services to corporate and institutional clients in four areas: mergers and acquisitions, structuring and raising debt, special situations and IPO advisory. The firm has an especially strong reputation in middle market transactions (with values up to €500 million), where it is one of the most active advisers in Europe on the basis of announced deals. Close Brothers' special situations team concentrates on one-of-a-kind deals and has notably been engaged in high-profile financial restructurings such as British Energy and Parmalat. While it holds its strongest presence in the UK, Close Brothers has expanded its corporate finance business into France, Germany, Spain and Italy. The bank operates further abroad through a series of exclusive alliances with investment banks in other countries, including Harris Williams in the US.

Changing chairmen

At its most recent annual meeting in November 2006, Close Brothers announced the retirement of David Scholey as chairman of the company. Scholey was succeeded by Rod Kent, who had led the management buyout of Close Brothers in 1979 and served as a managing director of the company from 1984 until 2002. Serving Close Brothers as chief executive is Colin Keogh, who joined the corporate finance division as a director in May 1985, after having previously been employed by Saudi International Bank and Arthur Andersen. Keogh was appointed a director of the company in August 1995 and chief executive in November 2002, having previously headed corporate finance and asset management divisions.

GETTING HIRED

Close Brothers does not have a central recruiting or HR department; candidates should directly contact departments of interest by visiting the group web site at www.closebrothers.co.uk.

Visit **Vault Europe's Finance Career Channel** at **www.vault.com/europe** for insider firm profiles, employee surveys of finance professionals in Europe, message boards, job listings, expert finance career advice, insider salary information and more.

VAULT CAREER LIBRARY 193

Commerzbank AG

Kaiserplatz
60261 Frankfurt
Germany
Phone: +49 69 136 20
Fax: +49 69 28 53 89
www.commerzbank.com

EUROPEAN LOCATIONS

Frankfurt (Global HQ)
Offices all over Europe.
Visit www.commerzbank.com for
regional breakdown

DEPARTMENTS

Retail Banking & Asset
Management
Commercial Real Estate, Public
Finance & Treasury
Corporate & Investment Banking

THE BUZZ
WHAT EMPLOYEES AT OTHER FIRMS ARE SAYING

"Strong in select countries"
"Looking for direction"
"Global player"
"Weak IB"

THE SCOOP

A German giant

Commerzbank AG is the second-largest bank in Germany after Deutsche Bank, and leads in Europe with over €138 billion in assets under management. The German giant provides financial services primarily catering to private customers and small to medium-sized companies in three major areas: retail banking and asset management; corporate and investment banking; and commercial real estate, public finance and treasury. In March 2006, Commerzbank acquired Eurohypo, Europe's largest institution specialising in financing real estate and public sector projects, increasing its assets by more than 50 per cent. Commerzbank is one of the DAX 30, a blue chip index of the leading 30 companies listed on the Frankfurt Stock Exchange. The company trades under the symbol CBK, and currently has around 290,000 shareholders, with more than 50 per cent of its capital in the hands of nonresident investors. The Italian-based insurance group Generali is its largest shareholder with an 8.6 per cent stake.

The "Relationship-Bank"

While Commerzbank's primary market is in Germany, where it has a nationwide network of roughly 820 branches, the bank conducts business worldwide, with corporate dealings in Western, Central and Eastern European markets, and activities in the Americas and Asia. The bank has outlets in more than 40 countries, operating through subsidiaries, branches and representative offices. At present, it runs a network of more than 5,000 correspondent banks worldwide.

Commerzbank's retail banking division focuses on providing investing services to its base of roughly five million customers. The division consists of private and business customers and asset management segments, which together offer services such as home loans, account management, an officially certified selection of funds and Eurocard and Visa credit cards. Its direct subsidiary, comdirect bank AG, is Germany's No. 1 online broker. The COMINVEST Group provides actively managed securities-based funds for retail and institutional investors, with an ebase subsidiary servicing and managing custody accounts.

Mittelstand

Mittelstand is the German term for small to medium-sized companies, a significant portion of Commerzbank's business. Strangely, it is the only major bank in Germany to devote an entire operational segment to Mittelstand business. Commerzbank provides services to over 50,000 small to medium-sized companies with an annual turnover of more than €2.5 million. In its corporate and investment banking division, Commerzbank's Mittelstand

Visit **Vault Europe's Finance Career Channel** at **www.vault.com/europe** for insider firm profiles, employee surveys of finance professionals in Europe, message boards, job listings, expert finance career advice, insider salary information and more.

V/\ULT CAREER LIBRARY **195**

business is concentrated in 166 branches, while its approximately 800 larger corporate clients are serviced in five specialised corporate centres.

Forged by European history

Commerzbank was founded in 1870 by individual and merchant bankers in Hamburg. It moved its headquarters to Berlin in 1905 after merging with Berliner Bank. After a succession of mergers with German banks, the name Commerzbank Aktiengesellschaft was officially adopted in 1940. The bank suffered a loss of 45 per cent of its premises with the division of Europe after World War II, and was divided into three regional banks. These entities were reunited in 1958 under a central headquarters in Düsseldorf. The bank gradually shifted its headquarters to Frankfurt in the 1970s, and established its centre of operations in Germany's financial center in 1990. Commerzbank was the first German bank to establish a branch in New York City in 1971. Throughout the 1970s, Commerzbank successfully opened offices in London, Chicago, Paris, Brussels, Tokyo, Hong Kong and Madrid.

The Tower

Commerzbank today holds its headquarters in Frankfurt, Germany, the wealthiest city in the EU according to GDP per capita. The head-office building is known as the Commerzbank Tower, an impressive structure designed by the British architect Norman Foster. The Commerzbank Tower holds over 2,500 Commerzbank employees, and was Europe's tallest skyscraper at a height of 301 metres from its completion in 1997 up until 2004, when it was surpassed by the Triumph-Palace in Moscow. The tower was also Europe's first ecological skyscraper, including features such as natural ventilation and lighting, multistory sky gardens and innovative eco-friendly heat and power systems. Heading the board of managing directors in the tower is Chairman Klaus-Peter Müller, formerly Commerzbank's executive vice president head of the corporate banking. Müller has worked for Commerzbank since 1966, and was appointed chairman in 2001. He also serves as president of the Association of German Banks, which is located in Berlin.

The Eurohypo acquisition

In March 2006, Commerzbank acquired Eurohypo, a Germany-based European real estate bank, purchasing the remaining 66.2 per cent of the company for a total price of €4.56 billion. The bank now owns a 98 per cent share in Europe's largest institution for public sector financing and real estate lending. Commerzbank purchased the Eurohypo interests from Deutsche Bank and Allianz/Dresdner Bank at an average price of €19.60 per share.

In order to finance the acquisition, Commerzbank issued new shares to institutional investors at the price of €23.50 per share, which was met with an overwhelming demand.

The bank was able to sell 57.7 million new shares in just two hours. The purchase was Commerzbank's largest acquisition in the last 50 years, increasing the bank's balance sheet total to almost €700 billion. The addition of Eurohypo not only increased the bank's balance sheet, but is expected by 2008 to create synergies in income and expenses valued at more than €100 million. Commerzbank reported a net profit of €1,597 million in the 2006 fiscal year.

GETTING HIRED

From all corners

Employees say the bank recruits from "different kinds of sources," from "universities" and "headhunters" to "competitors." Or if you prefer the electronic route, check out open positions or submit a "proactive application" in areas ranging from investment banking to asset management on the bank's website at www.commerzbank.com. Information about careers and graduate opportunities at Commerzbank can also be found on the site.

When you come in for an interview, you can expect as few as three meetings or as many as eight. One insider reports "two interviews at the group level and one at the decision level." The firm also offers internships, which provide "a small salary but the chance to see many different positions."

OUR SURVEY SAYS

That special something

The culture is "intense" but has a "special style," insiders report. The bank is also "changing a lot because of reorganizing." For the most part, though, the people are very "open" and "direct" but have "little tolerance for non-performers."

The perks get high marks from sources. There are "meal allowances," a "deferred compensation programme" and a "stock-option derivative programme" for employees who have reached a senior level within the firm.

Working for the weekend

Insiders report working anywhere from 40 to 70 hours per week (one says that "60 to 70 hours a week is normal, but working more hours happens quite frequently.") Working

Visit **Vault Europe's Finance Career Channel** at www.vault.com/europe for insider firm profiles, employee surveys of finance professionals in Europe, message boards, job listings, expert finance career advice, insider salary information and more.

VAULT CAREER LIBRARY **197**

weekends isn't unheard of, several respondents report that they come in "often" or "frequently" on weekends.

Offices receive mediocre marks. One source working in the Frankfurt office comments that there are "Too many people in one office with no efforts made to reduce noise" and, "No respect as far as the specific work environment we require." Another complains that there is "no adequate offering" of training for "Frankfurt-based colleagues," although "London receives plenty." However, the casual Friday dress policy doesn't meet with any staff protests.

Insiders give a wide range of marks regarding the bank's diversity efforts. One female source describes her experience, saying: "The firm stopped my promotions at the age of 26 — envisioning that one would drop out for family reasons."

Crédit Agricole

91-93 Blvd. Pasteur
Paris, 75015
FRANCE
Phone: +33 1 43 23 52 02
Fax: +33 1 43 23 34 48
www.credit-agricole.fr

EUROPEAN LOCATIONS

Paris (HQ)
Locations in France, Germany,
Greece, Portugal, Spain and
Turkey.

DEPARTMENTS

Asset Management
Corporate & Investment Banking
Insurance
Private Banking
Retail Banking
Specialised Services

THE STATS

Employer Type: Public Company
Ticker Symbol: ACA (Euronext Paris)
Chairman: René Carron
CEO; Chairman Credit Lyonnaise:
Georges Pauget
2006 Net Income: €4.9 billion
(FYE 12/06)
2005 Net Income: €3.8 billion
(FYE 12/05)
No. of Employees: 136,848
No. of Offices: 9,100 locations in 65
countries worldwide

PLUSES

France's largest bank

MINUSES

Ongoing restructuring

KEY COMPETITORS

BNP Paribas
Caisses d'Epargne
Société Générale

EMPLOYMENT CONTACT

www.credit-agricole.fr/ca/index.php?
ca=recrutement

THE BUZZ
WHAT EMPLOYEES AT OTHER FIRMS ARE SAYING

- "Strong in trade finance"
- "Difficult"

Visit the Vault Finance Career Channel at **www.vault.com/finance**—with insider firm
profiles, message boards, the Vault Finance Job Board and more.

VAULT CAREER LIBRARY 199

THE SCOOP

Growing a banking empire

Crédit Agricole S.A. was created in 2001 to represent the Crédit Agricole Group as a central body and central bank. When it became a listed company, it was organised to represent all of the group's business lines and entities — it owns 25 per cent of each regional bank, along with all of the group's holdings in specialist subsidiaries and foreign retail banks. It also offers retail and business banking, lending and deposit services at more than 9,000 locations throughout France, including those of subsidiary Le Crédit Lyonnais (LCL), which it acquired in 2003.

Despite its rather provincial name, Crédit Agricole is France's largest bank, with assets in excess of €913 billion. It owns a 25 per cent stake in each of about 40 regional banks, which own more than half of Crédit Agricole. It offers retail and business banking, and lending and deposit services at more than 9,000 locations throughout the country. The bank has approximately 9,100 locations in 65 countries. The bank also has a large presence in the Middle East and Southeast Asia.

French fare

With 5.7 million members, the firm's 2,599 local banks make up the backbone of its organisation. The local banks manage the capital of the regional banks, which act as fully fledged banks and cooperative organisations. With nearly 7,200 branches, the regional banks serve 16.1 million individual, professional and small business customers. Crédit Agricole S.A. was floated on the Paris exchange in December 2001 and represents all of the group business lines and entities. Crédit Agricole S.A. has three main roles within the group: lead institution, central banker and the entity responsible for ensuring consistent commercial development. It also owns 25 per cent of the regional bank's capital, along with all group interests in foreign banks.

Calyon, formed in 2004, combines the corporate and investment bank Crédit Agricole Indosuez and LCL's corresponding activities, allowing LCL to focus solely on retail operations. Calyon offers brokerage and investment banking services through regional offices in New York, Los Angeles, Chicago, Dallas and Houston, all part of Crédit Agricole's strategy to make further inroads into the lucrative US markets.

Surviving the worst of times

Crédit Lyonnais dates back to 1839, when the French banker, or banquier, Henri Germain founded a bank in Lyon, along with several other prominent local businessmen. The firm grew over the next 25 years and, in 1865, added branches in Paris and Marseilles. The company survived the Franco-Prussian War of 1870-1871, but after the siege of Paris by the Prussians in the winter of 1870, Germain felt Credit Lyonnais could benefit from geographical diversity and so a London office was promptly established.

Winning Euro-vision

By the end of the 1880s, Crédit Lyonnais was the leading bank in France and had branches in London, Constantinople (now Istanbul), Alexandria (Egypt), Geneva, Madrid and St. Petersburg. A new Paris headquarters opened in 1883, shortly after the firm led the French banking industry through a liquidity crisis. At the beginning of World War I, Crédit Lyonnais was the largest bank in the world with nearly 400 branches at the time — including 13 branches located in cities outside of France.

Like most of Europe, Crédit Lyonnais was devastated by the war; branches were closed and nearly 1,600 of the company's employees died in the fighting. The firm was touched by the tide of history again in the late 1910s, as revolutions in Russia and Turkey closed branches and put foreign debt in doubt. Crédit Lyonnais actually fared better in World War II than in the previous continent-wide conflict. Fewer branches were destroyed in the fighting, and the company focused on safer investments during the uncertain time. Post-war Crédit Lyonnais provided financial help to the rebuilding efforts. In the 1980s, the company benefited from deregulation mania, expanding its capital markets presence.

Italian expansion

In May 2005, Crédit Lyonnais bought a 63 per cent stake in Banca Intesa's asset management unit Nextra for €850 million. Crédit Lyonnais had been hoping to reinforce its links with Banca Intesa, in which it is the largest shareholder, while the Italian bank wished to sell its subsidiary, which suffered considerably as a result of the Parmalat scandal in 2004. In October 2006, Crédit Agricole bought 654 bank branches from Banca Intesa for €6 billion. Banca Intesa and Sanpaolo merged in January 2007, with Credit Agricole giving final approval only after being assured its Italian investments would be protected.

The merger diluted Crédit Agricole's stake in Intesa from 18 per cent to 10 per cent. The buy included Intesa's Cariparma and Friuladria regional savings banks. Intesa owned all of Cariparma and 76 per cent of Friuladria. Those banks had 450 branches, with the remainder of the acquired branches coming from the merged Intesa-Sanpaolo, which had to shed some of its holdings to comply with antitrust regulations.

International shopping trip

In March 2006, the bank signed a €220 million deal to buy JSC Index Bank, one of the Ukraine's leading banks. Crédit Agricole has had a 13-year presence in the country, and

Visit **Vault Europe's Finance Career Channel** at **www.vault.com/europe** for insider firm profiles, employee surveys of finance professionals in Europe, message boards, job listings, expert finance career advice, insider salary information and more.

VAULT CAREER LIBRARY **201**

was already one of the leading corporate and investment banks there, but the deal moves it into retail banking for the first time.

Crédit Agricole bought a majority stake in Greece's state-run Emporiki Bank in May 2005. The deal increased Crédit Agricole's stake in Emporiki, the nation's fourth-largest bank, from 11 per cent to 51 per cent. The bank boosted its stake to more than 70 per cent in September 2006, beating out the Central Bank of Cyprus. The same month Crédit Agricole made another regional play as part of a strategic partnership in the financial services market in Serbia, acquiring more than 70 per cent of Serbia's Meridian Bank for €34 million ($42 million).

Not all of Crédit Agricole's buys were focused on banking. It bought champagne producer Taittinger from Starwood Fund for €660 million ($849 million) in June 2006. The deal included California wine maker Domaine Carneros and French sparkling wine producer Bouvet-Ladubay.

Crédit Agricole broke into the Chinese banking market by forming a joint venture with the Agricultural Bank of China (ABC) in January 2007, taking a 33.7 per cent stake, with ABC holding 51.3 per cent and Chalco, the second-largest aluminum producer in the world, taking 15 per cent. However, not all of the bank's deals panned out. In May 2006, rumours hit the press that Crédit Agricole was planning a bid for the United Kingdom's seventh-largest bank, the building society Alliance & Leicester. But after looking at the books, Crédit Agricole decided not to bid on it.

Taking on a new approach

There was also significant reshuffling at Crédit Agricole in 2006 — in April, the firm announced that the bank's alternative investment products group would be rebranded as Crédit Agricole Asset Management. The division is a leader in the alternative funds industry, and manages €12.6 billion for both French and international investors.

The following June, CPR Private Equity was renamed Crédit Agricole Asset Management Capital Investors, and the bank committed to a drive to develop its business scope and client base. It is a business focused on the management of private equity fund of funds for institutional and retail investors and has €1.2 billion under management. That same month, Crédit Agricole announced the launch of a venture fund dedicated to investing in renewable energies, and a €400 million fund to invest in infrastructure financed by public-private partnerships.

GETTING HIRED

For more information on vacancies, graduate and career opportunities at Credit Agricole, check out the company's site at www.credit-agricole.fr and click on "Recrutement".

Visit **Vault Europe's Finance Career Channel** at **www.vault.com/europe** for insider firm profiles, employee surveys of finance professionals in Europe, message boards, job listings, expert finance career advice, insider salary information and more.

VAULT CAREER LIBRARY 203

Fortis SA/NV

Rue Royale 20
1000 Brussels,
Belgium
Phone: +32 (0)2 565 11 11
Fax: +32 (0)2 565 42 22

Fortis N.V.
Archimedeslaan 6
3584 BA Utrecht,
The Netherlands
Phone: +31 (0)30 226 62 22
Fax: +31 (0)30 226 98 35
www.fortis.com

DEPARTMENTS

Commercial & Private Banking
Insurance Belgium
Insurance International
Insurance Netherlands
Merchant Banking
Retail Banking

THE STATS

Employer Type: Public Company
Ticker Symbol: FOR (Euronext Brussels), FORA (Euronext Amsterdam)
CEO: Jean-Paul Votron
Chairman of the Board: Maurice Lippens
2006 Net Income: €4.41 billion (FYE 12/06)
2005 Net Income: €3.98 billion (FYE 12/05)
No. of Employees: 60,000
No. of Offices: Offices in more than 50 countries globally

PLUSES

Growing fast

MINUSES

Focus unclear

EMPLOYMENT CONTACT

www.fortis.com/career/index.asp

THE SCOOP

Twice as nice

At its core, Fortis provides a two-pronged service: banking and insurance. But that's not the only reason the firm might give you double vision - Fortis has dual offices in Belgium and The Netherlands, and its presence is strong in both countries as it continues to expand both across Europe and internationally. The bank even has a "twinned share" structure for its stocks, trading on the Brussels exchange as well as Amsterdam's.

The Benelux giant has been around in different incarnations for centuries, but it was in 1990 when Fortis really solidified as an entity. The Dutch insurer N.V. AMEV and Dutch bank VSB joined in a merger and were followed in financial matrimony by Belgian insurer AG Group. The uniting of the three units marked the first financial merger that crossed nations' borders.

Possible buy

Rumours swirled in April 2007 that Fortis, along with other European banks, may be heading to take over ABN Amro. Although the Dutch central bank warned the grouping, led by the Royal Bank of Scotland and including Santander in Spain, that a takeover may be "risky and complicated", the banks appear to be going ahead with the plan. (Fortis and ABN are not without their own slightly acrimonious history — Fortis beat out ABN in a bid for Belgium's Generale Bank in 1998.) The group has been planning to pit a bid against England's Barclays, which has been in talks with ABN about a possible merger.

Many happy returns

Financially, Fortis' future is looking bright. In full-year 2006, Fortis earned €10.1 billion in net revenue, up from €8.78 billion in 2005. Net profit jumped as well, to €3.16 billion in 2006 from €2.45 billion the year before. In a statement, the bank said it was "aided by a favourable economic environment in the Benelux countries and the rest of Europe and by buoyant commercial activity" in 2006.

Achieving across the globe

Fortis' expansion and achievements internationally have garnered the bank positive recognition as of late. In the *Financial Times* Banker Awards in 2006, the firm was acknowledged for its joint venture in China, where it was one of the only foreign groups to supervise China's new company pension schemes. CEO Jean-Paul Votron said the award "provides an important endorsement for our strategy and the excellent progress we are making against our 2005-2009 plans," adding that, "Our strategy focuses on growing

Visit **Vault Europe's Finance Career Channel** at www.vault.com/europe for insider firm profiles, employee surveys of finance professionals in Europe, message boards, job listings, expert finance career advice, insider salary information and more.

VAULT CAREER LIBRARY   205

our banking and insurance businesses across Europe, and selectively in Asia and North America, based on core competences and reflecting the needs and expectations of our customers."

GETTING HIRED

To find out more about employment opportunities and traineeships opportunities at Fortis, visit www.fortis.com/career/index.asp.

Fox-Pitt, Kelton

25 Copthall Avenue
London EC2R 7BP
United Kingdom
Phone: +44 (0) 207 663 6000
www.fpk.com

EUROPEAN LOCATION

London

DEPARTMENTS

Advisory Services
Capital Raising
Research
Sales, Sales Trading & Trading

THE STATS

Employer Type: Private Company
CEO: Giles Fitzpatrick
Number of Offices: 3 (Worldwide)

KEY COMPETITORS

Friedman, Billings, Ramsey Group
KBW
Sanford C. Bernstein

PLUSES

"Client first" philosophy

MINUSES

Small firm

EMPLOYMENT CONTACT

www.fpk.com (See "Careers" section)

THE BUZZ
WHAT EMPLOYEES AT OTHER FIRMS ARE SAYING

- "Great potential"
- "Who?"

Visit the Vault Finance Career Channel at **www.vault.com/finance**—with insider firm
profiles, message boards, the Vault Finance Job Board and more.

VAULT CAREER LIBRARY 207

THE SCOOP

A fox to be trusted

Fox-Pitt, Kelton, or FPK, is an investment bank well regarded for its equity research, which covers the stocks of more than 400 companies and institutions around the globe. The bank plays an important role in high-profile transactions worldwide as an investor, advisor, and as a researcher, specialising in banking, insurance and related industries. Services provided by FPK include equity brokerage and trading, capital markets services, and mergers and acquisitions advice. FPK clients consist of pension funds, mutual fund managers, insurance companies, bank investment departments, hedge funds and private client asset managers. The bank prides itself on its position as the only vertically integrated investment bank in the world specialising in the financial services industry.

Made in England

FPK was founded in 1971, by Oliver Fox-Pitt and Robin Kelton. The bank was originally built upon the idea of placing American bank and insurance equities with institutions in Europe. Nine years later, the founders opened two more offices in New York and Hartford, Connecticut. A corporate finance division was introduced in 1985 in the New York office, to manage the company's growing list of corporate clients. In 1988, FPK launched European Financials Product, to focus on European equities. The European corporate finance division was launched in London in 1996, to complement the company's US corporate finance offerings. FPK continued its global expansion in 1998 with the launch of an Asian Financials Product, and opened a corresponding office in Hong Kong in 2000. A Boston office was opened in 2004.

FPK today has offices in New York, Boston, Hartford, London and Hong Kong. At the helm in the London office is CEO Giles Fitzpatrick, who joined FPK in 2005 as the head of global equities, where he oversaw FPK's equity research, sales, sales trading and equity capital markets divisions. Prior to joining FPK, Fitzpatrick secured more than 20 years of equity markets experience running trading, heading up sales and then secondary equities at the UK broker Hoare Govett — and then at Dutch bank ABN AMRO as global head of trading and head of European equities. Fitzpatrick was also a member of the London Stock Exchange Markets Committee and The LIBA Securities Trading Committee.

Researchers to be reckoned with

The research team at FPK is consistently highly ranked in the main investor polls and is routinely quoted in financial newspapers, offering ratings and advice on dealings involving financial institutions and insurance companies. FPK research is distributed globally through a team of specialist salespeople and traders, with specialised research delivered to select clients. FPK currently has 41 publishing analysts covering equity research worldwide, in addition to its 151 front-line staff. With a "client first" philosophy, FPK aims to provide investors with a comparable view on the valuation of all the global financial institutions the firm covers. Analysts primarily focus on company-specific research, supported by a "rigorous approach" to valuation.

An efficiency-driven frontline

FPK has 16 sales traders at the "front and centre", responsible for aligning its research with sales and for driving commissions daily. Sales traders in New York, London and Hong Kong possess both specialisation and longevity, which they use to their advantage at buy-side trading desks, enjoying strong relationships with the dealing desks of investing clients. Traders practise instantaneous communication through smart electronic indicators-of-interest (IOI's) to undertake rapid order management and algorithmic trading. In 2004, FPK was the 11th most cost-efficient executor of trades around the world.

Trickle-down equity

In February of 2006, the owners of FPK, the reinsurer Swiss Re, announced their intention to sell FPK to a consortium led by private equity firm J.C. Flowers & Co. and FPK management. Swiss Re had acquired FPK in 1999 and now retains a minority stake in the company. Swiss Re, which is based in Zurich, provides reinsurance and risk management products to clients in over 30 countries. The transfer of ownership, which was completed in June of 2006, greatly reinforced the firm's independence by putting equity in the hands of FPK staff and managers, a crucial component of the firm's ability to deliver objective research and advice.

Eyes on Asia

Globally, FPK is considered a "Co-Lead of Choice" in the primary market for financial services equity issuance, where it has acted as the co-lead manager with companies such as Morgan Stanley, Goldman Sachs and Merrill Lynch. Fox-Pitt, Kelton has also been incredibly active as a securities underwriter in China, where it co-led the IPO of insurance company China Life, one of the largest IPO's in the world in 2003 at $3,500 million. FPK plans to continue serving as co-lead manager for Chinese financial institutions seeking international investors, hoping to take advantage of a crucial period in China's financial development.

FPK has been making significant increases in its Asia business, most recently adding three new upper-level staff to its Hong Kong office. In April of 2006, FPK announced the appointments of André Carey as head of sales trading, Warren Blight as senior banks analyst, and Jean-Marc Champagne, senior equity sales. FPK's Hong Kong office specialises in Chinese, Taiwanese and Korean markets and financial institutions.

GETTING HIRED

For more information on jobs and graduate opportunities at Fox-Pitt Kelton, visit the Careers section of the company web site at www.fpk.com.

Groupe Caisse d'Epargne

50 Avenue Pierre-Mendes
75201 Paris Cedex 13
France
Phone: +33 (0) 1 58 40 41 42
Fax: +33 (0) 1 58 40 48 00
www.groupe.caisse-epargne.com

EUROPEAN LOCATIONS

Paris (HQ)
Offices throughout France and
Europe

DEPARTMENTS

Retail Banking
Commercial Banking
Investment Banking via Natixis

THE STATS

Employer Type: Private Company
Chairman: Charles Milhaud
2006 Net Banking Income:
€11.3 .billion
2006 Gross Operating Income:
€2.8 billion
2005 Net Banking Income:
€10.0 billion
2005 Gross Operating Income:
€2.3 billion
No. of Employees: 55.800
No. of Offices: 4,700

KEY COMPETITORS

BNP Paribas
Crédit Agricole
Société Générale

PLUSES

Very big in France; lots of big deals

MINUSES

Not a top pan-European firm

EMPLOYMENT CONTACT

www.groupe.caisse-
epargne.fr/recrute

THE BUZZ
WHAT EMPLOYEES AT OTHER FIRMS ARE SAYING

- "French commercial bank"
- "Regional"

Visit the Vault Finance Career Channel at **www.vault.com/finance**—with insider firm
profiles, message boards, the Vault Finance Job Board and more.

VAULT CAREER LIBRARY **211**

THE SCOOP

Working together

Groupe Caisse d'Epargne (GCE) is one of the largest retail banking networks in France, comprised of the Caisses d'Epargne, Crédit Foncier, Banque Palatine and OCÉOR banks as well as its own specialised subsidiaries. As a huge full-service bank, GCE is popular among individuals and professionals in mainland France and the overseas territories, offering a full range of financial services through its various banners. The GCE boasts close to 56,000 employees spanning 4,700 branches and 26 million customers globally. The group's ambition is to play an active role in the consolidation of the European banking sector and continue to honor its founding pledge by expanding its commitment to social progress. Backed by €20 billion in consolidated equity, a net income of €3.8 billion and credit ratings that rank among the very best in the French banking sector, Groupe Caisse d'Epargne has a solid financial profile. In 2006, the bank was ranked 69th on the Fortune 500 list.

The regional Caisses d'Epargne own 80 per cent of CNCE, which is a limited or incorporated company (known in French as a "société anonyme") governed by a management board and a supervisory board. The Federation Nationale des Caisses d'Epargne is a nonprofit association representing the individual Caisses d'Epargne and their cooperative shareholders. Natixis, which is owned jointly by GCE and the Banque Populaire group, now spearheads the group's investment and corporate, asset management and financial services offering.

Growth frenzy

GCE experienced enormous growth in a slew of sectors, with several deals. In addition to the creation of a new IB sector in Natixis, 2006 saw some other big developments for GCE, with particular emphasis on Portugal. The group acquired an 80 per cent interest stake in the French and Luxembourg subsidiaries of Millenium bcp, a Portuguese bank. GCE also created two new banks, Banco Primus in Portugal, adding to its portfolio a specialist in loan restructuring, as well as its own joint subsidiary in Italy, which specialises in consumer credit. Also, GCE acquired interest in Crédit Immobilier et Hôtelier (CIH) in Morocco, in a joint transaction with Caisse de Dépôt et de Gestion. The acquired bank specialises in family banking services, adding still more diversity to GCE's practical services repertoire.

In April 2007, GCE signed a memorandum of understanding with Nexity for the purpose of generating power in the real estate market. The transaction between Nexity and the CNCE should be complete by the autumn of 2007. CNCE, by the terms of the memorandum, will contribute 25 per cent of Crédit Foncier, 100 per cent of GCE

Immobilier's services division and stakes in Eurosic, a real estate company. The idea is that Nexity will eventually ascend to leading shareholder of Eurosic, and therefore create a real estate stronghold between the company and GCE. CNCE would also become the key shareholder (upwards of 38 per cent) of Nexity, in exchange for its contributions.

Natixis in action

It did not take more than six months to bring this industrial project — of major importance for the future growth of Groupe Caisse d'Epargne — to a satisfactory conclusion. Created legally on November 17, 2006, Natixis, the new investment and project bank jointly owned by Groupe Caisse d'Epargne and Groupe Banque Populaire made its successful debut on the Paris Bourse on December 5, 2006.

As of spring 2007 Natixis has already attracted more than 2.86 million individual shareholders, according to the firm. As the largest operation in the French financial market in 2006 in terms of value, it was also the banking industry's most attractive investment since 1999. Close to 670,000 Groupe Caisse d'Epargne customers, including almost 390,000 Caisses d'Epargne cooperative shareholders, have bought shares in Natixis.

10,000 is the magic number

Like any corporation of integrity, GCE is not all business. It lays claim to the Caisses d'Epargne Foundation for Social Solidarity, which has become one of France's largest public-interest organisations. Created in 2001, the foundation celebrated its fifth anniversary by setting a number of goals to be completed by the end of the decade. CEFSS plans to procure 10,000 beds for the dependent elderly, provide 10,000 individuals with home support services, and reach 10,000 people with its literacy campaign.

GETTING HIRED

For more information about careers or graduate opportunities at Group Caisse d'Epargne, visit the company's website at www.groupe.caisse-epargne.fr/recrute.

Visit **Vault Europe's Finance Career Channel** at **www.vault.com/europe** for insider firm profiles, employee surveys of finance professionals in Europe, message boards, job listings, expert finance career advice, insider salary information and more.

VAULT CAREER LIBRARY 213

Grupo Santander

Banco Santander Central Hispano
Ciudad Grupo Santander
Boadilla del Monte
28660 Madrid
Spain
Phone: +34 91 659 75 17
www.santander.com

EUROPEAN LOCATIONS

Madrid (HQ)
Offices all over Europe

DEPARTMENTS

Asset Management
Financial Management
Global Markets & BBanking
Insurance
Private Banking
Retail Banking

THE STATS

Employer Type: Public Company
Ticker Symbol: STD (NYSE), Spanish: SAN
Chairman: Emilio Botin
Second Vice Chairman & CEO: Alfredo Saenz
2006 Net Income: €7.596 billion (FYE 12/06)
2005 Net Income: €6.220 billion (FYE 12/05)
No. of Employees: 129,749
No. of Offices: 5,772 branches in Europe

KEY COMPETITORS

BBVA
Citigroup
Grupo Banco Popular Espanol S.A.
HSBC Holdings

PLUSES

Going high tech and ongoing growth

MINUSES

Opportunities outside Spanish-speaking world are limited

EMPLOYMENT CONTACT

www.santander.com
Click on "Jobs at Santander" section

THE BUZZ
WHAT EMPLOYEES AT OTHER FIRMS ARE SAYING

- "Strong in Spanish speaking part of the world"
- "Very strong in Spain and South America but like BBVA, not known in EU"

THE SCOOP

Ruling Spain

Grupo Santander is the largest public company in Spain, the biggest bank in the Eurozone, and the fourth-largest bank in Europe. Born from the merger of the Santander and Central Hispanoamericano (BCH) banks, the group offers financial services in Spain, the UK (through Abbey), Portugal, where it is the third-largest banking group, and other parts of Europe. The bank had market cap of €88.4 billion at end-2006 and assets of €834 billion. The bank focuses on commercial banking, investment and pension funds, investment banking, corporate banking, internet and telephone banking, and treasury and capital markets.

Santander's subsidiaries offer a full range of asset management, private banking, corporate and investment banking, and insurance. The bank has more than 66 million customers at more than to 10,800 locations around the world. Santander's holdings include Banco Santander-Chile, Banco Rio in Argentina, Brazil's Santander Banespa and Mexico's Grupo Financiero Santander Mexico.

Through Santander Consumer Finance, the group is also a leading consumer finance franchise in Germany, Italy, Spain and nine other European countries. Santander entered the US market in 2006 by taking a share of 24.9 per cent in Sovereign Bancorp and bought about 90 per cent of Drive Financial Services, an American auto lender focused on the subprime market, for $651 million.

The Basque bank

Santander can trace its roots back to 1857, when a group of Basque businessmen launched Banco Santander to fund Latin American trade. The Botin family, has always played a major role in the bank. The current chairman, Emilio Botin-Sanz de Sautuola, took the reins in 1986 from his father, who had been chairman since 1950.

The bank weathered the Great Depression due to Spain's economic isolation and in the 1950s and 1960s it expanded into Latin America, as Franco's government regulated interest rates and mergers were simply not permitted. Clearly everything changed after the dictator's death in 1975 and the new Spanish government eased banking regulations, but by that point Santander's Latin American expansion had long been kicked off, and the bank continued expanding in the region.

It was not until the 1990s that the bank really became focused on its home market, acquiring troubled Banco Espanol de Credito. The Latin American economic crisis of 1998 took a heavy toll, forcing Santander to merge with BCH in 1999. The merger resulted

Visit Vault Europe's Finance Career Channel at www.vault.com/europe for insider firm profiles, employee surveys of finance professionals in Europe, message boards, job listings, expert finance career advice, insider salary information and more.

VAULT CAREER LIBRARY 215

in the layoffs of 10,000 employees and the shuttering of 20 per cent of its branches. Since then, growth has shifted back and forth between steady and accelerated.

Full steam ahead

In November 2004, after its €12.5 billion acquisition of Britain's Abbey National - which was rebranded as "Abbey" - Santander became the No. 1 bank in the Eurozone by market capitalisation. The deal created the fourth-largest bank in Europe, was the biggest ever cross-border purchase of a European retail bank, and made Santander the world's 10th-largest bank. The bank is moving to diversify its earnings stream away from Latin America. According to Santander, the Abbey acquisition will produce cost savings and revenue benefits worth €560 million within three years of the deal's completion. Prior to the deal, Abbey was suffering from two years of heavy losses caused by bad debt at the company's wholesale banking unit.

As part of a strategy to transform Abbey into a full-service bank, Santander announced in June 2006 that Abbey would be selling its life insurance business wholesale to Resolution for £3.6 billion, including Mutual, Scottish Provident and Abbey National Life. Abbey will retain all of its branch-based investment and asset management businesses. The gambit appears to be paying off. After negative growth in 2004 and zero growth in 2005, Abbey saw 5 per cent growth in 2006.

Going high tech

Santander's Partenon IT platform allows the bank to better respond to client needs and quickly measure the profitability of new products. The bank rolled out the system throughout its network in Spain and is being implemented in Abbey. In June 2006, The Banker's Technology Awards named Partenon Core Banking System Innovation of the Year. The bank also won other awards in 2006, including Bank of the Year in 2006 in Spain, Portugal, Chile and Puerto Rico by The Banker; Best Retail Bank in EMEA by Retail Banker International; and Best Bank in Latin America, Spain and Portugal by Euromoney magazine. Euromoney also named Santander Totta Best Bank in Portugal for the fifth year in a row and Best M&A House in Portugal. In 2005, *Euromoney* named Santander the "Best Bank in the world".

Italian dreams

Santander is eyeing expansion in Italy and in January 2007 the bank disclosed it had taken a stake of less than 2 per cent in Italian bank Capitalia. In May 2007, Santander joined forces with Royal Bank of Scotland and Fortis to study a possible bid for ABN AMRO. Under the plan, Santander would acquire ABN's units in Italy (Banca Antonveneta) and Brazil (Banco Real). Although it is looking to expand in the region, Santander, a shareholder in Sanpaolo, voted against the Intesa-Sanpaolo merger which created Italian banking giant SanPaolo-IMI, and in January 2007 sold a 4.8 per cent stake in the bank, leaving it 3.6 per cent, which will be diluted to 1.7 per cent after the merger is completed.

GETTING HIRED

For more information on current vacancies, traineeships, work experience and graduate opportunities at Santander, visit www.santander.com and click on "Jobs at Santander".

Visit **Vault Europe's Finance Career Channel** at **www.vault.com/europe** for insider firm profiles, employee surveys of finance professionals in Europe, message boards, job listings, expert finance career advice, insider salary information and more.

VAULT CAREER LIBRARY 217

Hawkpoint Partners

41 Lothbury
London EC2R 7AE
UK
Phone: +44 (0)20 7665 4500
Fax: +44 (0)20 7665 4600

Hawkpoint Partners Limited
(Succursale de Paris)
Washington Plaza, 29 rue de Berri
75008 Paris
France
Phone: +33 (0)1 56 69 66 66
Fax: +33 (0)1 56 69 66 67

www.hawkpoint.com

EUROPEAN LOCATIONS

London
Paris

DEPARTMENTS

Capital Markets
Mergers & Acquisitions
Restructuring
Strategic Services

THE STATS

Employer Type: Private Company
Chairman: David Reid Scott
Managing Partner: Paul Baines
No. of Employees: 120
No. of Offices: 2

KEY COMPETITORS

Close Brothers
CVC Capital
N.M. Rothschild

PLUSES

"Clients across diverse fields"

MINUSES

Small firm

EMPLOYMENT CONTACT

www.hawkpoint.com/careers

THE BUZZ
WHAT EMPLOYEES AT OTHER FIRMS ARE SAYING

- "Wealth"
- "Being left behind by its competitors"

THE SCOOP

Joining Forces with Collins Stewart

London-based Hawkpoint is a privately owned corporate finance advisory firm that bought out its parent, National Westminster Bank, in 1999. The majority of Hawkpoint's equity is owned by its staff, with 14 per cent held by Mezzanine Management. The firm advises private equity firms, corporate firms, financial institutions, government and quasi-government bodies throughout Europe, primarily in the UK, France and Germany. Hawkpoint's advisory services include mergers and acquisitions, capital markets, restructuring and strategic advice.

In October 2006, Collins Stewart Tullet's subsidiary Collins Stewart Europe Limited acquired the issued share capital of Hawkpoint, a deal that enabled Collins Stewart, an international financial services group, to expand into the M&A advisory business, while giving Hawkpoint access to mid-market stockbroking business. The two businesses operate from separate offices, and Hawkpoint continues to offer independent advice. Paul Baines, chief executive and managing partner of Hawkpoint, joined the board of Collins Stewart after the acquisition. Both David Reid Scott and Baines will remain as chairmen and chief executives of Hawkpoint, and will join the group's executive committee.

Swooping down on deals

Hawkpoint Partners is exclusively associated with Spain's Socios Financieros, an independent corporate finance house that serves both corporate and private interests. The two firms have collaborated on several cross-border European corporate finance transactions. In 2007, Hawkpoint advised Julius Baer Holdings Ltd. on a management buyout transaction of its currency and fixed income hedge fund management.

Hawkpoint also acted as sole advisory to the selling shareholders during Rentokil Initial PLC's acquisition of Target Express Holdings Limited for £210 million. Hawkpoint advised GE on the sale of its UK life insurance and pensions business, GE Life, to Swiss Re for £465 million in October 2006. In April 2006, Hawkpoint advised on the sale of New Media Spark's M&A online news service, Mergemarket. New Media Spark's initial intention was to simply restructure Mergemarket, but Hawkpoint encouraged the company to sell, in a deal that raised over €279 million.

Eggs in many baskets

In addition to its work advising banking and financial institutions, Hawkpoint has a number of clients across diverse fields. In the automotive industry, the firm advises Reynolds and Reynolds UK, as well as Stadco, the UK's largest supplier of car bodies. Acertec, maker of

Visit Vault Europe's Finance Career Channel at www.vault.com/europe for insider firm profiles, employee surveys of finance professionals in Europe, message boards, job listings, expert finance career advice, insider salary information and more.

VAULT CAREER LIBRARY 219

steel construction products, also hired the firm recently. And in 2006, Canadian media firm CanWest appointed Hawkpoint to sell its interest in TV3, a commercial Irish broadcasting company. Hawkpoint has also advised the Mansfield United football team and the Liverpool Football Club.

New blood

The last few years have seen personnel changes at Hawkpoint's top levels. In June 2006, life assurance company Paternoster lured away director Myles Pink. In January 2006, Michael Payan, head of French mergers and acquisitions, left Hawkpoint to join investment bank Société Générale as its global head of M&A.

In September 2006, Hawkpoint appointed Edouard Debost as a managing director of the firm, in the Paris office. Before joining Hawkpoint, Debost worked at Lazard Frères. In January 2005, the firm promoted Hugh Elwes from director to managing director. Elwes joined the firm from Deutsche Bank in 2002 and worked most notably on the sale of Pantheon to the Russell Group in 2005. In July 2005, Simon Gluckstein joined Hawkpoint as managing director, leaving Citigroup, where he was a managing director specialising in media. Finally, in September 2005, Hawkpoint snagged Michael Barnes from CIBC World Markets in London, offering him the role of director to the firm's debt advisory division.

Making rain

Hawkpoint Partners snagged multiple industry awards in 2006. The firm was named Financial Adviser of the Year 2006, at the BVCA/Real Deals Private Equity Awards, for the second time in three years. Hawkpoint was also named Independent House of the Year at the HGCapital Rainmaker Awards 2006.

Christopher Darlington, a managing director, was named Rainmaker of the Year at the same awards ceremony. Hawkpoint was named UK Independent Corporate Finance House of the Year at the Acquisitions Monthly Awards 2006. Finally, in February 2006, the firm was named Private Equity Boutique of the Year for the second year in a row at the EVCJ Private Equity Awards.

GETTING HIRED

While there are no actual job listings up on Hawkpoint's career site at www.hawkpoint.com/careers.html, there are a few clues about how to get in the door. The banks says potential candidates should "possess an excellent academic record, with strong numerical skills, and be able to demonstrate a keen interest in corporate activity." The firm also welcomes "graduate level and newly qualified ACA/MBA/law qualification level" candidates as well as those who have experience in "financial modeling." To inquire about any current vacancies or to submit your CV for consideration, contact the firm via email at: recruitment@hawkpoint.com.

Visit **Vault Europe's Finance Career Channel** at **www.vault.com/europe** for insider firm profiles, employee surveys of finance professionals in Europe, message boards, job listings, expert finance career advice, insider salary information and more.

VAULT CAREER LIBRARY 221

HBOS

The Mound
Edinburgh EH1 1YZ
United Kingdom
Phone: + 44 (0) 131 470 2000
Fax: +44 (0) 131 243 5437
www.hbosplc.com

EUROPEAN LOCATIONS

Edinburgh (HQ)
Offices and locations throughout
the UK, Ireland and Europe

DEPARTMENTS

Asset Management
Corporate Banking
Insurance
Investment
Retail Banking
Treasury Management

THE STATS

Employer Type: Public Company
Ticker Symbol: HBOS (London)
Chairman: Lord Dennis Stevenson
Group Executive Director: Andrew
Hornby
2006 Revenue: £11.9 billion
2006 Net Income: £5.3 billion
2005 Revenue: £10.9 billion
2005 Net Income: £4.7 billion
No. of Employees: 72,000

KEY COMPETITORS

Abbey
Deutsche Bank AG
HSBC Holdings
Lloyds TSB

PLUSES

"Good salary"

MINUSES

"More flexibility needed"

EMPLOYMENT CONTACT

www.hbosplc.com Click on
"Recruitment" link under "About
HBOS"

THE BUZZ
WHAT EMPLOYEES AT OTHER FIRMS ARE SAYING

- "Innovative"
- "Boring"

THE SCOOP

Building a giant

HBOS plc is the holding company of the HBOS Group, a UK-based banking and insurance company. HBOS was formed from Halifax's 2001 acquisition of Bank of Scotland, the UK's oldest commercial bank. Prior to the acquisition, Bank of Scotland had a strong retail banking business in Scotland, as well as a corporate banking business. At the time, Halifax was the largest provider of mortgages and savings in the UK and offered credit cards, life assurance and general insurance products among their services. The merger was heralded as creating a fifth force in UK banking, as HBOS was able to rival the established Big Four UK retail banks.

The firm is now the fourth-largest banking group in the UK by capitalisation and is currently the UK's No. 1 mortgage lender. Primarily active in the UK and Australian markets, the company operates in five business divisions: retail, corporate, insurance and investment, international, and treasury and asset management. In addition to Halifax and Bank of Scotland, some of HBOS' most recognisable brands include: Intelligent Finance, which offers consumer banking via the internet and phone; Birmingham Midshire, which offers lending, savings and general insurance; and Colleys, a surveying business.

The British banking giant is ranked No. 8 on the Commercial & Savings Banks — Top 45 Companies, which ranks companies by worldwide annual revenue. The company is ranked No. 44 on Dow Jones' list of Global 50 Titans, which tracks the market performance of large international companies. HBOS is also ranked No. 10 on the FTSE 350, which includes the most highly capitalised blue chip companies in the UK.

Feeding frenzy

In July 2005, in what was billed as "an absolute first," HBOS authorised its fund management wing, Insight, to begin a spending spree on European property that could reach £1.4 billion. The decision came at a time when other British firms began looking abroad for better yields.

In May 2006, HBOS announced that it would acquire a 50 per cent stake in Lex Vehicle Leasing from Aviva plc for £226.8 million. HBOS had previously held 50 per cent of the company that Halifax had acquired in 1998. This acquisition, combined with HBOS' Bank of Scotland Vehicle Finance, makes HBOS the top vehicle leasing company in the UK with 250,000 cars under contract. Also in 2006, the company agreed to sell its 90 per cent stake in US-based Drive Financial, a provider of subprime auto loans, to Banco Santander Central Hispano.

Visit **Vault Europe's Finance Career Channel** at **www.vault.com/europe** for insider firm profiles, employee surveys of finance professionals in Europe, message boards, job listings, expert finance career advice, insider salary information and more.

VAULT CAREER LIBRARY 223

In February 2007, the company announced that it had bought an additional 5 per cent of the shareholding in Sainsbury's Bank for £21 million from J Sainsbury plc. Sainsbury's is now a 50-50 joint venture between HBOS and Sainsbury's, as opposed to the previous 55-45 structure. The board of Sainsbury's will consist of eight directors; three from both HBOS and Sainsbury's and two executives from Sainsbury's Bank.

Giving back

Over the last 17 years, HBOS plc has donated more than £19.5 million through its charity credit cards through which HBOS donates to a charity of the customer's choice, every time the card is used and, in fact, in 2000, Halifax entered the Guinness Book of Records as the world's most successful charity card provider. In 2006, more than £1.5 million was donated by HBOS and its customers to three charities — Cancer Research UK, the National Society for the Prevention of Cruelty to Children and the Scottish Society for the Prevention of Cruelty to Animals. That same year, the company's foundation donated £100,000 to four homeless charities in the northwest England. In addition to its donations, HBOS has worked to help deprived areas in Scotland and England. In 2006, the company announced that it would install 100 new fee-free ATMs in poor and rural areas in Scotland and rural England.

HBOS also works to support its employees. In August 2006, the company announced that its 60,000 UK employees would be awarded free shares, worth approximately £67 million, bringing the total free shares and annual bonuses awarded to HBOS employees in 2006 to £289 million.

Great Scot!

HBOS' corporate headquarters is located in one of the most recognisable buildings in Scotland. Known as The Mound, the building is an important landmark in Edinburgh. Over 200 years old, The Mound displays specially commissioned works from contemporary Scottish artists.

In June of 2006, HBOS acquired the draft of the last will and testament of Scottish novelist and poet Sir Walter Scott, who is actually closely linked to the history of the Bank of Scotland. In 1826, Scott came to the defence of the bank when Parliament attempted to prevent the issue of notes for under £5. Scott wrote a series of letters to the Edinburgh Weekly Journal, which was reprinted as a pamphlet. The letters served to force the government to relent and allow banks to continue issuing £1 notes.

New blood

The year 2006 saw a spate of new hires for HBOS. In January of 2006, the company announced that Karen Jones, previously chief executive of Spirit Group, a pub and restaurant group, joined the company as a non-executive director. The following month, Jo Dawson was promoted from group risk director to chief executive, insurance and investment.

In May 2006, the company announced the appointment of George Grant as its new head of motor finance, replacing Tom Woolgrove, who was appointed managing director of HBOS General Insurance. In July 2006, James Crosby, then chief executive, left HBOS and was succeeded by Andy Hornby. Hornby has six years board experience at Halifax and HBOS, and is the former COO of HBOS. And, in January 2007, Ken Stannard, previously managing director of Capital One's UK credit card business, was appointed head of HBOS' credit card business.

GETTING HIRED

Stake out your personal page

Check out the "recruitment" link at www.hbosplc.com to learn about open positions for graduates and experienced professionals. And from there, you can use the "search and apply" function or register and receive your own "personal pages," where you'll have the opportunity to upload everything from a standard CV to a PowerPoint presentation for the firm to peruse.

Interview experiences run the gamut, sources report. One insider says that he "did not get asked job-specific questions" and that "they have the same questions for every vacancy." Another contact says "the interview process can be a nightmare" with "meaningless aptitude tests and endless streams of questions that make it nearly impossible not to repeat answers. By the end of the interview, the interviewer and the interviewee are totally exhausted." The insider goes on to add that "I learned later that some managers bypass normal procedures to make the interview process more effective and streamlined."

Visit **Vault Europe's Finance Career Channel** at **www.vault.com/europe** for insider firm profiles, employee surveys of finance professionals in Europe, message boards, job listings, expert finance career advice, insider salary information and more.

VAULT CAREER LIBRARY   225

OUR SURVEY SAYS

Average hours, decent perks

Sources report working hours run about "40 to 50" with weekend work averaging "about once a month." But perks such as a "company car" and the offer of shares seem to keep staffers' attention, and "casual Fridays" bode well, too. There aren't any complaints about diversity either — the firm's treatment of women, minorities, and gays and lesbians all receive high marks.

HypoVereinsbank AG (HVB)

Am Tucherpark 16
80538 Munich
Germany
Phone: +49 89 378 0
Fax: +49 89 378 27784
www.hvbgroup.com

EUROPEAN LOCATIONS

Munich (HQ)
Frankfurt
Luxembourg
Russia
780 subsidiaries worldwide of
which 732 are in Germany and
429 in Bavaria

DEPARTMENTS

Corporates
Retail
Markets & Investment Banking
Wealth Management

THE STATS

Employer Type: Public Company
Ticker Symbol: HVM (Frankfurt)
Chairman, Supervisory Board:
Alessandro Profumo
**CEO and Management Board
Spokesman:** Wolfgang Sprissler
2006 Revenue: €1,168m (FYE 06)
No. of Employees: 25,783
No. of Offices: 788

KEY COMPETITORS

Commerzbank
Deutsche Bank
Dresdner Bank

PLUSES

"I know my managers"
Good training programmes

MINUSES

"Needs greater transparency"
Long hours

EMPLOYMENT CONTACT

See "Jobs & Karriere" section on
www.hvbgroup.com

THE BUZZ
WHAT EMPLOYEES AT OTHER FIRMS ARE SAYING

- "Strong in real estate"
- "Old style German story"

Visit the Vault Finance Career Channel at **www.vault.com/finance**—with insider firm
profiles, message boards, the Vault Finance Job Board and more.

VAULT CAREER LIBRARY 227

THE SCOOP

Number two in Deutschland

HVB Group is the second-largest German bank behind Deutsche Bank and has 7,000 branches around the world, including 700 in Germany. The firm has more than 25,000 employees, 2,489 branch offices and 4.3 million customers. HVB focuses on European retail and mid-cap customers and provides capital market activities. It is also a leading real estate lender in Europe, with a loan portfolio of €325 billion. HVB is divided — as is its parent company UniCredit — into four divisions: retail, corporate, wealth management and multinationals/investment banking. The Italian bank UniCredit bought HVB for about $18 billion in 2005. HVB spun off its commercial real estate financing unit as Hypo Real Estate Holding.

As a result of the sale, HVB began offering free cashpoint withdrawals in January 2006 from UniCredit Banca cashpoints in Italy and from all Bank Austria Creditanstalt cashpoints in Austria. HVB now has approximately 11,000 cashpoints available for use free of charge, knocking out the regular surcharge of at least €3.95.

Fit for a king

The bank can trace its roots back to 1835 when King Ludwig I of Bavaria created Bayerische Hypotheken- und Wechsel-Bank (BHWB) to offer real estate loans, insurance and to issue currency. In 1869, Bavarian investors formed Bayerische Vereinsbank as a commercial bank. The two banks teamed up after World War I to protect themselves from being gobbled up by larger banks. After the end of World War II, they benefited from the breakup of national banks as punishment for helping the Nazi government. But in the late 1950s the national banks had recovered and eventually Deutsche Bank, Dresdner Bank and Commerzbank were back again ruling the roost.

The two banks discussed merging in 1969, but the government mandated that any merger include the Bavarian state bank Bayerische Staatsbank, squashing the deal. Vereinsbank ended up buying the state bank in 1971. BHWB and Vereinsbank finally merged in 1998 and stayed regionally focused to fend off the superbanks.

Buying and selling

In July 2006, HVB announced that it will sell its three Activest companies to Pioneer Global Asset Management, a UniCredit subsidiary, for €600 million. HVB will still maintain a partnership with the transferred Activest companies. Pioneer also agreed to buy investment fund NORDINVEST Norddeutsche Investment-Gesellschaft from HVB in January 2007.

Though it is selling off the Activest companies, HVB is still investing. In June 2006, in an acquisition for the UniCredit network, HVB entered into an agreement with Nordea Bank

Finland plc to purchase an additional 20 per cent stake in ZAO International Moscow Bank (IMB) for roughly $395 million. Acquiring Nordea's stake will increase HVB's participation from 52.9 per cent to 79.3 per cent of IMB's voting capital, thereby solidifying HVB's controlling position on the bank. HVB will sell its IMB holdings to UniCredit in future. In May HVB and IMB jointly tendered a structured export finance loan of €77 million to OAO Ural Steel, to fund the construction of a new steel mill and allow Ural Steel to finally tap into the international export market.

HVB has other interests in Eastern Europe. In June 2006, the bank announced that it would be advising the Croatian government on the restructuring and privatisation of its shipyards. Shipping is the Balkan state's second-highest grossing industry, and Croatia is hoping to make its shipyards internationally competitive. HVB's global shipping branch in Hamburg is one of the world's leading ship financiers, with a portfolio of over €5.5 billion. HVB bought a 26.44 per cent stake in International Moscow Bank from Nordea Bank in October 2006 for $395 million, boosting the 50 per cent stake it already held. IMB is Russia's first joint-venture bank, formed in 1989 with Nordea, a financial services group in the Nordic and Baltic regions.

In January 2007, HVB transferred its 77.53 per cent stake in Bank Austria Creditansalt (BA-CA) to its parent UniCredit for about €12.5 billion. HVB also sold its 100 per cent stake in HVB Latvia to BA-CA for €35 million plus €40 million of capital it invested in August 2006. The deal also included selling a 70 per cent stake in International Moscow Bank for €1 million, with the option to buy 5 per cent more. HVB also unloaded HVB Bank Ukraine to UniCredit for €83 million.

Selling some real estate

HVB sold a real estate portfolio with 86 properties to Varde Partners in December 2006 to shed non-core holdings. Most of the buildings were offices space that weren't being used by HVB. The bank said at the time of the deal that it didn't want to hold real estate used by third parties, and that the buildings were non-strategic holdings. The same month the bank sold a €960 million real estate loan portfolio to Goldman Sachs after an auction. The deal includes loans to 1,100 HVB borrowers.

GETTING HIRED

Moving up from the inside

Getting in the door initially might be your biggest hurdle at HVB. The bank recruits "internally" as well as "at the universities in Germany and Italy." But insiders say landing a position is "neither very easy nor nearly impossible," although current candidates have the best

Visit **Vault Europe's Finance Career Channel** at www.vault.com/europe for insider firm profiles, employee surveys of finance professionals in Europe, message boards, job listings, expert finance career advice, insider salary information and more.

VAULT CAREER LIBRARY 229

shot at filling open slots-one insider says that "for the hiring of many jobs, we promote juniors to the intermediate level."

To apply for a position, click on the jobs link on the main site at www.hypovereinsbank.de. If your CV makes a good impression, prepare to stick around for a long haul if they like you. Past the "initial interviews," you can expect a "full round of six to eight interviews in one day," says one source.

OUR SURVEY SAYS

A growing culture

The bank's culture "is evolving because of the takeover and merger into a larger group," "but it is clearly shaping into a better one." However, the hours can "sometimes be long," reports a contact, who adds that he typically works "two to four extra hours each weekend".

Benefits get middling marks from sources. There are perks available such as "company cars," says an insider, adding: "it's not meaningful because it's taxable." But managers do receive mostly positive reactions. One contact has "an excellent relationship with my immediate superior" and "[I'm] well respected and treated well by managers and subordinates." The dress code gets a thumbs-up as well — one insider describes it as: "formal always with an unwritten rule of business casual on Fridays or just before holidays." And in the way of training, the bank offers a "formal trainee program, on-the-job-training for newcomers, participation in external seminars and conferences."

Making progress

Diversity at the bank is "improving". It was "previously a male-dominated world, but more and more women are coming," although currently, there are "very few or no women on top levels". One respondent says that in terms of ethnic diversity, the bank is "getting more diversified over the years" with "lots of German, Austrian, Italian and British workers."

ICAP

2 Broadgate
London EC2M 7UR
United Kingdom
Phone: + 44 (0) 20 7000 5000
Fax: + 44 (0) 20 7000 5975
www.icap.com

EUROPEAN LOCATIONS

London (HQ)
Amsterdam
Bergen
Copenhagen
Frankfurt
Madrid
Warsaw

DEPARTMENTS

Information Services
Interdealer Broker

THE BUZZ
WHAT EMPLOYEES AT OTHER FIRMS ARE SAYING

- "Biggest Broker"
- "Who?"

Visit the Vault Finance Career Channel at **www.vault.com/finance** — with insider firm
profiles, message boards, the Vault Finance Job Board and more.

VAULT CAREER LIBRARY 231

THE SCOOP

Leader of the pack

ICAP is the world's premier voice and electronic interdealer money broker and the source of global market information and commentary for professionals in the international financial markets. ICAP provides a specialist broking service to trading professionals in the global wholesale financial markets. Its customers include investment and commercial banks . ICAP covers a broad range of OTC financial products and services in energy, FX, interest rates, credit and equity markets. The electronic networks deliver global connectivity to customers seeking unparalleled liquidity and flow in an orderly marketplace.

ICAP was formed in 1999 when Garban plc and Intercapital plc merged, combining Garban's strength in government and corporate bonds, interest rate products and money market instruments with Intercapital's expertise in interest rate swaps and options, commodity swaps, illiquid securities and foreign exchange options. Initially called Garban-Intercapital plc, the joint entity was renamed ICAP in 2001. Today ICAP is led by Intercapital Founder Michael Spencer and employs more than 3,400 people in 25 offices around the world.

Working across Europe

ICAP's head office in London is home to 1,250 employees, including 740 brokers. The firm has six other offices in Europe, each providing unique services to its region. ICAP's Copenhagen office was established in 1968 and has expanded to include approximately 40 staffers that focus on money market products, foreign exchange and derivatives, with an emphasis on Scandinavian currencies. In Spain ICAP operates via a 25 per cent shareholding in Grupo Corrataje e Informacion Monetaria y de Divisas — its office is in Madrid. ICAP's Dutch arm is APB Energy, located in Amsterdam, which offers full-service energy brokerage. It's a leading electricity and energy broker in natural gas, coal and weather derivatives in seven countries. Nordic operations (in Bergen, Norway) are also conducted through APB Energy.

In Germany ICAP's business was built by a series of acquisitions, starting with Intercapital's 1998 takeover of Exco plc. ICAP's Frankfurt office focuses on money markets, fixed income, and interbank deposits. Frankfurt works in close collaboration with London. It also offers execution in spot transactions, switches, spread trades and orders on the Frankfurt Stock Exchange. Finally, ICAP's Polish office, in Warsaw, traces its roots to 1998, when it was known as Harlow Butler Sp.zo.o. Today it covers the Polish government bond market, swaps, forward rate agreement, foreign exchange and money markets, and is active in both local currency and deposits in US dollars as well as major European currencies — and it's staffed by only 14 people.

A share of EBS

In April 2006 ICAP agreed to acquire the total share capital of EBS Group Limited, a leading provider of foreign exchange trading and market data solutions to the professional spot foreign exchange community. ICAP CEO Michael Spencer said the acquisition "takes us further toward our goal of offering comprehensive electronic execution and post-trade services for liquid, commoditised markets." ICAP reportedly paid $775 million in cash for 100 per cent of EBS' share capital. For fiscal 2005 EBS reported revenue of $206 million, with operating profit of $37 million.

ICAP makes the list

ICAP joined the UK's FTSE 100 Index in June 2006, replacing BAA, the world's biggest airport owner, which had been on the index for almost 19 years. BAA was removed following its acquisition by Spain's Grupo Ferrovial SA. At the time of its indexing, ICAP reported a market value of £3.18 billion.

Off to China

Not wanting to miss the boat of opportunity in the fast-growing Asian markets, in July 2006 ICAP announced a joint venture with the China Foreign Exchange Trade System and National Interbank Funding Center (CFETS). The new entity, Shanghai CFETS-ICAP International Money Broking Co. Ltd., will provide voice broking services to the money, bond and derivatives markets in both the Chinese currency and international markets. The move — and the opening of the CFETS-ICAP office in Shanghai — is part of ICAP's strategy to gain a foothold in Chinese interbank financial markets.

Winning at risk

ICAP picked up several awards in 2006. It was voted interdealer broker of the year in Risk magazine's annual interdealer rankings, which survey over 1,000 market experts and covered 120 derivative products in the interest rate, foreign exchange, credit and equity markets. ICAP was the placed in first position in more products — 48 to be precise — than any other broker, and scored particularly well in interest rates, winning 60 per cent of the categories. ICAP was also named the 2006 broker of the year at the annual Energy Risk Awards.

Visit **Vault Europe's Finance Career Channel** at **www.vault.com/europe** for insider firm profiles, employee surveys of finance professionals in Europe, message boards, job listings, expert finance career advice, insider salary information and more.

VAULT CAREER LIBRARY 233

Scoping the market for an exchange

As rumours of a possible takeover of the London Stock Exchange swirled in 2006, ICAP's name emerged as a potential buyer. Although Nasdaq owns 25 per cent of the London exchange, the LSE rejected Nasdaq's $4.2 billion takeover offer in March 2006. In September ICAP revealed that it had held merger talks with the LSE, which had already turned down offers from Deutsche Borse, Euronext, Macquarie Bank and the New York Stock Exchange. The initial round of ICAP-LSE talks didn't result in a deal, though, because the LSE's £2.6 billion valuation was too pricey for ICAP. That may not be ICAP's final attempt at the exchange, however. In October 2006 CEO Michael Spencer addressed the UK Conservative Party conference and noted that "in the right alliance, the LSE could be broadened from being just a very, very strong UK exchange to potentially being the global equity exchange ... and that really is the ambition we discussed."

One day's work

ICAP holds an annual Charity Day — "a day on which all revenues and commissions would be given away to just a few charities." In December 2006 it celebrated the 14th anniversary of Charity Day by raising a record £7.1 million. On Charity Day, the proceeds from the firm's global broking activities go to approximately 80 selected charities worldwide. Since Charity Day began in 1992, ICAP has raised more than £33 million for various good causes.

GETTING HIRED

For more information about careers and graduate opportunities at ICAP, visit the careers section of the company's web site at www.icap.com/careers.

Intesa Sanpaolo S.p.A.

Via Monte di Pieta, 8
Milan, 20121
Italy
Phone: +39 (0) 2 879 11
Fax: +39 (0) 2 88 44 36 38
www.intesasanpaolo.com

EUROPEAN LOCATIONS

Milan (HQ)
Offices across Europe and
worldwide

BUSINESSES

Banca dei Territori Division
Corporate & Investment Banking
Division
Eurizon Financial Group
Foreign Banks Division
Group's Finance
Public Finance Division

DEPARTMENTS

Corporate
International
Retail

THE STATS

Employer Type: Public Company
Ticker Symbol: ISP (Borsa Italia)
Chairman: Giovanni Bazoli
Managing Director and CEO: Corrado
Passera
2006-07 Net Income: €4.68bn
(FYE 03/07)
2005-06 Net Income: €4.48bn
(FYE 03/06)* restated on a
consistent basis, considering the
merger between Banca Intesa and
Sanpaolo IMI and the connected
transactions with Crédit Agricole and
the changes in the consolidation area.
Number of Employees: 58,703
No. of Offices: 6,249 (Worldwide)

KEY COMPETITORS

Banca Nazionale del Lavoro
Capitalia
UniCredit

PLUSES

New structure

MINUSES

Employee cuts

EMPLOYMENT CONTACT

www.bancaintesa.it/piu/jsp/Editorial

THE BUZZ
WHAT EMPLOYEES AT OTHER FIRMS ARE SAYING

- "Strong retail presence"
- "Regional"

Visit the Vault Finance Career Channel at **www.vault.com/finance**—with insider firm
profiles, message boards, the Vault Finance Job Board and more.

VAULT CAREER LIBRARY 235

THE SCOOP

Italian banking's biggest meatball

Intesa-Sanpaolo S.p.A. was born in January 2007 following the merger of Italy's No. 2 and No. 3 banks, Banca Intesa S.p.A. and Sanpaolo IMI. The deal, which was announced in late August 2006, closed quickly, earning approval from shareholders and Italian bank regulators alike. Although the transaction was officially described as a "merger of equals," it had all the hallmarks of a takeover — Milan-based Banca Intesa took over the smaller Turin-based Sanpaolo, offering 3.115 of its own shares for each Sanpaolo share. Citigroup advised on the €29.6 billion deal ($38 billion), which created Italy's largest bank, surpassing UniCredit S.p.A. in size and assets. Intesa- Sanpaolo now boasts approximately 6,000 branches and control of more than one-fifth of the Italian retail market.

The deal — the biggest since Royal Bank of Scotland's takeover of National Westminster Bank in 2000 — could result in €1.6 billion in savings and new revenue over three years. Furthermore, the deal has enabled Intesa Saopaolo to draw even with rival Italian banking group UniCredito, which merged with Germany's HypoVereinsbank in 2005, putting it in second place behind French bank BNP Paribas in Italy. Based on market cap, Intesa Sanpaolo is one of the top-10 largest banks in the world.

The new Intesa-Sanpaolo is legally incorporated in Turin, Sanpaolo's home, with operating headquarters in Milan. At the close of the merger, Intesa-Sanpaolo held €541 billion ($690 billion) in assets and represented 13 million customers in 30 countries, including Russia, China and India. The combination of two Italian superpowers boosted the confidence of analysts in the Italian banking world — Fitch Ratings upgraded its rating of Intesa-Sanpaolo from 2 to 1.

Building a new bank

Post-merger reorganisations resulted in a new structure for Intesa-Sanpaolo, which has six business units and 16 head office departments. Its six business units are the Banca dei Territori (which includes retail and small business banking in Italy), corporate and investment banking, foreign banks, public finance (which combines the operations of two subsidiaries, BIIS and Banca OPI), Eurizon Financial Group and group's finance. The 16 head office departments include a number of corporate support operations, such as legal affairs, audit, IT and tax.

As the reorganisation winds down, Intesa-Sanpaolo may go through with its plan to spin off Eurizon Financial Group, which offers life insurance and mutual funds and includes the subsidiary financial planner Banca Fideuram. Former Banca Intesa CEO Corrado Passera was named CEO of the new bank. Sanpaolo Chairman Enrico Salza leads the management board, and Banca Intesa Chairman Giovanni Bazoli now heads the supervisory board.

Major European player

The bank provides a range of services, including investment banking, public and infrastructure finance, factoring and trade financing services. The retail division serves individuals, small businesses, micro enterprises, SMEs and nonprofits. It offers retail banking, wealth management, private banking and industrial credit via Banca Intesa Mediocredito, which has a leading position in Italy.

The corporate division serves midsized and large corporations, financial institutions and public administrations. Its main activities include mergers and acquisitions, structured finance services, merchant banking, capital markets (through Banca Caboto), global custody and an international network focused on corporate banking, which includes ZAO Banca Intesa, the only Italian banking subsidiary licensed to operate in Russia.

The specialised subsidiary Banca Intesa Infrastrutture e Sviluppo supports the public and infrastructure sectors. Its fields of action range from public work lending to securitisations for public entities and project finance. The Italian subsidiary banks division includes regional banking subsidiaries Cariparma & Piacenza, Banca Popolare FriulAdria, Biverbanca, Banca di Trento e Bolzano and Intesa Casse del Centro. The international subsidiary banks division is composed of subsidiaries abroad, mainly in Central Eastern Europe, that offer retail and commercial banking services.

Let the cuts begin!

In a statement about their merger, Banca Intesa and Sanpaolo announced that they would cut their combined operations by up to 10 per cent "to avoid duplication." A few days later the two banks released another statement saying they had reached an agreement with all nine trade unions of the Italian banking industry. Under this agreement, employees of both banks who qualified for retirement within 60 months would take their Solidarity Allowance — retirement payout — by January 2007.

After the employee cuts are finalised, Intesa-Sanpaolo has disclosed plans to hire new staff while admitting that there won't be a full replacement of lost staff. Only 50 per cent of the eliminated positions will be filled. The number of employees expected to take early retirement is approximately 5,200 (2,400 from Banca Intesa and 2,800 from Sanpaolo). At the time of the merger, Banca Intesa had a workforce of 60,788 while Sanpaolo's total headcount was 42,872.

Visit **Vault Europe's Finance Career Channel** at www.vault.com/europe for insider firm profiles, employee surveys of finance professionals in Europe, message boards, job listings, expert finance career advice, insider salary information and more.

VAULT CAREER LIBRARY   237

Jet set investing

In April 2006, Banca Intesa and Lazard Group finalised a breakup of their Italian joint venture, with Lazard paying $146 million to buy back its Milan-based rival's 40 per cent stake. Intesa will get the payout in debt securities, which will mature in February 2008, and has also has an interest in Lazard Group through a $150 million convertible debt security it bought when the joint venture was formed.

It was originally scheduled to expire in December 2007, but Lazard terminated the deal early following a number of senior departures from its own Italian operation. Also in 2006, Banca Intesa purchased a 5 per cent stake in fashion house Prada for €2 billion, also lending the high-fashion brand another €200 million. In the beginning of 2007, the bank, financier Carlo De Benedetti's Management & Capitali and Air were rumoured to be considering a bid for Italy's unprofitable airline, Alitalia.

Building for the future

In January 2007, as expected, Sanpaolo Chairman Enrico Salza and Banca Intesa CEO Corrado Passera assumed the same posts at Intesa Sanpaolo. Integrating the two banks will be a difficult task as Passera's team will have to create a clear management structure to avoid infighting between former rivals. The leadership will also have to decide how to integrate the banks' IT systems, by either combining the old systems or going with new technology. Dealing with the staffing redundancies will also be an issue because Italian unions won't allow the kind of massive layoffs common in mergers in the US and UK.

GETTING HIRED

For more information about career opportunities at Intesa-Sanpaolo S.p.A., visit the company's website at www.bancaintesa.it/piu/jsp/Editorial.

Jefferies & Company

Jefferies International Ltd.
Bracken House, Floor 4
1 Friday Street
London EC4M 9JA
United Kingdom
Phone: +44 (0) 20 7618 3500
www.jefferies.com

EUROPEAN LOCATIONS

London (European HQ)
Paris
Zurich

DEPARTMENTS

Asset Management
Investment Banking
Private Client Services
Research
Sales & Trading

THE STATS

Employer Type: Public Company
Ticker Symbol: JEF (NYSE)
Chairman and CEO: Richard B. Handler
2006 Net Revenue: $1.5 billion (FYE 12/06)
2005 Net Revenue: $1.2 billion (FYE 12/05)
2006 Employees: 2,257
No. of Offices: 25

PLUSES

Strong in global financial markets
Good perks

MINUSES

"A 'one-size fits all' policy for the firm in terms of process and systems"
More transparent compensation structure needed

EMPLOYMENT CONTACT

www.jefferies.com/careers

THE BUZZ
WHAT EMPLOYEES AT OTHER FIRMS ARE SAYING

- "Excellent niche player"
- "Not exceptional"

Visit the Vault Finance Career Channel at **www.vault.com/finance**—with insider firm profiles, message boards, the Vault Finance Job Board and more.

VAULT CAREER LIBRARY 239

THE SCOOP

Pretty good-looking, for a mid-sized firm

Boyd Jefferies' eponymous firm has come a long way since its founding in 1962, when it focused almost exclusively on institutional trading. Today Jefferies Group Inc. is a full-service investment bank and institutional securities firm serving midsized companies in the United States, Europe and Asia. The firm's business arms provide investment banking, sales and trading, research and asset management to corporate clients, institutional investors and high-net-worth individuals.

Jefferies specialises in a broad range of industries such as aerospace and defence, energy, financial and business services, gaming and leisure, health care, industrials, maritime and oil service, media and communications, retail and consumer and technology and a dedicated private equity coverage group. Jefferies & Company, Inc. is the firm's principal operating subsidiary. Business at Jefferies is broken into five divisions: investment banking (including specialised industry groups), sales and trading, research, asset management and private client services. As of 2006 Jefferies employed more than 2,200 people at its 25 offices around the world.

International operations

Jefferies International Ltd. (JIL) is the primary operating subsidiary for Jefferies Group Inc. in Europe as well as the hub for the European divisions of Jefferies Broadview, Jefferies Quarterdeck and Randall & Dewey (the firm's technology, aerospace and defence and energy investment banking groups, respectively). JIL is based in London, and is a member of the London Stock Exchange, the Frankfurt Xetra, Euronext and the Dubai exchange.

A subsidiary, Helix Associates Limited, is a major independent placement agent for private equity funds. Jefferies' focus in Europe is on aerospace and defence, energy, health care, media, technology and maritime, infrastructure and logistics. Its European equity research includes consumer, energy, gaming, health care, media, telecommunications and technology and France country coverage. The London office is also home to a UK sales team dedicated to providing US securities and research to European clients.

Elsewhere in Europe, Jefferies (Switzerland) Ltd. operates in Zurich, conducting sales, trading and investment management of global convertibles, and it is one of the world's largest providers of asset management services for global convertible bonds for institutional investors; JIL has approximately $2 billion (€1.55 billion) of investment assets under management. Finally, Jefferies' Paris office contains a sales and research team that conducts French and European equity research for domestic and international clients.

Being part of the equation

Employees of Jefferies are not just employees — they are described as "employee-owners", because Jefferies employees and board members own approximately 50 per cent of the firm's equity. In a contest sponsored by the online financial news publication Here Is The City, Jefferies' employee-owners turned out in record numbers to vote their firm Best Place to Work in the Global Financial Markets. More than 86 per cent of Jefferies' global staff of 2,247 people voted for their employer. In response, CEO Richard Handler thanked his fellow employee-owners, saying their dedication and passion are the firm's biggest assets. He added, "We still have much work to do in accomplishing our worldwide goals in the middle market, and [we] are continually looking for good partners. If you work at another financial services firm and want a career at a company where one person can still make a difference, please think of us."

Building infrastructure

In December 2006 Jefferies International Limited expanded its European investment banking capabilities, hiring three top bankers to be managing directors in the firm's transportation, oil service and infrastructure group. Anne-Christin Dovigen, Nick Davies and Andrew Meigh joined Jefferies from HSBC. Jefferies noted that in 2005 it completed nearly 20 transactions in the oil services, maritime and offshore industries group — the deals had a combined value of $4.8 billion. Deals in this sector were up for 2006, as Jefferies completed 25 transactions valued at $5 billion. As further proof of Jefferies' commitment to global growth, the firm acquired Nomad accreditation on the Alternative Investment Market (AIM) of the London Stock Exchange in 2006.

The proof is in the tables

Jefferies' expertise in the mid-market was reflected in the 2006 mid-market league tables. It was ranked No. 8 in worldwide announced M&A deals up to $50 million, No. 4 in announced deals up to $100 million, No. 13 in announced deals up to $200 million and No. 12 in announced deals up to $500 million. On the European regional mid-market tables, Jefferies ranked No. 24 in announced deals up to $100 million, No. 14 in UK announced deals up to $100 million, and No. 16 in UK announced deals up to $200 million.

Eyes on Asia

Jefferies had something to celebrate even before the 2007 new year began. In December 2006 it announced the opening of its first office in mainland China. According to the bank, this Shanghai office "represents the next step in an ongoing expansion of the Jefferies investment bank."

Visit **Vault Europe's Finance Career Channel** at www.vault.com/europe for insider firm profiles, employee surveys of finance professionals in Europe, message boards, job listings, expert finance career advice, insider salary information and more.

VAULT CAREER LIBRARY 241

But Jefferies was no stranger to Asia. It is an established underwriter and advisor in the region and has worked on several cross-border M&A transactions involving Asian companies. Since 2004 Jefferies has raised almost $3 billion in equity and debt transactions for Asia-based companies, and its M&A advisory fees in the region totaled $2.5 billion. It has also worked with several China-focused private equity and venture capital funds.

In August 2006 Jefferies made its debut on the Dubai International Financial Exchange (DIFX). The Dubai exchange leaders persuaded Jefferies to join 13 other groups on the list, which was launched in September 2005; Jefferies joined as a securities trading manager. Analysts said Dubai's new exchange is a signal that the country is determined to compete with neighbouring Abu Dhabi for financial prominence in the region. Jefferies' presence on the DIFX helped lend the exchange some credibility — and it has put Jefferies in the midst of a growing market.

GETTING HIRED

Establish your ability

The firm recruits from a long list of schools, but if you prefer the direct route, you can also submit a resume via www.jefferies.com/careers. If you are called into the offices, expect "two to three rounds of interviews." And anticipate "a series of interviews with an analyst/associate, then a vice president and finally a managing director." But be ready to prove yourself. Jefferies has a "strong entrepreneurial culture, and this is often the hardest criteria to meet — and to demonstrate that you have these skills," notes one respondent.

OUR SURVEY SAYS

Own it

The Jefferies culture emphasises "common ownership" where "partnership is key." They're also "aggressive" and "client- and solution-oriented," say sources. Insiders also enjoy some very employee-oriented perks. The bank offers "reduced gym membership," "breakfast provided," "lunch allowance," "car service home," "a 5 per cent discount when buying Jefferies stock" and even "showers at the office." But one contact says that Jefferies should "reinstate the 15 per cent discount for employee stock purchases-the change to 5 per cent was one of the worst decisions in terms of morale-building in the firm." The insider goes on to add that the bank "needs to make their compensation structure more transparent and reward/promote individuals based on their ability rather than headline their years of experience."

As far as day-to-day life in the Jefferies offices, expect to be dressing "formal always" in the office and clocking in about "60 to 70" hours per week — one insider reports coming in on the weekends "about once a month."

Visit **Vault Europe's Finance Career Channel** at **www.vault.com/europe** for insider firm profiles, employee surveys of finance professionals in Europe, message boards, job listings, expert finance career advice, insider salary information and more.

VAULT CAREER LIBRARY **243**

Lexicon Partners

No. 1 Paternoster Square
London, EC4M 7DX
United Kingdom
Phone: + 44 (0) 20 7653 6000
Fax: +44 (0) 20 7653 6001
www.lexiconpartners.com

EUROPEAN LOCATION

London (Global HQ)

DEPARTMENTS

Capital Raising
Corporate Strategy
Mergers & Acquisitions
Utilities and Infrastructure

THE STATS

Employer Type: Private Company
Chairman: Cliff Hampton
2006 Employees: 66
No. of Offices: 2

PLUSES

Plenty of business
Good reputation

MINUSES

Young
Small firm

EMPLOYMENT CONTACT

www.lexiconpartners.com/contact.htm

THE BUZZ
WHAT EMPLOYEES AT OTHER FIRMS ARE SAYING

- "Superior boutique"
- "Obscure"

THE SCOOP

One office, three sectors, six principles

The small, closely-held Lexicon Partners is relatively young. It was formed in 2000 as an independent corporate advisory firm focusing on the financial services sector; its founders had worked together at Phoenix Securities Limited and in the Financial Institutions Group at Donaldson, Lufkin & Jenrette International. Lexicon's business expanded in 2004 when it hired a utilities team to lead the firm into the utilities and infrastructure sectors. Since its inception, Lexicon has advised on more than 80 completed transactions with a combined market value of more than £20 billion. Although it operates from its head office in London, Lexicon has worked on global transactions for clients in the UK, US, continental Europe, Africa, Asia and Australia.

Wholly owned by its partners and employees, Lexicon focuses on six principles: industry specialisation, independence, personal touch, experience, flexibility and partnership. Lexicon's services include public and private M&A advisory, equity and debit capital raising, and other corporate finance advisory services. It was ranked the Number Four European M&A Boutique of 2006 by *Financial News*.

Law and order

In June 2006 Lexicon teamed with one of the legal market's most respected management consultants, Alan Hodgart, to form a joint venture aimed at advising firms on potential IPOs and fundraisings. Together Hodgart and Lexicon developed a three-step process for an IPO, private placement or private equity sale. The process starts with an initial assessment, followed by advice on structural reorganisation (including changes to partner remunerations). The last step would be a "road show," a series of presentations designed to inform and attract potential investors. According to Hodgart, the model's strength lies in the addition of his legal market knowledge — a factor missing from many other advisory services.

Big deal (s)

Focusing on three industry sectors still gives Lexicon plenty of business. Among its notable transactions in 2006: the £5.7 billion acquisition of AWG by Lexicon client Osprey Consortium; the £211 million float of LSL Property Services plc on the London Stock Exchange; the £2.8 billion acquisition of Associated British Ports by Lexicon client Admiral Consortium; the $825 million acquisition of EBS by Lexicon client ICAP; and the £200 million sale by Barclays Private Equity of Cabot Financial to Nikko Principal Investments (Lexicon advised Cabot, a Barclays holding).

sit **Vault Europe's Finance Career Channel** at **www.vault.com/europe** for insider firm ofiles, employee surveys of finance professionals in Europe, message boards, job tings, expert finance career advice, insider salary information and more.

VAULT CAREER LIBRARY 245

When buyers began nosing around Provident Financial plc, a UK lender to low-income households, it brought Lexicon on board for advice. Buyers have specifically targeted Provident's UK auto insurance operation, which Provident considers a non-core business. Still, it covers 455,000 policyholders and is valued at approximately £188 million. Anxious to boost profits and stock prices, analysts suggest that Provident — with Lexicon's help — is likely to go forward with the sale in spring 2007.

GETTING HIRED

To find out more about career opportunities at Lexicon Partners, visit the company's web site at www.lexiconpartners.com/contact.htm.

Lloyds TSB Group plc

25 Gresham Street
London, EC2V 7HN
United Kingdom
Phone: +44 (0) 20 7626 1500
Fax: +44 (0) 20 7489 3484
www.lloydstsbgroup.co.uk

EUROPEAN LOCATIONS

Offices worldwide

DEPARTMENTS

Central Support Functions
Group Finance
Insurance & Investments
IT & Operations
Retail Bank
Wholesale & International Bank

THE STATS

Employer Type: Public Company
Ticker Symbol: LLOY (LSE); LYG (NYSE)
Chairman: Sir Victor Blank
2006 Net Income: £5,537 million (FYE 12/06)
2005 Net Income: £5,671 million (FYE 12/05)
2006 Employees: 67,000
No. of Offices: 2,000 branches

KEY COMPETITORS

Abbey
Barclays Bank
HBOS
HSBC Holdings
RBS

PLUSES

"Progressive and entrepreneurial culture"

MINUSES

"Hierarchical"

EMPLOYMENT CONTACT

www.lloydstsbjobs.com/career_oppor
tunities.asp

THE BUZZ
WHAT EMPLOYEES AT OTHER FIRMS ARE SAYING

- "Very good for retail and insurance"
- "Not a prestigious image"

Visit the Vault Finance Career Channel at **www.vault.com/finance** — with insider firm profiles, message boards, the Vault Finance Job Board and more.

VAULT CAREER LIBRARY 247

THE SCOOP

A world history lesson

Lloyds TSB Group was formed in 1995 with the merger of Lloyds Bank and the Trustee Savings Bank. Lloyds Bank was first started in 1765 by John Taylor and Sampson Lloyd in Birmingham, England. Two sons of the original partners formed Barnetts Hoares Hanbury and Lloyd in London, which became a part of the Lloyds Banking Company.

By 1923, Lloyds Bank had made dozens of takeovers and by the early 1990s, Lloyds had offices in 30 countries around the world — from Argentina to the United States. The bank's significant role as the National Bank of New Zealand was reinforced by the 1994 takeover of the Rural Bank, making Lloyds the leading provider of agricultural finance. Trustee Savings Bank (TSB) was created in 1985 by an Act of Parliament that merged all UK savings banks under TSB Bank plc, but had older origins in a savings bank founded in 1810 by Henry Duncan in Ruthwell, Dumfriesshire, Scotland.

Shakers and deal-makers

In August 1995, Cheltenham & Gloucester (C&G) joined the Lloyds Bank Group, which merged with TSB Group to form what is now known as the Lloyds TSB Group plc. All of the TSB and Lloyds Bank branches in England and Wales were rebranded Lloyds TSB in June 1999, while bank branches in Scotland came under the new brand of Lloyds TSB Scotland. The insurance provider Scottish Widows joined the Group in March 2000, creating one of the United Kingdom's largest providers of life, pensions and unit trust products.

Then, in October 2003, Lloyds TSB Group sold subsidiary NBNZ Holdings Limited, comprising the Group's New Zealand banking and insurance operations, to Australia and New Zealand Banking Group Limited. It also sold its Argentinean business to Banco Patagonia Sudameris S.A and its Colombian business to Primer Banco del Istmo, S.A. in July 2004. In December 2005, the firm announced a deal to sell its credit card business Goldfish to Morgan Stanley Bank for £175 million in cash.

Fast-growing Islamic banking market

Lloyds TSB became Britain's first high street bank, in March 2005, to offer mortgage services compatible with Islamic Shar'ia law. The firm clearly sought a piece of the country's massive market of Muslim customers, following in the footsteps of the Islamic Bank of Britain that opened in London in September 2004, offering the same service.

Then, less than a year later, in June 2006, following a successful test run, Lloyds TSB launched a range of Islamic financial services across Britain, enabling the country's population of two million Muslims to access current accounts and mortgages and observe Islamic Shar'ia law in all of the bank's 2,000 branches. Muslims are forbidden to earn interest, or Riba, and similar financial services catering to their needs will follow, including an Islamic student account.

Paul Sherrin, head of Islamic financial services at Lloyds TSB, said "Muslims across Britain will be able to use our Islamic banking services wherever they live. We're now the largest provider of Islamic banking across the UK." The Islamic current account and Islamic mortgage comply with Islamic law by avoiding the payment of interest. The current account offers no credit interest and no overdraft facility, but provides a debit card and does not charge a fee or require a minimum balance.

The funds held by Lloyds TSB on all Islamic current accounts will be held in accordance with Islamic law and will not be invested in industries that are not permitted in Islam. In order to ensure that the current account and mortgage are fully compliant with Islamic law, Lloyds TSB has consulted with a board of renowned Islamic scholars who have advised on all aspects of Islamic finance law. Also, in January 2007, Lloyds TSB Corporate Markets completed one of the largest Islamic finance deals in the UK to date by refinancing the purchase by two Kuwaiti investment firms of a prestigious London building, providing funding of at least £100 million.

Philanthropy and the community

The Lloyds TSB Foundation for England and Wales is a grant-making trust that works with charities and charitable organisations "to play a fuller role in communities throughout England and Wales" — focusing on smaller, community-based charities. Officially stated exclusions are individuals and "the promotion of religion". Also, the trust does not fund animals and animal welfare, the environment or medical research. In 2006, the organisation announced an income of £24.8 million, a 10 per cent gain from the foundation's 2005 income.

As one of the largest charitable causes for grant endowments in the UK, The Lloyds TSB Foundation takes a "local approach, focusing on assisting charities aimed at helping handicapped and low-income citizens to more actively participate in their communities through social projects, education and training."

The customer is always right

In January 2006, Lloyds TSB clearly improved customer relations by canceling the use of scripted dialogues by call centre staff. Prior to the move, a whopping 90 per cent of Lloyds TSB customers had indicated that they would prefer if the bank's call centre staff did not read from prepared prompts. Since then, Lloyds call centre workers have been engaging in actual conversations with customers.

GETTING HIRED

Foot in the door

There are a number of routes into Lloyds TSB. For graduates, industrial placements and interns, applications are taken online from September. For more general roles and positions adverts are placed on the Lloyds TSB web site at www.lloydstsbjobs.com/career_opportunities.asp. Insiders agree it is easier to land a job at Lloyds after having a summer internship, but it is far from required, as many current graduates and employees did not intern at Lloyds TSB. However those that did intern spoke highly of the experience. One contact says his internship involved working on the management of private banking clients portfolios (and overall) the work was quite diverse." The experience, he adds, "certainly helped me in getting back into the organisation, as I knew how the bank operated."

While some insiders maintain that Lloyds TSB is not an overly selective firm, one associate says the company is "in an aggressive growth phase — arguably UK's fastest growing institution — so their recruitment is very selective at present." Sources say the interview and selection process is relatively standard and potential hires are subject to competency tests. A contact describes his hiring experience as a "very straightforward process."

OUR SURVEY SAYS

The real deal

The culture within the firm is widely described as "serious" and "hierarchical." But one insider says, "The culture is one of change and progression - this has developed over the last two years. Previously, a more reactive culture existed." An associate adds that it's a "progressive and entrepreneurial culture that embraces change (and an) intellectually challenging working environment."

Money talks

The level of satisfaction with work hours is high among those surveyed. One associate says, "Lloyds TSB has a very good work/life balance. There is little pressure (for) the need to work long hours, and the culture dictates that very often it is a 9 a.m. to 5 p.m. (experience)." Overall, sources rank their compensation as average and are satisfied with their benefits options.

Always room for change

One contact says maternity pay is an area the bank could improve upon and needs to offer "better maternity leave pay and more flexibility around return to work- [such as] two days a week for a month and then so on." Another employee thinks more attention should be paid to commuters, and banks should "take people's commuting times into consideration and arrange hours around this — or pay travel," he suggests. However, as one junior associate succinctly says, "The hours are reasonable [and the] money is okay for starting out."

One survey respondent says: "The bank needs to focus on becoming more international in reach and focus on developing its investment bank product expertise."

Meet the bosses

Overall, the managerial side of Lloyds TSB is highly rated. As one associate puts it, "The new senior management that the firm is bringing in is making for a more proactive, challenging environment. The (new) talent coming through will benefit immensely."

A relatively new hire describes his experience positively, saying, "There is very good exposure to senior members of the organisation and these people are more than willing to take time out of their hectic schedules to meet with us." As one insider reports, "Everyone I have ever met (here) has been very helpful and friendly."

Training is an important part of working for a big firm and the opportunity for further training is highly rated at Lloyds. But, as one associate notes, "You don't always get the time to attend." The firm is, however, given high marks for diversity across the board in terms of hiring, treatment and opportunities based on gender or ethnicity. One insider shares, "There are many women in senior management and at the executive level and I feel in no way penalised for being female." Another associate feels encouraged by the "diversity of activity available to work on".

Visit Vault Europe's Finance Career Channel at www.vault.com/europe for insider firm profiles, employee surveys of finance professionals in Europe, message boards, job listings, expert finance career advice, insider salary information and more.

VAULT CAREER LIBRARY 251

MCC SpA

Via Piemonte, 51
Rome, 00187
Italy
Phone: +39 (0) 6 47 911
Fax: +39 (0) 6 47 913130
www.mcc.it

DEPARTMENTS

Factoring
Industrial Credit
Leasing
Structured Finance

THE STATS

Employer Type: Subsidiary of
CAPITALIA Group
Ticker Symbol: CAP (Borsa Italia)
CEO: Cesare Caletti
No. of Offices: 2

KEY COMPETITORS

Intesa Sanpaolo
Mediobanca
UniCredit

PLUSES

Sophisticated

MINUSES

Little opportunity outside Italy

EMPLOYMENT CONTACT

www.mcc.it/english_version/pagina_
curriculum/

THE BUZZ
WHAT EMPLOYEES AT OTHER FIRMS ARE SAYING

- "Wealth"
- "Unknown"

Visit the Vault Finance Career Channel at **www.vault.com/finance**—with insider firm
profiles, message boards, the Vault Finance Job Board and more.

V/\ULT CAREER LIBRARY 253

THE SCOOP

A long and winding road

Post WWII industrialisation in Italy created the need for a banking system that would support small and medium-sized companies. In 1952 the Italian government established a state agency suitably named Mediocredito Centrale and charged with the all-important task of providing financing for businesses. Mediocredito Centrale managed the government's subsidized loan programs and helped Italian companies with financing for exports and international business.

In 1994 Mediocredito Centrale shifted from a public development bank to a market financial services bank, becoming a joint-stock company. Five years later, after Italy's banks were privatised, it was acquired by Banca di Roma (later Bancaroma), one of Italy's biggest banking groups. Renamed Mediocredito di Roma, the bank continued to develop its capital market and structured finance activities.

In 2000 the bank underwent another name change, becoming Mediocredito Centrale. Then, in 2002, the bank holding company known as Capitalia Gruppo Bancario was created through the merger of Gruppo Bancaroma and Bipop-Carire Group — and Mediocredito became known as MCC, a wholly owned subsidiary of Capitalia. Today Capitalia is Italy's fourth-largest banking group, with 28,203 employees and 1,948 branches around the world.

Capitalia's other subsidiaries include Banca di Roma, Bipop Carire and Banco di Sicilia. It also owns the asset management and insurance businesses of FinecoGroup. The Capitalia Group is partially owned by Dutch bank ABN AMRO, which is part of a shareholder's pact that holds approximately 30 per cent of the group. MCC has only two offices, in Rome and Milan.

Getting it together

Reorganisation was on Capitalia's agenda for 2005 and 2006. At the beginning of 2007, the group declared its "operational synergy improvement" was in place for the coming year. At MCC these changes included operational integrations with Fineco's leasing business and incorporation of Capitalia's leasing and factoring businesses. The aim was to create a specialty bank, focused on corporate credit activities. MCC was also realigned to focus on sophisticated credit services like project and acquisition finance, industrial credit, subsidised credit, leasing and factoring, especially for mid-corporate customers. To lighten its load, Capitalia relieved MCC of its capital market, investment banking and M&A advisory activities.

Four plus one

MCC's business is divided into four main sectors. Industrial credit provides assistance, consulting and financial support for small and medium-sized investment programs in Italy and elsewhere. Leasing offers medium-term financing for clients renting capital goods and real estate for entrepreneurial purposes. In its factoring sector MCC acts as an account receivable, carrying out cash flow and receivables operations for its clients. Finally, structured finance provides servicing and advisory for the structuring of corporate, shipping, acquisition finance and real estate finance operations, as well as project and export finance.

Since coming under Capitalia's umbrella MCC has also developed a strong research division, which focuses on in-depth economic, industrial and company analysis linked to MCC's business and development. The research department uses its industry sector expertise to understand national and international economic trends and to identify new business opportunities for the bank.

Holding hands with Holland

Dutch banking giant ABN AMRO faced a big decision in September 2006: should it remain part of the shareholder pact that holds a significant stake in MCC's parent company Capitalia, or should it sell its shares? Waiting until three days before the decision deadline, ABN AMRO — Capitalia's largest investor — finally decided to hold its 7.7 per cent within the shareholder pact. It will remain a shareholder until July 2008, when it may again consider a share sale. ABN AMRO CEO Rijkman Groenink issued a statement saying his decision to hold on to Capitalia shares "underlines the importance of Italy to ABN AMRO."

Ask the factoring experts

Although much of its M&A advisory business has been spun off into Capitalia's hands, MCC still uses its expertise to advise corporations on deals. It made news in December 2006 when it was hired by Apax Partners, an international private equity group, to advise on its purchase of a majority stake in Confarma. As a holding company, Confarma controls 60 per cent of Farmafactoring, a leader in the factoring of non-recourse receivables toward the Italian public healthcare system. At the close of the deal, Apax — who also brought Merrill Lynch in for advice - owned 87 per cent of Confarma's share capital.

Movin' on up

In January 2007 MCC announced that Standard & Poor's had upgraded its long- and short-term ratings, to A from A-1 and to A-1 from A-2, respectively. At the same time, parent company Capitalia's ratings — both long- and short-term — moved from A-1 to A.

Visit **Vault** Europe's Finance Career Channel at www.vault.com/europe for insider firm profiles, employee surveys of finance professionals in Europe, message boards, job listings, expert finance career advice, insider salary information and more.

VAULT CAREER LIBRARY 255

According to MCC and Capitalia, these ratings changes were based on the group's streamlining and operating improvement. Both MCC and Capitalia's outlook ratings were listed as Stable.

Marco? Fanno.

Economist Marco Fanno's legacy lives on in Italy, thanks to a prominent scholarship programme in his name. MCC runs the Associazione Borsisti Marco Fanno, a nonprofit operation that organises the winners of the Marco Fanno scholarship, past and present. The Associazione — or the Association — keeps winners in touch with each other, providing opportunities for idea exchanges and national debates on topics of economics, finance and business. It also holds conferences and seminars, publishes scholarly papers, launches economic study initiatives and sponsors research.

GETTING HIRED

For more information about career opportunities at Mediocredito Centrale, visit the company's web site at www.mcc.it/english_version/pagina_curriculum.

VAULT CAREER LIBRARY

Mediobanca Banca di Credito Finanziario S.p.A

Piazzetta E. Cuccia, 1
20121 Milan
Italy
Phone: +39 (0) 2 882 91
Fax: +39 (0) 2 882 93 67
www.mediobanca.it

EUROPEAN LOCATIONS

Frankfurt
Milan
Paris
Rome

DEPARTMENTS

Equity Investment
Private Banking
Private Equity
Retail Financial Services
Trust Business
Wholesale Banking

THE STATS

Employer Type: Public Company
Ticker Symbol: MB (Borsa Italia)
Chairman: Gabriele Galateri di Genola
General Manager: Alberto Nagel
2006 Revenue: € 1.511,7 (FYE 6/06)
2005 Revenue: € 1.156,6 (FYE 6/05)
2006 Employees: 415
No. of Offices: 4

PLUSES

Specialised in midsized firms

MINUSES

Regional

EMPLOYMENT CONTACT

www.mediobanca.it

THE BUZZ
WHAT EMPLOYEES AT OTHER FIRMS ARE SAYING

- "Local superstar"
- "Unknown" [outside of Europe]

Visit the Vault Finance Career Channel at **www.vault.com/finance**—with insider firm
profiles, message boards, the Vault Finance Job Board and more.

VAULT CAREER LIBRARY 257

THE SCOOP

Postwar banking

As part of Italy's post-WWII rebuilding, Mediobanca was created by a joint initiative organised by Banca Commerciale Italiana, Credito Italiano and Banco di Roma. Their goal was to provide medium-term financing for Italian manufacturers and to create a link between investors and Italian industries struggling to recover from the war. From its birth in 1944 to 1973, Mediobanca was limited to medium-term credit. Then, in October 1973, the bank changed its mission to include financing on terms of up to 20 years.

Admitted to the Italian stock market in 1956, Mediobanca revamped its ownership structure in 1988, splitting its shares between the public and private sectors. Founding banks BCI, Credito Italiano and Banco di Roma reduced their combined holding from 56.9 per cent of the share capital to 25 per cent. Then, in 2000, BCI sold its interest in Mediobanca to other members of a block shareholders' syndicate, which currently includes such major Italian finance houses as Capitalia and UniCredit. Today Mediobanca offers underwriting, M&A advisory, wholesale banking and financial advisory to its corporate clients. It provides loans, credit and retail banking services to individual clients. In addition to its main office in Milan, Mediobanca has offices in Frankfurt, Rome and Paris and business interests in Germany, in addition to France and Spain.

Expansion planned

In March 2006 Mediobanca officials told investors the bank planned to expand its retail financial services and private banking sectors by acquiring other companies and had no plans to acquire competing investment banks. The growth plan is focused mainly on France, where Mediobanca has been present since 2004, but will include targets in Spain and Germany.

Compass, Mediobanca's retail financial services unit, is said to be investigating possible acquisition targets. In the private banking arena, Mediobanca launched Banca Esperia, a joint venture with Mediolanum S.p.A. In November 2006 Mediobanca bought ABN Amro Holdings NV's private banking operations in Monaco for an estimated €40 million. However, corporate and investment banking won't be left out of the expansion plans. Mediobanca officials say they plan to expand those businesses into France, Spain and Germany, after which they will look at possible partnerships in the United Kingdom.

Mediobanca is on a three-year business plan aimed at growth and higher profits. For 2006, the first year of the plan, the bank said it exceeded its own expectations, reporting a 31 per cent increase in income and a 40 per cent increase in profit as compared to the previous year. The three-year plan had set target growth of 13 and 15 per cent, respectively, for these figures. Wholesale banking was the growth leader for 2006, generating 45 per cent of Mediobanca's consolidated income.

Fiat takes off

Automaker Fiat, a significant member of Mediobanca's shareholders' syndicate, sold a 34 per cent interest in Ferrari to the bank in 2002. Mediobanca, in turn, sold the shares to other financial institutions and investors. In September 2006 Fiat exercised its call option to buy back the Ferrari shares, paying Mediobanca €590.4 million to claim an 85 per cent stake in Ferrari. That deal netted Mediobanca more than €150 million.

Studying hard

Mediobanca's robust research division turns out a number of reports, studies and surveys focused on Italian and European business, including analysis of Italian privatisation, small business reports and competitiveness reports. In October 2006 it released the 2006 edition of Le Principali Societa Italiane, which provides two years' worth of data about prominent Italian companies in industry, trading, public services, banking, insurance, leasing, factoring and finance.

Cases closed

In December 2006 Mediobanca Deputy Chairman Cesare Geronzi and Director Roberto Colaninno were suspended from the board of directors following their convictions in a bankruptcy case related to collapse of real estate company Italcase-Bagaglino in the late 1990s. A Brescian court sentenced Colaninno to four years and one month in jail. Geronzi got off with just one year and eight months. Prosecutors argued that the Italian bankers knew Italcase-Bagaglino was in financial straits, but said nothing so they could gain property as collateral. However, at a general meeting in January 2007, Mediobanca's shareholders' syndicate unanimously voted to reinstate Geronzi and Colaninno, saying, "The events hitherto were not such as to prejudice the relationship of trust" between the bank and the convicted executives.

Also in January 2007, a Milanese court upheld Mediobanca's appeal against a 2005 ruling in which the bank and co-defendant Fondiaria-SAI were ordered to pay €3.4 million in damages to Italian company Promofinan for alleged failure to launch a compulsory takeover bid for Fondiaria. The damages part of the ruling was reversed and Promofinan was ordered to refund Mediobanca's legal expenses in the matter.

Visit **Vault Europe's Finance Career Channel** at www.vault.com/europe for insider firm profiles, employee surveys of finance professionals in Europe, message boards, job listings, expert finance career advice, insider salary information and more.

VAULT CAREER LIBRARY 259

Eyes on the prize

Each year Mediobanca offers the Mediobanca Prize, awarded to medium-sized Italian companies with the best growth rates. According to the bank, the prize is meant to identify and reward Italy's most dynamic midsized companies, especially those with the potential to become larger corporations. Applications for the prize are reviewed by Mediobanca's research department, which makes recommendations to an independent committee. Of course, Mediobanca isn't just trying to reward others — its commitment to Italy's midsized companies underscores its plan to boost its own growth in the mid-corporate segment. Mediobanca says it plans to build an integrated, dedicated platform of services for midsized businesses, offering specialised expertise from its headquarters in Milan.

GETTING HIRED

For more information about careers and graduate opportunities at Mediobanca, visit the company's web site at www.mediobanca.it.

Natixis

45, rue Saint-Dominique
75007, Paris
France
Phone: +33 1 58 32 30 00
www.natixis.com

EUROPEAN LOCATIONS

Paris (Global HQ)
Locations in: Austria, Belgium,
Bulgaria, Croatia, Czech Republic,
Denmark, Estonia, Germany,
Hungary, Ireland, Italy, Latvia,
Lithuania, Luxembourg,
Netherlands, Poland, Portugal,
Romania, Russia, Slovakia,
Slovenia, Spain, Sweden,
Switzerland, Turkey, Ukraine

DEPARTMENTS

Corporate & Investment Banking
Asset Management
Private Equity and Private Banking
Services
Receivables management
Retail Banking

THE STATS

Employer Type: Public Company
Ticker Symbol: KN (Euronext Paris)
Chairman of the Supervisory Board:
Charles Milhaud
Executive Chairman: Philippe Dupont
CEO: Dominique Ferrero
2006 Net Banking Income:
€7,322m
2006 Gross Operating Income:
€2,354m
2006 Net Income (Group share):
€2,158m
2005 Net Banking Income:
€6,006m
2005 Gross Operating Income:
€1,921m
2005 Net Income (Group share):
€1,727m
No. of Employees: 23,000

KEY COMPETITORS

ABN AMRO
HSBC France
Société Générale

PLUSES

Firm has environmental
consciousness

MINUSES

Regional reputation despite global
footprint

THE BUZZ
WHAT EMPLOYEES AT OTHER FIRMS ARE SAYING

(Click on Human Resources link)
• "Wealth"
• "Have not heard of"

EMPLOYMENT CONTACT

www.natixis.com

Visit the Vault Finance Career Channel at **www.vault.com/finance**—with insider firm
profiles, message boards, the Vault Finance Job Board and more.

VAULT CAREER LIBRARY 261

THE SCOOP

Product of France

Despite a name that one company information site says "sounds Greek", Paris-based Natixis is rather French. The firm was formed in November 2006 when Groupe Banque Populaire, one of France's largest retail banking networks, and Groupe Caisse d'Epargne inked a deal to form Natixis. What they created is as a joint subsidiary that combines Natexis Banques Populaires, a leader in the French property leasing market and a bookrunner for both syndicated loans and acquisition financing in France, and various Caisse Nationale des Caisses d'Epargne subsidiaries in finance and investment banking, specialist banking services and private asset management sectors.

The result of the deal, Natixis, is controlled by the banks' two holding companies, each holding 34.4 per cent. The bank focuses on mid- and large-sized European companies. Subsidiary Natixis Interepargne provides employee savings plan management services to French companies. Coface, another subsidiary, is one of the world's leading providers of credit insurance and credit management services. Natixis operates in 68 countries, including the Americas, Africa, Asia and Oceania.

Groupe Banque Populaire and Groupe Caisse d'Epargne have equal presence on a supervisory board. Chairmanship of Natixis will alternate between executives from each company; the first chairman of the supervisory board is Caisse d'Epargne's chairman, Charles Milhaud, while Banque Populaire's chairman, Philippe Dupont, is the first chairman of the management board.

Aiming high

Natixis participated in several major airline financing deals in 2006. Natixis Transport Finance (a wholly owned Natixis subsidiary) joined with Calyon to finance the down payment of seven Airbus A321 aircraft for the Russian national airline Aeroflot in April 2006. The plan calls for a long-term financing programme combining export credits and commercial loans, allowing Aeroflot to fully finance the cost of the planes. Natixis Transport Finance will also act as the deal's transaction agent. The $400 million deal represents the first down-payment financing arrangement ever implemented for a Russian airline. Natixis Transport Finance was also a joint arranger with HSH Nordbank for the $250 million loan to easyJet to finance Airbus A320s delivered between 2005 and 2011.

In October 2006, Natixis Transport Finance and DVB bank teamed up to arrange the $96 million financing of three Boeing 737s to Alaska Airlines. Natixis Transport Finance was the sole lead arranger in a $120 million 10-year financing for China Southern Airlines for three Airbus A320-200s. The bank also makes more down-to-earth investments, such as taking the lead with Standard Chartered Bank in the $810 million funding of the Ghana Cocoa Board in September 2006 in the largest structured soft commodity deal in Africa.

The world is our oyster

Before the creation of Natixis, Natexis Banques Populaires decided to make sustainable development issues a part of its corporate and institutional banking and markets sector, creating a team responsible for buying and selling European carbon dioxide quotas on the Amsterdam Stock Exchange. Natexis Banques Populaires also increased its financing of environmentally-friendly wind energy parks at home and abroad.

Natixis has continued this trend, serving as lead arranger with Caja Madrid to finance the construction of two thermoelectric solar plants developed by Abengola that will be built near Seville. The project will have a 302MW capacity, making it one of the largest European solar power plants. The bank also served as lead financer with Caixa BI, funding the construction of two wind farm portfolios in France in September 2006. The bank also practises what it funds, promoting waste reduction programmes for its offices, researching carpooling systems for its workers and focusing on purchasing Earth-friendly products.

French laundry

Natixis signed a €1 million deal with Norkom Technologies to implement Norkom financial crime and compliance software, thus strengthening bank security against money laundering and scams in early 2006. The bank has been rolling out the software throughout its French branch offices and will rely on behavioural analysis, customer profiling and case management to prevent fraud. The Norkom technology will instantly detect suspicious banking activity and send alerts to a special team of bank investigators. Implementing the software is part of Natixis' overall strategy to comply with tough European anti-money laundering rules and will allow it to streamline its compliance systems.

Don't jump the gun

After the merger, Natixis is looking to expand overseas, which should include organic growth as well as retail banking acquisitions funded by its parent banks. In 2005, Natixis generated $3.2 billion in revenue outside France, and looks to have foreign revenue account for more than half of revenue by 2010. Natixis is also open to other European banks joining the group, but has denied rumours that the joint venture is a precursor to a merger of Banques Populaires and Caisses d'Epargne.

Visit **Vault Europe's Finance Career Channel** at www.vault.com/europe for insider firm profiles, employee surveys of finance professionals in Europe, message boards, job listings, expert finance career advice, insider salary information and more.

VAULT CAREER LIBRARY **263**

GETTING HIRED

To find out how to pursue a career at Natixis, go www.natixis.com and click on the Human Resources link. Here, you can find useful information, such as career development and training opportunities at Natixis, current vacancies, internships and work placements as well as entry-level positions for students and recent graduates, applications, information about events where prospective applicants can meet employees and recruiters of the firm, and valuable information on Natixis' business area and its diversified lines of work.

Petercam

Place Sainte-Gudule 19
Brussels, 1000
Belgium
Phone: +32 2229 6311
Fax: +32 2229 6598
www.petercam.be

DEPARTMENTS

Corporate Finance
Institutional Asset Management
Institutional Sales & Research
Private Banking

THE STATS

Employer Type: Private Company
Chairman: Jean Peterbroeck
2006 Net Revenue: N/A
2005 Net Revenue: $189 million
2005 Employees: 364
No. of Offices: 10

KEY COMPETITORS

ABN AMRO Belgium
BACOB Bank
Fortis

PLUSES

Growing fast

MINUSES

Regional

EMPLOYMENT CONTACT

www.petercam.com (See "jobs" link)

THE BUZZ
WHAT EMPLOYEES AT OTHER FIRMS ARE SAYING

- "Strong"
- "Have not heard of"

Visit the Vault Finance Career Channel at **www.vault.com/finance**—with insider firm profiles, message boards, the Vault Finance Job Board and more.

VAULT CAREER LIBRARY 265

THE SCOOP

Assets in motion

Owned by 17 active partners, Petercam is one of the leading banks in the Benelux region. The firm comprises four sectors: institutional sales and research, asset management, corporate finance and private banking. The firm acts as an institutional sales and markets advisor for both Belgian and international clients, and handles trading, execution and settlement of orders in stocks, bonds and derivatives products.

The institutional sales team boasts an extensive client base drawn from the UK, France, Germany, Luxembourg, Switzerland, Italy, Scandinavia, US and Canada — a base that allows Petercam the strongest placing capacity for Belgian equities. The asset management department does portfolio management for private and institutional clients, as well as creation and management of investment funds.

In recent years, the institutional asset management sector has seen tremendous growth, with €8.5 billion assets under management by the end of 2005. At the end of October 2006, the Petercam Group had €15 billion in total assets under management, approximately €9 billion of which were managed on behalf of private clients. Among its other offerings, the corporate finance sector deals with stock exchange acquisitions, M&A and advisory services.

Upwardly mobile

Headquartered in Brussels, Petercam has multiple branches throughout Europe, as well as an office in New York on Madison Avenue. And plans for growth are underway. In the firm's 2005 annual report, Corporate Finance Managing Director Pierre Drion said, "From our New York office, we are observing growing interest from US investors for Belgian and Dutch securities. This is the reason why we are planning to strengthen our presence in New York."

In 2005, asset management was Petercam's strongest business unit. As for corporate finance, 2005, according to the firm's annual report, "was a good year … but not a record year, unlike our private and institutional asset management activities." For 2005, Petercam made a net profit of more than €40 million, double what the firm made in 2004. The annual report cites a number of significant transactions in 2005, such as the floatation of Elia, Zetes and Telenet. Petercam also advised Keytrade Bank on its sale to Crédit Agricole.

Near the end of 2005, Mergermarket completed a ranking of the top-10 largest European M&A deals of the last five years. Petercam made an appearance at No.5 for co-advising (with Goldman Sachs) Almanij NV on its sale to KBC Bank & Verzekering NV.

Circa 1968

The Petercam Group was formed by the merger of two foreign exchange brokers, Peterbroeck and van Campenhout, which in 1968 became the firm S.C.S. Peterbroeck, van Campenhout & CIE. The merged firm focused on stock broking and fund management, with a secondary interest in running foreign currency exchange outlets set up in several Belgian railway stations.

In 1990, one year after the firm entered the US market with the opening of a New York office, S.C.S. Peterbroeck, van Campenhout & CIE decided to transfer its stock market and foreign currency activities to two new and distinct limited liability companies called Petercam and Camrail. In 1994, the group took majority control of stockbrokers Pitti & Co s.a., thus gaining a presence in the city of Liege.

In 1995, after the takeover of activities of the stockbrokers Beeckmans Van Gaver, Petercam opened an office in Antwerp. In 1999, the firm sold its participation in KBC Petercam Derivatives to KBC, opening two new offices one in Ghent and one in Hasselt. The same year, Petercam extended its activities to the Netherlands by setting up Petercam Nederland N.V., an institutional sales and research and corporate finance firm.

In 2000, Petercam took full control of CEPA in Geneva, which became Petercam Banque Privée Suisse in 2002. Also that year, Petercam acquired a majority interest in Concerto Capital Ltd, a company based in both London and New York that specialises in hedge fund management and consultancy. The firm also opened an office in Paris that year. And in 2003, Petercam Nederland acquired a bank status in The Netherlands. That same year, Petercam S.A. took over Petercam Securities.

Recognition

The firm's mutual funds have won numerous accolades, including the Super Tijd Award for the best overall performance over five years and Standard & Poor's Ten Year Internationally Marketed Funds (Smaller Group) for best overall performance over 10 years. Petercam's other honours include the De Tijd Award for Best Fixed Income Manager over five years; Most Improved Benelux mid/small cap firm; first place in the Thomson Extel survey of Benelux mid/small caps sales; a second place ranking in the Thomson Extel survey of Benelux mid/small cap trading and a second place ranking for Benelux mid/small caps research.

In France, Investir magazine named Petercam the 2005 Best Foreign Fund Manager over five years. In March 2006, in its first year of attendance, Petercam also snagged two general banking awards at the annual Victoires des Sicav. At the top of the niche banking division, Petercam took the big prizes, coming in second behind SPGP. Also in 2006, Institutional Investor magazine ranked Petercam the No. 1 firm in the Benelux.

Visit Vault Europe's Finance Career Channel at www.vault.com/europe for insider firm profiles, employee surveys of finance professionals in Europe, message boards, job listings, expert finance career advice, insider salary information and more.

VAULT CAREER LIBRARY 267

Dedicated to its homeland

Petercam Partner Guy Lerminiaux believes that, on its own turf, Petercam has that special "savoir faire." In a March 2006 interview with De Standaard, Lerminiaux explained that few investment banks focus on Belgium, preferring to take their business to big banking centers like London and Paris - that's why Petercam comprises the vast majority of the Belgian banking market.

The Belgian equity funds that Petercam offers are definitely "European," as the euro has become universal and European stock markets have fused to form Euronext, but its mutual funds comprise anywhere from 30 to 75 per cent Belgian companies. Lerminiaux explains that, while the EU makes for a universal European banking scene, banking in Belgium is, "What we know." He adds: "It's the benchmark by which we measure our success."

As some industries simply don't exist in Belgium (i.e., energy, mining and certain luxury products), Petercam does invest beyond Belgium's borders. Nevertheless, where it can, Petercam tries to stay local. And, as Lerminiaux puts it: "Why invest in an Italian giant, when Belgium has a small, similar enterprise that performs better?"

Despite fluctuations in the European stock markets and a slowdown in the US market, as of June 2006 Petercam wasn't really changing its strategy. According to an interview with Boursorama, Jan Leroy, upper manager with Petercam Equity Management, said, "Au contraire. If we do that, it would cost us in terms of performance." The firm prides itself on paying close attention to business cycles and industries that have global development implications such as energy. As for investments in agriculture and telecom, Petercam tempers its involvement, claiming that those industries are no longer "riding high" within Europe.

Well-rounded M&A shop

Petercam also prides itself on offering comprehensive M&A advisory. From the evaluation of strategic alternatives to negotiating the final terms of a deal, the firm counsels clients in all kinds of transactions: trade sales, leveraged buyouts, acquisitions or disposals of minority or majority shareholdings, and public takeover bids. In addition to sell-side and buy-side assignments, Petercam's M&A advisory services include advice on shareholders structure, and assistance in the structuring and execution of public bids.

In March 2006, the firm served as financial advisor to The Mond Group — provider of logistics solutions to the chemical sector in the Benelux, Germany and France — when it was sold for €26.9 million to TDG Plc, a leading European logistics provider, listed on the London Stock Exchange. Only one month earlier, Petercam played a critical role in another deal — Club, a Belgian retail chain specialising in books and stationery, and

Proxis, Belgium's main web site for the sale of books and multimedia products, were sold to Distripar, a company owned by CNP, for €21,6 million.

As advisor to the selling shareholders, including Net Fund Europe and KBC Private Equity, Petercam counseled to organise a controlled auction procedure with a strict timetable to preserve a maximum of control over the sales process. And in January 2006, Petercam stood by Belgacom's side when it completed its acquisition of Telindus. Belgacom announced a public tender offer on all shares of Telindus back in September 2005. Telindus initially rejected Belgacom's approach and, in December 2005, France Telecom announced a counter offer. After Belgacom made a number of commitments to Telindus and increased its bid price to €594 million for 100 per cent of the shares, it successfully completed the acquisition.

GETTING HIRED

For more information on careers and graduate opportunities at Petercam, visit the company's web site at www.petercam.com and click on the Jobs link.

Visit **Vault Europe's Finance Career Channel** at **www.vault.com/europe** for insider firm profiles, employee surveys of finance professionals in Europe, message boards, job listings, expert finance career advice, insider salary information and more.

VAULT CAREER LIBRARY 269

RBC Capital Markets

One Queenhithe,
Thames Court
London EC4V 4DE
United Kingdom
Phone: +44 (0) 207 653 4000
71 Queen Victoria Street
London EC4V 4DE
United Kingdom
Phone: +44 (0) 207 489 1188
www.rbccm.com

EUROPEAN LOCATIONS

London (European HQ)
Amsterdam
Lausanne
Madrid

DEPARTMENTS

Global Credit
Global Investment Banking &
Equity
Global Markets
Global Research
National Clients Group

THE STATS

Employer Type: Subsidiary of RBC
Chairman: Anthony S. Fell
CEO: Charles Winograd
Co-Presidents: Doug McGregor and
Mark Standish
2006 Total Revenue: CAD$4.69
billion
2005 Total Revenue: CAD$4.06
billion
2006 Employees: 3,700
No. of Offices: 75 worldwide

KEY COMPETITORS

Morgan Stanley
Citigroup Global Markets
Credit Suisse

PLUSES

Lots of opportunity

MINUSES

Still establishing ground in Europe

EMPLOYMENT CONTACT

www.rbccm.com
(Click on "Careers" link in "About
Us" menu)

THE BUZZ
WHAT EMPLOYEES AT OTHER FIRMS ARE SAYING

- "Wealth"
- "Too regional"

THE SCOOP

R-E-S-P-E-C-T

Born in the Great White North, RBC Capital Markets is the corporate and investment banking arm of RBC, one of the largest diversified financial services companies in Canada and one of the top banks in North America. In February 2006, RBC was named Canada's Most Respected Corporation for the fourth year in a row in an annual survey conducted by Ipsos Reid for KPMG. In addition, RBC was ranked No. 1 in six of the nine categories measured by the survey Top of Mind Most Respected, Best Long Term Investment, Human Resources Management, Financial Performance, Corporate Social Responsibility and Corporate Governance. And, for the 11th consecutive year, RBC was named the top corporation in the category of Corporate Social Responsibility.

RBC Capital Markets offers products and services through five key business divisions: global investment banking and equity markets (corporate finance, mergers and acquisitions, equity capital markets, leveraged finance, syndicated finance, equity private placements), global markets (debt markets, foreign exchange, structured products, commodities), global credit, global research and a national clients group. The firm is well known for its middle-market investment banking and capital markets services, which include corporate finance; equity and debt origination; merger and acquisition advisory; equity, debt and foreign exchange; sales and trading; and a complete range of structured products.

RBC Capital Markets has 3,700 employees in 75 offices located around the world, in North America, the UK, Europe, Asia and Australia. RBC's employee numbers in the US have more than tripled since 2001, growing from 500 to more than 1,700. In 2006, RBC Capital Markets generated a net income of CAD$1.4 billion and CAD$4.69 billion in total revenue. Parent company, RBC had total revenue of CAD$20.6 billion in 2006 and one of the highest credit ratings of any financial institution.

As the leading underwriter in Canadian league tables for the year, the firm received the Financial Post's 2006 Dealmaker of the Year/Top Canadian Underwriter award. The newspaper also named RBC Capital Markets top debt and equity underwriter for 2006. Global Finance magazine recently named the firm the Best Bank in Canada as part of its listing of the World's Best Developed Market Banks in 2007. In July 2006, RBC was named Euromoney's Best Canadian Debt House, Best Canadian M&A House and Best Canadian Equity House.

Big shots

In 2006, for the third successive year, RBC Capital Markets was ranked by Bloomberg as one of the top-20 investment banks globally. The firm is 17th in the 2006 rankings, up one spot from the previous year. RBC Capital Markets is the only Canadian bank on the list. Specific to bond underwriting, Bloomberg ranks the firm 14th in the world, up from 15th a year prior. In equity underwriting, RBC ranks 14th, up from 18th in 2005. At the Euroweek Magazine Awards in 2006, RBC Capital Markets tied for the Best Lead Manager of Non-Core Dollar Bonds award and won the Most Impressive Bank in Other Currencies award.

RBC Capital Markets led the Canadian market taking seven first place rankings in Bloomberg's 2006 Canadian Capital Markets league tables. RBC Capital Markets ranked No. 1 in Canada Corporate Bonds, Canada Government Bonds, Maple Bonds, Canada Equity, Equity Linked & Preferred Offerings, Canada Equity Offerings, Canada IPO and Canada Syndicated Loans.

In 2006, the firm was ranked No. 40, out of 100, on Here Is The City's Best Places to Work in the Global Financial Markets 2006 survey. As lead underwriter on the largest IPO in North America in the summer of 2006, RBC Capital Markets gave its North American competitors a run for their money. The firm was lead underwriter on the hugely successful Canadian coffee and doughnut franchise Tim Hortons' $672 million IPO. Tim Hortons was spun off by Wendy's International. The Tim Horton score came on the heels of Southwestern Energy Corporation's $600 million follow-on offering, for which RBC Capital Markets also acted as lead underwriter.

Growth is excellent

In 2006 RBC Capital Markets became an approved nominated adviser (NOMAD) to the Alternative Investment Market (AIM), which is owned by the LSE and caters to junior mining, oil and gas companies. The firm quickly sprung into action closing its first AIM transaction in December, advising Australian-based uranium miner Berkeley Resources Ltd. on its new listing on the London exchange.

In Europe, RBC Capital Markets' infrastructure team is firing on all cylinders. In addition to landmark mandates such as the £8 billion Thames Water acquisition in the UK in early 2007, the team is focused on expanding into targeted European countries and developing its product platform. The firm's US investment banking business is operating at its highest performance levels ever. RBC Capital Markets acted as exclusive financial advisor to American organic grocery giant Whole Foods in its recent acquisition of Wild Oats Markets. This transaction is a huge win for RBC Capital Markets as it builds its US franchise and is an indication of how far the firm has progressed in the eyes of the US mid-market.

Revenue from RBC's UK and US operations exceed revenue from the firm's homeland Canadian operations. The firm has strong global capabilities in energy, mining, fixed income, structured products, infrastructure finance and alternative dollars. RBC says it has an active global US dollar investor base of over 4,700 accounts.

GETTING HIRED

For more information about careers or graduate opportunities at RBC, visit the company's web site at www.rbccm.com and click on the Careers link listed in the "About Us" menu.

Visit **Vault Europe's Finance Career Channel** at **www.vault.com/europe** for insider firm profiles, employee surveys of finance professionals in Europe, message boards, job listings, expert finance career advice, insider salary information and more.

VAULT CAREER LIBRARY 273

Sal. Oppenheim jr. & Cie

Unter Sachsenhausen 4
D-50667 Cologne
Germany
Phone: +49 (0) 221 145 01
Fax: +49 (0) 221 145 1512
www.oppenheim.de

EUROPEAN LOCATIONS

Cologne (HQ)
Austria
Belgium
Czech Republic
France
Germany
Ireland
Italy
Luxembourg
Netherlands
Portugal
Spain
Switzerland
United Kingdom

DEPARTMENTS

Asset Management
Corporate Finance
Financial Markets
Investment Banking
Private Banking

THE STATS

Employer Type: Private Company
Chairman: Georg Baron von Ullmann
First Deputy Chairman: Friedrich Carl
Freiherr von Oppenheim
2006 Net Income: €309 million
(FYE 12/06)
2005 Net Income: €283 million
(FYE 12/05)
No. of Employees: 3,490
No. of Offices: 20

KEY COMPETITORS

Berenberg
Julius Bär
Metzler seel Sohn & Co.
Pictet & Cie
UBS

PLUSES

Growing fast

MINUSES

"Compensation could be improved"

EMPLOYMENT CONTACT

www.oppenheim.com
(Click on "Careers" link)

THE BUZZ
WHAT EMPLOYEES AT OTHER FIRMS ARE SAYING

- "Meaningful player in the mid-German scene"
- "Snobby culture"

THE SCOOP

200 years of history

The largest family-owned private bank in Europe, Sal. Oppenheim jr. & Cie offers asset management and investment banking services to corporations and high-net-worth individuals. The Cologne, Germany-based bank has more than 20 offices in Germany and other European countries. In 2005, the 200 year-old-company started a period of enormous expansion, nearly doubling in size, both in terms of assets and employees, following its acquisition of BHF-BANK early that year.

Founded in 1789, Sal. Oppenheim began as a Bonn, Germany-based commissions and exchange house, which extended credit, dealt in commodities and provided foreign currency exchange. Nine years later, Sal. Oppenheim relocated its headquarters to Cologne. The bank's enterprising founder, Salomon Oppenheim Jr., was only 17 years old when he began his banking career, and successfully managed operations for most of his life. Upon his death in 1828, a tight succession plan saw management responsibilities shift to his wife, Therese, and their two sons, Simon and Abraham.

In 1904, though the bank shifted in structure from a general partnership to a limited partnership, it nevertheless remained firmly within the family. During the Nazi period, the bank was forced to adopt a new identity due to the Jewish origins of the founding family-this in spite of the fact that the family had converted to Christianity in the 1850s. The firm was renamed after Partner Robert Pfedmenges, who acted as a trustee for the Oppenheims, withdrawing to the background while the ownership structure remained intact. In 1947, the original family name was restored. Christopher Freiherr von Oppenheim, personally liable partner since January 2000, represents the seventh generation of Oppenheim bankers to serve as head of private banking.

Building (and rebuilding) Deutschland

Sal. Oppenheim has been involved in many of the most significant economic developments in Germany over the past 200 years. The firm has provided financing for many key infrastructure projects, including the construction of Germany's railway system and steam shipping on the Rhine, in addition to much of the country's 19th-century industrialisation.

The years after World War II were difficult for Germany's private bankers, whose numbers were reduced from more than 800 to a mere 225. Sal. Oppenheim, however, reemerged successfully. Its post-war activities included financing the German Auto Union, which later became Audi AG; the mining and steel industries of the Ruhr area; and the German insurance industry.

Visit **Vault Europe's Finance Career Channel** at **www.vault.com/europe** for insider firm profiles, employee surveys of finance professionals in Europe, message boards, job listings, expert finance career advice, insider salary information and more.

VAULT CAREER LIBRARY 275

Sal. Oppenheim scored a major deal in 1989 when it sold its majority holdings in the Colonia Insurance Company, the second-largest in Germany. Part of the proceeds flowed into its equity, which leapt from 180 million to one billion Deutschmarks. In 1999 the bank redefined its strategies, identifying investment banking and asset management as its core businesses. Due to its recent internationalisation policies, Sal. Oppenheim now boasts offices and subsidiaries in Luxembourg, Switzerland, Austria, the Czech Republic, the United Kingdom and Ireland.

Dutch treat

In early 2005, Sal. Oppenheim made what ranks as one of the most significant acquisitions in the history of German private banking, purchasing the core business of BHF-BANK from the Dutch ING group for €600 million, effectively doubling in size overnight. However, the bank has been careful to emphasise that the combined firm will not lose any of the individual strengths that it had been built upon. To this end, Sal. Oppenheim announced the integration would be accompanied by the launch of a "two-bank strategy," whereby both banks would retain their identities, decision-making authority and employees, along with a distinct market presence.

This dynamic growth strategy continued in 2006, taking key steps in Sal. Oppenheim's internationalisation strategy over the past 12 months. These include the investment in Prader Bank, Bolzano, which gives the bank access to clients in northern Italy. In the alternative investments segment, Sal. Oppenheim was able to boost its presence in London through the acquisition of the Attica Group and an investment in Integrated Assets Management (IAM). In Paris, the bank opened an office to set up an equity sales services team, further boosting its presence in France with the 100 per cent takeover of the asset management specialist Financière Atlas. In Belgium, Sal. Oppenheim also formed a joint venture with a holding company of the Frère-Bourgeois Group.

With the 10 per cent stake in the US investment bank Miller Buckfire, based in New York, Sal. Oppenheim has entered into an exclusive partnership that will open up further market potential for cross-border M&A transactions between the US and the German-speaking world.

217 years of success

2006 saw the bank post record results across the board. In fact, Sal. Oppenheim announced that its 218th financial year was the bank's most successful year in history. Consolidated income before takes was up by 9.2 per cent to €309 million. The bank saw an increase in equity to €1,935 million, and a growth in assets under management to €138 billion.

Sal. Oppenheim generates around one-third of its income outside of Germany at present, with this figure expected to increase to approximately 50 per cent in the medium term. As a result, the bank's growth strategy aims to create a balanced relationship between its German and international business. In the future, the basis for international growth will continue to lie in Sal. Oppenheim's strong market position in Germany. In financial year 2006, Sal. Oppenheim boosted the operating income generated in Germany by 25 per cent. It plans to considerably expand its German workforce by the end of 2007, recruiting 200 new employees.

Additionally, the Sal. Oppenheim Group will be merging its subsidiary bank in Luxembourg with its international holding company, Sal. Oppenheim International S.A., to form the new group parent company, Sal. Oppenheim jr. & Cie. S.C.A., and provide a basis for further international expansion. Sal. Oppenheim jr. & Cie. KGaA will remain responsible for the bank's domestic business, and aims to further expand and strengthen its solid market position.

GETTING HIRED

Finding the best

The bank recruits potential candidates everywhere from universities to "executive search" agencies, insiders report. And although the career section of the firm's web site at www.oppenheim.com is only available in German, you can still submit a resume to personal@oppenheim.de. If you end up getting to the next stage, "two to three interviews" isn't uncommon, says one source.

OUR SURVEY SAYS

Open culture

The bank's culture receives high marks from insiders — one calls it "open and results-driven." Benefits get high marks as well, and include perks like a "lease car". That said, n the realm of the daily grind, dress is formal and hours have a tendency to run about "50 to 60" per week — but weekend work is a rarity.

Visit **Vault Europe's Finance Career Channel** at **www.vault.com/europe** for insider firm profiles, employee surveys of finance professionals in Europe, message boards, job listings, expert finance career advice, insider salary information and more.

VAULT CAREER LIBRARY 277

Standard Chartered Bank

1 Aldermanbury Square
London EC2V 7SB
United Kingdom
Phone: +44 (0) 207 280 7500
Fax: +44 (0) 207 280 7791
www.standardchartered.com

EUROPEAN LOCATIONS

London (Global HQ)
Jersey
Switzerland
Turkey
UK
*90 percent of the firm's business is in Asia, Africa and the Middle East

DEPARTMENTS

Consumer Banking
    Private
    Priority
    Islamic banking)

Wholesale Banking
    Global Markets
    Trade Finance
    Export Finance
    Funds Management
    Transactional Banking

THE BUZZ
WHAT EMPLOYEES AT OTHER FIRMS ARE SAYING

- "Improving"
- "Second-tier bank"

THE STATS

Employer Type: Public Company
Ticker Symbol: STAN (LSE)
Chairman: Mervyn Davies
2006 Income: $8.62bn (FYE 12/06)
2006 Profit: $2.35 billion
2005 Income: $6.86 billion (FYE 12/05)
2005 Profit: $1.97 billion
2006 Employees: 60,000
No. of Branches and Offices: 1,400

PLUSES

"Laid-back" culture
Very multicultural

MINUSES

"Need more compensation for long hours"
"More understanding needed in regards to women's problems"

EMPLOYMENT CONTACT

www.careers.standardchartered.com

THE SCOOP

Think globally

Standard Chartered (StanChart) in its current form was created in 1969 by the merger of the Standard Bank of British South Africa and the Chartered Bank of India, Australia and China. Both banks traced their roots to the 1800s, when British trade activities created a need for banking and financial institutions throughout the far reaches of the British Empire. A period of peaceful growth lasted into modern times, until 1986, when Britain's Lloyds Bank attempted a hostile takeover. StanChart fought off the bid, but was prompted to make some business changes as a result of the threat. First it reduced its shaky debt exposure (especially in the Third World). Then it began divesting itself of assets, including businesses in the United States and South Africa. Today StanChart focuses its operations on Asia, Africa and the Middle East. More than 90 per cent of its profits are derived from these regions. The bank's European operations serve as a bridge to emerging markets. Based in London, StanChart offers consumer, corporate and institutional banking, as well as treasury services. It has more than 1,400 branches in 50 countries and employs approximately 60,000 people.

Go, go gallup

StanChart staff are familiar with Q12, an annual Gallup survey unveiled in 2000. This in-depth report is an independent external survey designed to measure employee engagement on a number of indices and thus make employee responses a central part of StanChart's agenda. Results of the Q12 survey are used by line managers to plan the next year's course of action. In 2005 the survey was distributed to every country in which StanChart operates and a whopping 96 per cent of employees chose to participate.

Mervyn's moment

Welshman Mervyn Davies became chairman of StanChart in November 2006, replacing Bryan Sanderson. Previously, Davies had been StanChart's chief executive and a group executive director. Soon after taking office, Davies had to fend off rumours that StanChart (like so many British banks) was ripe for a takeover. Its presence and growth sets it apart from other UK rivals, and with a market cap of $47.27 billion, a mega-bank could easily make a bid. "A lot of banks would like to have this franchise," Davies admitted in an interview. But he reaffirmed his intention to focus on StanChart's business, not hypothetical deals. "My job is to create value," he said.

Visit **Vault Europe's Finance Career Channel** at **www.vault.com/europe** for insider firm profiles, employee surveys of finance professionals in Europe, message boards, job listings, expert finance career advice, insider salary information and more.

VAULT CAREER LIBRARY   279

On to Taiwan

In November 2006 StanChart announced that it would purchase Taiwanese bank Hsinchu International, gobbling up its 2.5 million customer accounts. The move made sense in many ways (Hong Kong represents StanChart's largest concentration of customers and profits and Taiwan is home to many international companies with rapidly increasing investments), but Hsinchu brought a shaky record to the table. Beset with bad loans — Hsinchu had one of the lower Non-Performing Loan (NPL) ratios in Taiwan — the bank had been losing money. Still, StanChart said the purchase was part of a larger plan to build its presence in Taiwan, where Hsinchu has locations throughout the republic. According to officials at both banks, no employees would be cut as a result of the acquisition.

People are people

The bank has a 13-member Group Diversity & Inclusion Council representing all levels and markets of the Bank with 53 Diversity & Inclusion Champions globally appointed, the bank says, to help achieve its D&I agenda. The firm adds: "An in-country council supports these Champions to evaluate and measure the environments we work in and suggest and implement key enablers to improve the way the firm works." Standard Chartered has a formal flexible working structure in the UK with job sharing options to help promote work-life balance. The bank also has other networks to help support women in the workplace, including networking events with senior managers.

International intrigue

Although StanChart is known for its forays into Asia and the Middle East, in October 2006 a Dubai-based investment company paid $1 billion for a 2.7 per cent stake in the British bank. Istithmar (the name means investment in Arabic) is an investment company owned by Dubai's ruling Maktoum family. Even with its 2.7 per cent share, Istithmar is the second-largest StanChart shareholder (Temasek, a Singapore government entity, owns 13 per cent). Analysts suggested that the Dubai group would slowly raise its ownership of StanChart, perhaps in part to one-up Singapore. StanChart had no comment on these speculations, but a spokesman noted that "We view any interest shown by investors as an endorsement of our growth strategy and performance."

Performance rewarded

At the 2006 Banker Awards in London StanChart nabbed a total of 9 awards, including Global Bank of the Year. This top award recognised the bank's performance in Asia, Africa and the Middle East and its "prudent acquisition strategy." StanChart also won top regional awards for Africa and the Asia-Pacific region. It took home six country awards for its operations in Afghanistan, Botswana, Cote d'Ivoire, Gambia, Kenya and Sierra Leone. It also won the award for Best Corporate and Social Responsibility Bank.

Building the road to trade

In December 2006 StanChart launched something it called a China-Africa Trade Corridor, an initiative designed to offer financial solutions to small- and medium-sized enterprises (SMEs) in China and Africa making their first strides into international business. The initiative was kicked off with a two-day seminar in Shenzhen, China, giving SMEs from both regions an opportunity to exchange ideas and explore cooperation. The Trade Corridor initiative will offer capital management services and financing solutions to SMEs, and will assist them in their globalisation processes.

GETTING HIRED

Going global

At careers.standardchartered.com, you can search globally for open positions or learn about the firm's intern recruitment as well as graduate and MBA recruitment programmes. The bank also offers FAQs regarding the application process along with a list of "hints and tips". Once you're called in, insiders say you can expect at least "three interviews", adding, "Questions were minimal. They just asked what I had been doing and seemed quite keen to recruit at the time." The insider adds, "They also needed people with experience on certain products within the marketplace."

OUR SURVEY SAYS

Laid-back, but long hours

The firm is "very multicultural and laid-back," reports one source. At the same time, another says, "The bank has no concept of work/life balance. I left one department because I was working from 7 a.m. to 10 p.m. every day and they did not seem to care about this. If they did care, they did not show it." Hours can be long and weekend work occurs "about once a month". A contact adds "compensation for these long hours worked was dreadful."

Visit **Vault Europe's Finance Career Channel** at **www.vault.com/europe** for insider firm profiles, employee surveys of finance professionals in Europe, message boards, job listings, expert finance career advice, insider salary information and more.

VAULT CAREER LIBRARY 281

WestLB AG

Herzogstraße 15
40217 Düsseldorf
Germany
Phone: +49 211 826 01
Fax: +49 211 826 6119
www.westlb.de

EUROPEAN LOCATIONS

Dusseldorf (HQ)
Czech Republic • France •
Hungary • Ireland • Italy •
Luxembourg • Poland • Russia •
Serbia • Spain • Turkey • Ukraine
• United Kingdom.

DEPARTMENTS

Asset Management
Corporate Banking
Investment Banking
Private Banking

THE STATS

Employer Type: Government Entity
Chairman: Dr. Thomas R. Fischer
2006 Revenues: €1.14bn (FYE 12/06)
2005 Revenues: €1.33bn (FYE 12/05)
2006 Employees: 6,353
No. of Offices: 20 (Worldwide)

PLUSES

"Work/life balance"

MINUSES

"Lack of extra monetary benefits"

EMPLOYMENT CONTACT

www.westlbcareers.com

THE BUZZ
WHAT EMPLOYEES AT OTHER FIRMS ARE SAYING

• "Strong local player"
• "Disappeared"

THE SCOOP

Old bank with a new future

With total assets of €292.1 billion as of mid-2006, WestLB is one of Germany's biggest financial services companies. It serves as a central bank for the sparkassen, or savings banks, in North Rhine-Westphalia and Brandenburg. It's also an international commercial bank that links its home turf to global financial markets. WestLB offers lending, structured finance, capital market and private equity products, asset management, transaction services and real estate finance.

The bank has dual headquarters in Düsseldorf and Münster, in addition to German branch offices in Berlin, Cologne, Dortmund, Frankfurt am Main, Hamburg and Munich. Throughout the rest of Europe, WestLB maintains branches in Istanbul, London, Madrid, Milan and Paris. It also has branches in Asia, Australia and New York, as well as representative offices and subsidiaries around the world.

WestLB was created in 1969 by the merger of Landesbank für Westfalen Girozentrale, a Münster institution founded in 1832, and Rheinische Girozentrale und Provinzialbank, a Düsseldorf firm founded in 1854. In 2002 WestLB became a joint stock company and in July 2005, government support for the bank's institutional liability and guarantor liability was abolished, forcing WestLB to operate without state guarantees. WestLB is still partially owned by the government of North Rhine-Westphalia, Germany's largest federal state.

Germany's next top model

Although its roots go back to the 1800s, WestLB is going through some growing pains thanks to recent changes in German banking regulations and new requirements of the European Commission. The close of fiscal 2005 marked the first year of WestLB's new business model, which was created when the bank lost its state liability guarantees — the traditional foundation for its credit ratings. Pushed into independence, WestLB scrambled to become more competitive by setting high profit targets and improving its market capitalisation. It also boosted its transactions with the sparkassen and restructured its investment banking activities to focus on client-driven and fee-based business — a move that brought investment banking profits up 57 per cent in the first half of 2006. Structured finance, syndicated lending, equity issues and structured trading turned in especially strong performances.

In fiscal 2006 WestLB announced that it was still "in the midst of a transformation process," which included the resumption of private German banking business (under the Weberbank brand) and the formation of strategic partnerships with Mellon, DekaBank,

Visit **Vault Europe's Finance Career Channel** at **www.vault.com/europe** for insider firm profiles, employee surveys of finance professionals in Europe, message boards, job listings, expert finance career advice, insider salary information and more.

VAULT CAREER LIBRARY 283

Sachsen LB and Sachsen-Finanzgruppe. WestLB also spent 2006 executing its "Lean Bank programme," a cost-cutting initiative designed to bring costs and expenditure processes in line with those of competitors by 2008.

Opening investment doors

In August 2006 WestLB paved the way for the first significant private equity investment in Germany's public banking sector. The bank agreed to sell its stake in fellow bank HSH Nordbank to a consortium of five institutional investors led by American firm JC Flowers. The consortium paid WestLB $1.6 billion for its 24.1 per cent of HSH Nordbank's share capital and 26.6 per cent of its voting rights. This purchase came as HSH Nordbank readied itself for a stock market listing — it planned to spend 2007 preparing for an IPO to launch in 2008 or 2009.

WestLB was also among the German banks that, in November 2006, entered talks to buy a significant stake in European Aeronautic Defense & Space (EADS). German automaker DaimlerChrysler, which owns a major part of EADS, had plans to reduce its holding. Other German banks named in the deal were Commerzbank, Deutsche Bank and KfW, and a German government spokesman said the transaction would likely go through sometime in 2007.

It's PAYBACK time

WestLB's partnership with PAYBACK, a customer loyalty program, is slated to begin in early 2007. Announced in March 2006, the collaboration will provide joint products for customers who enroll in PAYBACK, including loyalty cards with cost-free payment functions. All WestLB banks and partners will be able to offer their products and services to PAYBACK customers. The program will be managed by Abc Privatkunden-Bank, which WestLB acquired in 2006.

Moving up the ranks

In December 2006 Investment Dealer's Digest published its list of 40 bankers and traders under the age of 40 who are making an impact on financial markets. WestLB's Thomas Murray, global head of energy, was included on that list. WestLB ranked No. 404 on the 2006 Fortune 500 list, climbing up from No. 460 in 2005.

Expansion and a sale?

WestLB's international growth strategy for 2007 will include an expansion into the United States, a company spokesman said, explaining that plans for the expansion are set to be unveiled later in the year. In late 2006, WestLB ventured into new territory in Asia, opening offices in China and India. Sometime in 2007 the bank is expected to add another top partner to its Latin American business, perhaps indicating future growth in that region.

Despite the bank's efforts to become a global competitor, North Rhine-Westphalia finance minister Helmut Linssen announced in January 2007 that his government was considering selling its 38 per cent stake in WestLB. "But we are not in a hurry," he said, citing WestLB's strong performance — which, if it continues, will make the government's share of the bank even more valuable. As of early 2007, WestLB was valued at approximately €7 to €8 billion. In addition, Linssen went on to say that selling the state's share to another major European bank was a possibility.

GETTING HIRED

All levels

In the "job forum" section at www.westlb.de, you can apply for positions that require experience in the field. But you don't necessarily have to have years of experience under your belt to work at West LB - at www.westlbcareers.com, you can check out opportunities specifically targeted to graduates and potential interns. And if you're hoping to work in a specific location, you may be in luck as the firm recruits "globally." Expect at least three interviews once you're called in — "one with a team head, one with team members and one with HR."

OUR SURVEY SAYS

Balancing act

There is a "good work/life balance" at the bank, one insider says. Perks include a "gym membership," "flexible working hours," "casual Fridays" and "working from home," insiders report. And to boot, working hours generally run from "50 to 60" per week but "rarely or never" on weekends.

Visit **Vault Europe's Finance Career Channel** at www.vault.com/europe for insider firm profiles, employee surveys of finance professionals in Europe, message boards, job listings, expert finance career advice, insider salary information and more.

VAULT CAREER LIBRARY 285

APPENDIX

About the Editor

Saba Haider is the editor of Vault Europe. Prior to joining Vault, she spent more than eight years working as a journalist and editor in Toronto, San Diego, London, Dubai, Amsterdam and New York. She has a BA in Political Science from the University of Guelph in Canada and is a Masters candidate at the University of London. She would like to one day retire in Argentina.

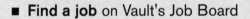

As a responsible publishing company, Vault is proud to work with printers who source materials from well managed sustainable forests: this ensures long term timber supplies and helps protect the environment.

We aim to grow our business while minimizing our impact on the environment.

We encourage readers to download and read the electronic versions of our guides available on our web sites, www.vault.com and www.vault.com/europe.

We are also proud to have installed the Vault Online Career Library at 850 universities worldwide. With the Online Career Library, students worldwide can download electronic versions of our guides as part of their job search preparation. By providing this service to students, Vault and its university partners help reduce the printing and shipping of our guides

By leveraging the latest technology, we aim to contribute responsibly to the world in which we live.

Thomas Nutt
General Manager
Vault Europe.